# Violent Crimes in Aid of Racketeering 18 U.S.C. § 1959

# A Manual for Federal Prosecutors

December 2006

Prepared by the Staff of the Organized Crime and Racketeering Section
U.S. Department of Justice, Washington, DC 20005       (202) 514-3594

Frank J. Marine, Consultant
Douglas E. Crow, Principal Deputy Chief
Amy Chang Lee, Assistant Chief

Robert C. Dalton
Merv Hamburg
Gregory C.J. Lisa
Melissa Marquez-Oliver
David J. Stander
Catherine M. Weinstock

# PREFACE

This manual is intended to assist federal prosecutors in the preparation and litigation of cases involving the Violent Crimes in Aid of Racketeering Statute, 18 U.S.C. § 1959. Prosecutors are encouraged to contact the Organized Crime and Racketeering Section (OCRS) early in the preparation of their case for advice and assistance.

All pleadings alleging a violation of 18 U.S.C. § 1959 including any indictment, information, or criminal complaint, and a prosecution memorandum must be submitted to OCRS for review and approval before being filed with the court. The submission should be approved by the prosecutor's office before being submitted to OCRS. Due to the volume of submissions received by OCRS, prosecutors should submit the proposal three weeks prior to the date final approval is needed. Prosecutors should contact OCRS regarding the status of the proposed submission before finally scheduling arrests or other time-sensitive actions relating to the submission. Moreover, prosecutors should refrain from finalizing any guilty plea agreement containing a Section 1959 charge until final approval has been obtained from OCRS.

The policies and procedures set forth in this manual and elsewhere relating to 18 U.S.C. § 1959 are internal Department of Justice policies and guidance only. They are not intended to, do not, and may not be relied upon to, create any right, substantive or procedural, enforceable at law by any party in any matter civil or criminal. Nor are any limitations hereby placed on otherwise lawful litigative prerogatives of the Department of Justice.

## TABLE OF CONTENTS

**PAGE**

PREFACE..................................................................

TABLE OF CONTENTS......................................................

TABLE OF AUTHORITIES...................................................

I. INTRODUCTION AND OVERVIEW......................................................1

    A. Introduction..................................................................1
    B. Prior Approval by the Organized Crime and Racketeering Section Is Required..................................................................2

        1. Approval Authority..................................................................2
        2. Guidelines for Section 1959 Prosecutions..................................................................3
        3. Prosecution Memorandum..................................................................4
        4. Post-Indictment Duties..................................................................5

    C. Legislative History Of Section 1959 and Its Relationship To RICO..................................................................5
    D. Liberal Construction Rule..................................................................7

II. ELEMENTS OF SECTION 1959 OFFENSES..................................................................7

    A. Overview of Elements and Mens Rea..................................................................7
    B. The Existence of An Enterprise..................................................................10
    C. The Enterprise Engaged in, or its Activities Affected, Interstate or Foreign Commerce..................................................................13
    D. The Enterprise Engaged in Racketeering Activity..................................................................15
    E. Generic Offenses - Determining Whether A Particular Statutory Offense Qualifies as A Section 1959 Predicate Offense..................................................................18
    F. Murder..................................................................26

        1. The Federal Murder Statute -- 18 U.S.C. § 1111..................................................................27

            (a) Elements..................................................................28
            (b) "Unlawful" killing..................................................................30
            (c) Malice Aforethought..................................................................30
            (d) Premeditation..................................................................31

|  |  | (e) | Felony Murder. | 33 |
|---|---|---|---|---|
|  |  | (f) | Jurisdiction. | 36 |

      2.    Generic Murder. ................................................ 38
      3.    Section 1959 Cases Charging Murder. ........................... 43

G.    Kidnapping. ............................................................ 44

      1.    Federal Kidnapping Statute, 18 U.S.C. § 1201. ................... 44

          (a)    Elements. ............................................. 48
          (b)    Kidnapping by force (seizure, confinement, kidnapping, abduction, or carrying away) or seduction (decoying and inveigling). ........................................... 49
          (c)    Transportation in interstate commerce. ................ 50
          (d)    For "Ransom or Reward or Otherwise" Requirement. ..... 51

      2.    Generic Kidnapping.. ........................................... 53
      3.    Section 1959 Cases Charging Kidnapping.. ...................... 55

H.    Maiming. .............................................................. 56

      1.    Generic Maiming. .............................................. 56
      2.    Section 1959 Prosecutions Charging Maiming. .................. 65

I.     Assault With A Dangerous Weapon.. .................................... 65

      1.    Federal Definition Under 18 U.S.C. § 113. ...................... 65
      2.    Generic Assault With A Dangerous Weapon. .................... 67
      3.    Section 1959 Cases Charging Assault With A Dangerous Weapon. . 72

J.     Assaults Resulting in Serious Bodily Injury. ........................... 74

      1.    Federal Definitions Under 18 U.S.C. §§ 113 and 1365. ............ 74
      2.    Generic Assault Resulting in Serious Bodily Injury. .............. 78
      3.    Section 1959 Cases Charging Assault Resulting in Serious Bodily Injury ........................................................ 80

K.    Threats To Commit A Crime of Violence. ............................... 81

      1.    Federal Definition of a Crime of Violence under 18 U.S.C. § 16 ................................................. 81

|      |      | a. | Section 16(a) – the Use, Attempted Use, or Threatened Use of Physical Force Against the Person or Property of Another . . . . . . . . . . . . . . . . . . . . . . . . . . . . . . . . . . . . . . . 86 |
|------|------|----|---|

                                b.     Section 16(b) --Felony Offenses Involving a Substantial Risk that Physical Force Against the Person or Property of Another May Be Used. . . . . . . . . . . . . . . . . . . . . . . . . . . . 88

               2.     Section 1959 Cases Charging a Threat to Commit a Crime of Violence. . . . . . . . . . . . . . . . . . . . . . . . . . . . . . . . . . . . . . . . . . . . . . 91

    L.     Attempts and Conspiracies. . . . . . . . . . . . . . . . . . . . . . . . . . . . . . . . . . . . . . . . 93

    M.    The Underlying Crimes of Violence Must Be Committed For One of Two Purposes. . . . . . . . . . . . . . . . . . . . . . . . . . . . . . . . . . . . . . . . . . . . . 102

               1.     Receipt of, or as Consideration for A Promise or Agreement to Pay, Anything of Pecuniary Value From An Enterprise. . . . . . . 102
               2.     Gaining Entrance to or Maintaining or Increasing Position in an Enterprise. . . . . . . . . . . . . . . . . . . . . . . . . . . . . . . . . . . . . . . . . . . . 104

III.    ALTERNATIVE THEORIES OF LIABILITY. . . . . . . . . . . . . . . . . . . . . . . . . . 111

    A.     Aiding and Abetting. . . . . . . . . . . . . . . . . . . . . . . . . . . . . . . . . . . . . . . . . . . . . 111
    B.     Pinkerton Liability. . . . . . . . . . . . . . . . . . . . . . . . . . . . . . . . . . . . . . . . . . . . . . 114
    C.     Accessory After the Fact. . . . . . . . . . . . . . . . . . . . . . . . . . . . . . . . . . . . . . . . . 115

IV.    MISCELLANEOUS LEGAL ISSUES AND PROCEDURAL MATTERS. . . . . . 116

    A.     Venue. . . . . . . . . . . . . . . . . . . . . . . . . . . . . . . . . . . . . . . . . . . . . . . . . . . . . . . . 116
    B.     Extraterritorial Application of Section 1959. . . . . . . . . . . . . . . . . . . . . . . . . . 119
    C.     Drafting the Indictment and Related Issues. . . . . . . . . . . . . . . . . . . . . . . . . . . 123
    D.    Double Jeopardy and Collateral Estoppel. . . . . . . . . . . . . . . . . . . . . . . . . . . . 126

               1.     Double Jeopardy. . . . . . . . . . . . . . . . . . . . . . . . . . . . . . . . . . . . . . . . 126
               2.     Collateral Estoppel. . . . . . . . . . . . . . . . . . . . . . . . . . . . . . . . . . . . . . 128

    E.     Joinder and Severance. . . . . . . . . . . . . . . . . . . . . . . . . . . . . . . . . . . . . . . . . . . 133
    F.     Statute of Limitations. . . . . . . . . . . . . . . . . . . . . . . . . . . . . . . . . . . . . . . . . . . . 134
    G.    Sentencing and Punishment in Non-Capital Cases. . . . . . . . . . . . . . . . . . . . . 135

               1.     Murder and Kidnapping. . . . . . . . . . . . . . . . . . . . . . . . . . . . . . . . . . 135
               2.     Maiming. . . . . . . . . . . . . . . . . . . . . . . . . . . . . . . . . . . . . . . . . . . . . . 136
               3.     Assault Offenses. . . . . . . . . . . . . . . . . . . . . . . . . . . . . . . . . . . . . . . . 136

|   |   |   |
|---|---|---|
|   | 4. | Threats to Commit A Crime of Violence........................ 137 |
|   | 5. | Attempts or Conspiracies to Commit Murder or Kidnapping..... 137 |
|   | 6. | Attempts or Conspiracies to Commit Maiming or Assault Offenses................................................................. 138 |

H. Jury Instructions................................................................. 138
I. Admission of Uncharged Crimes.......................................... 139
J. Constitutional Challenges.................................................... 140

      1. Vagueness Challenges................................................ 140
      2. Ex Post Facto Challenges............................................ 142
      3. Tenth Amendment Challenges..................................... 142

**APPENDIX A -** Excerpts of Senate Report No. 98-225, 98th Cong. 1st Sess. pp. 1-2, 304-314, 322-323.

**APPENDIX B -** United States Attorneys' Manual Sections 9-110.010 to 9-110.8161

**APPENDIX C -** State Assault Statutes

**APPENDIX D -** Model Section 1959 Indictments

# TABLE OF AUTHORITIES

**SUPREME COURT CASES**

                                                **PAGE**

Abbate v. United States, 359 U.S. 187 (1959). ............................................................. 128

Apprendi v. New Jersey, 530 U.S. 466 (2000). ............................................................. 136

Ashe v. Swenson, 397 U.S. 436 (1970). ................................................................ 128, 129

Bartkus v. Illinois, 359 U.S. 121 (1959). ........................................................................ 128

Blockburger v. United States, 284 U.S. 299 (1932). ..................................................... 127

Heath v. Alabama, 474 U.S. 82 (1985). ......................................................................... 128

Chatwin v. United States, 326 U.S. 455 (1946). .............................................................. 49

Dowling v. United States, 493 U.S. 342 (1990). ........................................................... 129

EEOC v. Arabian American Oil Co., 499 U.S. 244 (1991). .......................................... 119

Foley Brothers, Inc. v. Filardo, 336 U.S. 281 (1949). ................................................... 119

Gooch v. United States, 297 U.S. 124 (1936). .......................................................... 51, 52

Johnson v. Louisiana, 406 U.S. 356 (1972). .................................................................. 131

Leocal v. Ashcroft, 543 U.S. 1 (2004). ....................................................................... *Passim*

McCulloch v. Sociedad Nacional de Marineros de Honduras, 372 U.S. 10 (1963). ...... 120

Morissette v. United States, 342 U.S. 246 (1952). .......................................................... 68

Mullaney v. Wilbur, 421 U.S. 684 (1975). ....................................................................... 31

Nardello v. United States, 393 U.S. 286 (1969). ............................................................. 19

Nash v. United States, 229 U.S. 373 (1913). ................................................................... 94

Nye & Nissen v. United States, 336 U.S. 613 (1949). ................................................... 115

Pereira v. United States, 347 U.S. 1 (1954). .................................................................. 115

Perrin v. United States, 444 U.S. 37 (1979) ............................................................. 19

Petite v. United States, 361 U.S. 529 (1960) ........................................................... 128

Pinkerton v. United States, 328 U.S. 640 (1946) ............................................. 114, 115

Richardson v. United States, 468 U.S. 317 (1984) ................................................. 131

Rutledge v. United States, 517 U.S. 292 (1996) ...................................................... 101

Salinas v. United States, 522 U.S. 52 (1977) ........................................................... 112

Schad v. Arizona, 501 U.S. 624 (1991) ................................................................ 35, 41

Scheidler v. National Organization for Women, Inc., 537 U.S. 409 ................... 18, 19

Sedima, S.P.R.L. v. Imrex Co., 473 U.S. 479 (1985) ................................................ 16

Shepard v. United States, 544 U.S. 13 (2005) ............................................... 21, 22, 26

Singer v. United States, 323 U.S. 338 (1945) ............................................................ 94

Taylor v. United States, 495 U.S. 575 (1990) ................................................ 20, 21, 26

United States v. Bowman, 260 U.S. 94 (1922) ................................................ 119, 120

United States v. Cabrales, 524 U.S. 1 (1998) .......................................................... 117

United States v. Dixon, 509 U.S. 688 (1993) .......................................................... 127

United States v. Healy, 376 U.S. 75 (1964) ........................................... 51, 52, 53, 54

United States v. Lanza, 260 U.S. 377 (1922) .......................................................... 128

United States v. Rabinovich, 238 U.S. 78 (1915) ................................................... 112

United States v. Rodriquez-Moreno, 526 U.S. 275 (1999) ..................................... 117

United States v. Shabani, 513 U.S. 10 (1994) ........................................................... 94

United States v. Turkette, 452 U.S. 576 (1981) ................................... 10, 12, 17, 117

United States v. Turley, 352 U.S. 407 (1957) ........................................................... 68

United States v. Wheeler, 435 U.S. 1313 (1978) .................................................... 128

Whitfield v. United States, 543 U.S. 209 (2005). .................................................... 94

**FEDERAL CASES**

Bazan-Reyes v. INS, 256 F.3d 600 (CA 7 2001). ........................................................ 85

Beardslee v. United States, 387 F.2d 280 (8th Cir. 1967). ........................................... 29

Bostic v. United States, 94 F. 2d 636 (D.C. Cir. 1937). ............................................... 32

Bovkun v. Ashcroft, 283 F.3d 166 (3d Cir. 2002). .................................................. 86, 87

Brackett v. Peters, 11 F.3d 78 (7th Cir. 1993). ............................................................ 36

Brundage v. United States, 365 F.2d 616 (10th Cir. 1966). ......................................... 68

Chery v. Ashcroft, 347 F.3d 404 (2d Cir. 2003). ..................................................... 86, 89

Chrzanoski v. Ashcroft, 327 F.3d 18 (2d Cir. 2003). ............................................... 86, 88

Chua Han Mow v. United States, 730 F.2d 1308 (9th Cir. 1984). ....................... 119, 121

De Herrera v. United States, 339 F.2d 587 (10th Cir. 1964). .................................. 52, 92

Dickson v. Ashcroft, 346 F.3d 44 (2d Cir. 2003). ........................................................ 87

Duarte v. United States, 289 F. Supp. 2d 487 (S.D.N.Y. 2003). ................................. 136

Flores v. Ashcroft, 350 F.3d 666 (7th Cir. 2003). ................................................... 86, 87

Gawne v. United States, 409 F.2d 1399 (9th Cir. 1969). .............................................. 51

Guzman v. United States, 277 F. Supp. 2d 255 (S.D.N.Y. 2003). ........................ 136, 142

Hess v. United States, 254 F.2d 578 (8th Cir. 1958). ................................................... 52

Hongsathirath v. Ashcroft, 322 F. Supp. 2d 203 (D. Conn. 2004). ............................... 90

Jobson v. Ashcroft, 326 F.3d 367 (2d Cir. 2003). .................................................. 86, 90

United States v. Katona, 204 F. Supp. 2d at 412. ............................................... 115, 138

Nguyen v. Ashcroft, 366 F.3d 386 (5th Cir. 2004). ................................................ 86, 89

Ornelas v. United States, 236 F.2d 392 (9th Cir. 1956)................................................. 32

Owens v. United States, 236 F. Supp. 2d 137 (D. Mass 2002).............................. 43, 125

Ramirez v. Ashcroft, 361 F. Supp. 2d 650 (S.D. Texas 2005). ....................................... 89

Reyes-Alcaraz v. Ashcroft, 363 F.3d 937 (9th Cir. 2004). ........................................... 86

Santapaola v. Ashcroft, 249 F. Supp. 2d 181 (D. Conn. 2003). .............................. 86, 90

Smith v. Berg, 247 F.3d 532 (3d Cir. 2001). ................................................................ 112

Stantini v. United States, 268 F. Supp. 2d 168 (E.D.N.Y. 2003). ................................... 1

Szucz-Toldy v. Gonzales, 400 F.3d 978 (7th Cir. 2005). ......................................... 86, 87

Tabas v. Tabas, 47 F.3d 1280 (3d Cir. 1995)................................................................ 139

Tatta v. Mitchell, 962 F. Supp. 21 (E.D.N.Y. 1997)....................................................... 80

Tran v. Gonzales, 414 F.3d 464 (3d Cir. 2005). ............................................................. 90

Tse v. United States, 112 F. Supp. 2d 189 (D.Mass. 2000)............................................ 14

Tse v. United States, 290 F.3d 462 (1st Cir. 2002)................................................... 13, 14

United States v. Adams, 83 F.3d 1371 (11th Cir. 1996)........................................... 49, 51

United States v. Agostini, 365 F. Supp. 530 (S.D.N.Y. 2005). ..................................... 137

United State v. Aguilar-Aranceta, 957 F.2d 18 (1st Cir. 1992). ................................... 129

United States v. Aiken, 76 F. Supp. 2d 1346 (S.D. Fla. 1999). ............................. 117, 134

United States v. Aiken, 76 F. Supp. 2d 1346 (S.D. Fla. 1999). ................................... 133

United States v. Alkins, 925 F.2d 552 (2d. Cir. 1991). ................................................ 139

United States v. Alvarez, 755 F.2d 830 (11th Cir. 1985). .............................................. 30

United States v. Andino, 101 F. Supp. 2d at 175 (S.D.N.Y. 2000). ..................... 103, 104

United States v. Aragon, 983 F.2d 1306 (4th Cir. 1993). ................................... 86, 89, 91

United States v. Atchinson, 524 F.2d 367 (7th Cir. 1975).............................................. 52

United States v. Baez, 62 F. Supp. 2d 557 (D. Conn. 1999). ........................ 123

United States v. Baez, 349 F.3d 90 (2d Cir. 2003). ...................................... 140

United States v. Bagaric, 706 F.2d 42 (2d Cir. 1983). .................................... 24

United States v. Barton, 257 F.3d 433 (5th Cir. 2001). ................................... 48

United States v. Bell, 505 F.2d 539 (7th Cir. 1974). ................................. 67, 68

United States v. Benton, 852 F.2d 1456 (6th Cir. 1988). .............................. 129

United States v. Bey, 667 F.2d 7 (5th Cir. 1982). .......................................... 67

United States v. Biaggi, 675 F. Supp. 790 (S.D.N.Y. 1987). ........................ 125

United States v. Bin Laden, 92 F. Supp. 2d 189 (S.D.N.Y. 2000)(3). ........... 121

United States v. Black Elk, 579 F.2d 49 (8th Cir. 1978). ................................ 30

United States v. Bledsoe, 674 F.2d 647 (8th Cir. 1982). ................................. 11

United States v. Blue Thunder, 604 F.3d 550 (8th Cir. 1979). ........................ 31

United States v. Boldin, 818 F.2d 771 (11th Cir. 1987). ............................... 129

United States v. Boone, 959 F.2d 1550 (11th Cir. 1992). ............................... 50

United States v. Bordeaux, 84 F.3d 1544 (8th Cir. 1996). ......................... 50, 52

United States v. Bracy, 67 F.3d 1421 (9th Cir. 1995). ............................. *Passim*

United States v. Broadwell, 870 F.2d 594 (11th Cir. 1989). ......................... 114

United States v. Brown, 330 F.3d 1073 (8th Cir. 2003). ................................. 52

United States v. Brown, 518 F.2d 821 (7th Cir. 1975). ............................. 31, 32

United States v. Browner, 889 F.2d 549 (5th Cir. 1989). ................................ 35

United States v. Bruno, 383 F.3d 65 (2d Cir. 2004). ................................ *Passim*

United States v. Carrillo, 229 F.3d 177 (2d Cir. 2000). ........................... *Passim*

United States v. Carrozza, 55 F. Supp. 2d 84 (D. Mass. 1999). ............................... 115

United States v. Celestine, 510 F.2d 457 (9th Cir. 1975). ....................................... 30

United States v. Cervantez-Nava, 281 F.3d 501 (5th Cir. 2002). ............................. 90

United States v. Chancery, 715 F.2d 543 (11th Cir. 1983). ...................................... 49

United States v. Chanthadara, 230 F.3d 1237 (10th Cir. 2000). ......................... 33, 34

United States v. Chen, 2 F.3d 330 (9th Cir. 1993). ................................................ 121

United States v. Chischilly, 30 F.3d 1144 (9th Cir. 1994). ......................... 29, 33, 35

United States v. Christopher, 956 F.2d 536 (6th Cir. 1991). .................................... 76

United States v. Claiborne, 92 F. Supp. 2d 503 (E.D. Va. 2000). .......................... 128

United States v. Clemente, 22 F.3d 477 (2d Cir. 1994). ......................................... 140

United States v. Cobb, 558 F.2d 486 (8th Cir. 1977). ............................................ 101

United States v. Cohen, 427 F.3d 164 (2d Cir. 2005). ........................................... 121

United State v. Collins, 78 F.3d 1021 (6th Cir. 1992). ........................................... 112

Untied States v. Colon, 2005 WL 2764820 3 (D. Conn. October 21, 2005). ........... 44

Untied States v. Coiro, 922 F.2d 1008 (2d Cir. 1991). .......................................... 139

United States v. Concepcion, 983 F.2d 369 (2d Cir. 1992). ............................. *Passim*

United States v. Console, 13 F.3d 641 (3d Cir. 1993). ........................... 128, 129, 131

United States v. Coonan, 938 F.2d 1553 (2d Cir. 1991). ....................................... 140

United States v. Corrigan, 548 F.2d 879 (10th Cir. 1977). ...................................... 30

United States v. Crenshaw, 359 F.3d 977 (8th Cir. 2004). ............................... *Passim*

United States v. Crosby, 713 F.2d 1066 (5th Cir. 1983). .................................. 51, 52

United States v. Crowley, 318 F.3d 401 (2d Cir. 2003). .......................................... 95

United States v. Cruz, 805 F.2d 1464 (11th Cir. 1996). ..................................... 88, 90

United States v. Cruz-Jiminez, 977 F.2d 95 (3d Cir. 1992). ............................................ 95

United States v. Cuong Gia Le, 310 F. Supp. 2d 763 (E.D.Va. 2004)...................... *Passim*

United States v. Cuong Gia Le, 316 F. Supp. 2d 355 (E.D.Va. 2004)...................... *Passim*

United States v. Cutolo, 861 F. Supp. 1142 (E.D.N.Y. 1994). ........................... 17, 18, 26

United States v. Darden, 70 F.3d 1507 (8th Cir. 1995). ............................................. 134

United States v. DeJesus, 48 F. Supp. 2d 275 (S.D.N.Y. 1998). ................................ 117

United States v. DeJesus, 75 F. Supp. 2d 141 (S.D.N.Y. 1999). ................................ 138

United States v. De La Motte, 434 F.2d 289 (2d Cir. 1970). ....................................... 52

United States v. Delatorre, 157 F.3d 1205 (10th Cir. 1998). ..................................... 140

United States v. Demery, 980 F.2d 1187 (8th Cir. 1992). ............................................ 76

United States v. Dennison, 937 F.2d 559 (10th Cir. 1991)........................................... 76

United States v. Desena, 287 F.3d 170 (2d Cir. 2002). ........................................ *Passim*

United States v. Dhinsa, 243 F.3d 635 (2d Cir. 2001)........................................... *Passim*

United States v. DiGiorgio, 193 F.3d 1175 (11th Cir. 1999)...................................... 138

United States v. DiSalvo, 34 F.3d 1204 (3d Cir. 1994). ............................................ 140

United States v. Diaz, 176 F.3d 52 (2d Cir. 1999).............................................. *Passim*

United States v. Diaz, 778 F.2d 86 (2d Cir. 1985)....................................................... 91

United States v. Dixon, 273 F.3d 636 (5th Cir. 2001). ................................................ 51

United States v. Doyon, 194 F.3d 207 (1st Cir. 1999).................................................. 95

United States v. Dupree, 544 F.2d 1050 (9th Cir. 1976). .................................. 66, 67, 38

United State v. Duran, 1998 WL 115865 (10th Cir. March 16, 1998). ...................... 101

United States v. Eagle Thunder, 893 F.2d 950 (8th Cir. 1990). ................................... 51

United States v. Ellison, 793 F.2d 942 (8th Cir. 1986)................................................. 140

United States v. Engle, 586 F.2d 1193 (8th Cir. 1978)..................................................... 76

United States v. Eufrasio, 935 F.2d 553 (3d. Cir. 1991).................................................. 140

United States v. Feliciano, 223 F.3d 102 (2d Cir. 2000). ......................................... *Passim*

United States v. Felipe, 148 F.3d 101 (2d Cir. 1998). .................................................. 137

United States v. Felix-Gutierrez, 940 F.2d 1200 (9th Cir. 1991). ................. 119, 122, 134

United States v. Ferguson, 49 F. Supp. 2d 321 (S.D.N.Y. 1999). ................................ 103

United States v. Fernandez, 388 F.3d 1199 (9th Cir. 2004). .................................... *Passim*

United States v. Fiel, 35 F.3d 997 (4th Cir. 1994)..................................................... *Passim*

United States v. Flores, 63 F.3d 1342 (5th Cir. 1995). .................................................. 33

United States v. Forbrich, 758 F.2d 555 (11th Cir. 1985). ............................................ 95

United States v. Frampton, 382 F.3d 213 (2d Cir. 2004).......................................... *Passim*

United States v. Galvan-Rodriguez, 169 F.3d 217 (5th Cir. 1999)........................... 86, 89

United States v. Garcia, 68 F. Supp. 2d 802 (E.D. Mich. 1999)...................... 13, 14, 15

United States v. Garcia-Meza, 403 F.3d 364 (6th Cir. 2005). ....................................... 32

United States v. Garfinkle, 842 F. Supp. 1284 (D. Nev. 1993). ....................... 16, 17, 142

United States v. Gibson, 896 F.2d 206 (6th Cir. 1990). ................................................ 67

United States v. Gigante, 982 F. Supp. 140 (E.D.N.Y. 1997). .................................... 134

United States v. Gonzalez, 921 F.2d 1530 (11th Cir. 1991)................................... 139, 140

United States v. Gracia-Cantu, 302 F.3d 308 (5th Cir. 2002)............................ 86, 88, 90

United States v. Gray, 137 F.3d 765 (4th Cir. 1998). ............................................... *Passim*

United States v. Guadaro, 40 F.3d 102 (5th Cir. 1994). ............................................... 89

United States v. Guilbert, 692 F.2d 1340 (11th Cir. 1982)................................ 66, 67, 68

United States v. Hayes, 827 F.2d 469 (9th Cir. 1987). ................................................ 112

United States v. Healy, 376 U.S. 75 (1964). ................................................................ 50

United States v. Hernandez-Fundora, 58 F.3d 802 (2d Cir. 1995). ............................. 37

United States v. Hicks, 389 F.3d 514 (5th Cir. 2004). ................................................. 31

United States v. Hollow, 747 F.2d 481 (8th Cir. 1984). .............................................. 67

United States v. Hoog, 504 F.2d 45 (8th Cir. 1974). ................................................... 50

United States v. Houlihan, 92 F.3d 1271 (1st Cir. 1996). ............................... 9, 111, 134

United States v. Hoyte, 51 F.3d 1239 (4th Cir. 1995). ....................................... 107, 111

United States v. Hughes, 716 F.2d 234 (4th Cir. 1983). .............................................. 50

United States v. Hunt, 129 F.3d 739 (5th Cir. 1997). ................................................. 101

United State v. Hunt, 1998 WL 732475 (6th Cir. July 15, 1998). .............................. 101

United States v. Innie, 7 F.3d 840 (9th Cir. 1993). ...................................................... 92

United States v. Irwin, 787 F.2d 1506 (11th Cir. 1986). ............................................ 129

United States v. Jackson, 978 F.2d 903 (5th Cir. 1992). .............................................. 48

United States v. Jacobs, 632 F.2d 695 (7th Cir. 1980). ................................................ 75

United States v. James, 239 F.3d 120 (2d Cir. 2000). ...................... 93, 102, 105, 135

United States v. Johnson, 219 F.3d 349 (4th Cir. 2000). .............................. 43, 102, 127

United States v. Johnson, 324 F.2d 264 (4th Cir. 1963). ................................ 66, 76, 77

United State v. Johnson, 637 F.2d 1224 (9th Cir. 1980). ............................................ 75

United States v. Jones, 808 F.2d 561 (7th Cir. 1986). .................................................. 52

United States v. Jones, 938 F.2d 737 (7th Cir. 1991). ................................................ 112

United States v. Jourdain, 433 F.3d 652 (8th Cir. 2006). ............................................. 77

United States v. Juvenile Male, 930 F.2d 727 (9th Cir. 1991). ......................................... 76

United States v. Kaplan, 866 F.2d 536 (2d Cir. 1989). ................................................. 139

United States v. Keltner, 147 F.3d 662 (8th Cir. 1998). ................................................ 139

United States v. Khalil, 279 F.3d 358 (6th Cir. 2002). ............................................. *Passim*

United State v. Kehoe, 310 F.3d 579 (8th Cir. 2002). ...................................... 5, 7, 18, 43

United States v. Kim, 246 F.3d 186 (2d Cir. 2001). ...................................................... 119

United States v. King, 850 F. Supp. 750 (C.D. Ill. 1994). ................................................. 6

United States v. Knife, 592 F.2d 472 (8th Cir. 1979). ..................................................... 76

United States v. Krout, 66 F.3d 1420 (5th Cir. 1995). ................................................... 140

United States v. Lamartina, 584 F.2d 764 (6th Cir. 1978). ........................................... 101

United States v. Lanoue, 137 F.3d 656 (1st Cir. 1998). ................................................ 129

United States v. Layton, 855 F.2d 1388 (9th Cir. 1988). .............................................. 121

United States v. LeCompte, 108 F.3d 948 (8th Cir. 1997). ....................................... 66, 67

United States v. Lentz, 383 F.3d 191 (4th Cir. 2004). .................................................... 49

United States v. Lepore, 304 F. Supp. 2d 183 (D. Mass 2004). ................................ 89, 90

United States v. Levesque, 681 F.2d 75 (1st Cir. 1982). ................................................ 38

United States v. Lewis, 115 F.3d 1531 (11th Cir. 1997). ................................................ 50

United States v. Lilly, 512 F.2d 1259 (9th Cir. 1975). .................................................... 33

United States v. Link, 921 F.2d 1523 (11th Cir. 1991). ................................................ 139

United States v. Loera, 923 F.2d 727 (9th Cir. 1991). .................................................... 76

United States v. Lopez-Alvarez, 970 F.2d 583 (9th Cir. 1992). ...................... 55, 56, 122

United States v. Lowe, 145 F.3d 45 (1st Cir. 1998). ....................................................... 52

United States v. Lucio-Lucio, 347 F.3d 1202 (10th Cir. 2003). ........................ 82, 85, 90

United States v. Lutz, 420 F.2d 414 (3rd Cir. 1970)........................................................... 52

United States v. Macklin, 671 F.2d 60 (2d Cir. 1982)......................................................... 49

United States v. Maddalena, 893 F.2d 815 (6th Cir. 1990). ............................. 87, 89, 107

United States v. Malpeso, 115 F.3d 155 (2d Cir, 1997). ................................................. 116

United States v. Mandujano, 499 F.2d 370 (5th Cir. 1974)............................................... 95

United States v. Manely, 632 F.2d 978 (2d Cir. 1980). ..................................................... 95

United States v. Mapp, 170 F.3d 328 (2d Cir. 1999)................................................. Passim

United States v. Marcy, 777 F. Supp. 1393 (N.D. Ill. 1991). ......................................... 112

United States v. Marino, 277 F.3d 11 (1st Cir. 2002)................................................ Passim

United States v. Martell, 335 F.2d 764 (4th Cir. 1964). .................................................... 52

United States v. Martin, 920 F.2d 345 (6th Cir. 1990). .................................................. 112

United States v. Martinez, 16 F.3d 202 (7th Cir. 1994)..................................................... 36

United States v. Martinez, 136 F.3d 972 (4th Cir. 1998)................................................. 123

United States v. Matta-Ballesteros, 71 F.3d 754 (9th Cir. 1995)............................. Passim

United States v. McBryar, 553 F.2d 433 (5th Cir. 1997)................................................... 52

United States v. McCabe, 812 F.2d 1060 (8th Cir. 1987). ................................... 48, 49, 52

United States v. McCall, 915 F.2d 811 (2d Cir. 1990). .................................................. 137

United States v. Melton, 883 F.2d 336 (5th Cir. 1989). .................................................... 51

United States v. Merlino, 310 F.3d 137 (3rd Cir. 2002)...................................... 130, 131

United States v. Miguel, 338 F.3d 995 (9th Cir. 2003). ...................................... 29, 35, 36

United States v. Miller, 116 F.3d 641 (2d Cir. 1997). ............................................ 25, 139

United States v. Moore, 846 F.2d 1163 (8th Cir. 1988). .................................................. 67

United States v. Morales, 185 F.3d 74 (2d Cir. 1999). ................................... 6, 10, 11, 12

United States v. Morales, 881 F. Supp. 769 (D. Conn. 1995). ............................. *Passim*

United States v. Morgan, 380 F.3d 698 (2d Cir. 2004)...................................... 86

United States v. Murphy, 768 F.2d 1518 (7th Cir. 1985). ............................................ 140

United States v. Muyet, 943 F. Supp. 586 (S.D.N.Y. 1996)........................................ 134

United State v. Muyet, 994 F.Supp. 501 (S.D.N.Y. 1998). ............................... 80, 81, 104

United States v. Nelson, 66 F.3d 1036 (9th Cir. 1995)............................................ 95

United States v. Nguyen, 155 F.3d 1219 (10th Cir. 1998)........................................ 33

United States v. Noriega, 746 F. Supp. 1506 (S.D. Florida 1990).............................. 121

United States v. Nosov, 153 F. Supp. 2d 477 (S.D.N.Y. 2001)................................... 140

United States v. Orena, 32 F.3d 704 (2d Cir. 1994). ........................... 18, 24, 93, 123

United States v. Owens, 965 F. Supp. 158 (D. Mass. 1997)............................... 134, 135

United States v. Parker, 103 F.2d 857 (3d Cir. 1939)...................................... 51

United States v. Parker, 622 F.2d 298 (8th Cir. 1980)...................................... 37

United States v. Patrick, 248 F.3d 11 (1st Cir. 2000). ............................................ 10, 12

United States v. Paul, 37 F.3d 496 (9th Cir. 1994)......................................... 30

United States v. Pearson, 159 F.3d 480 (10th Cir. 1998). ........................................ 33, 35

United States v. Pearson, 203 F.3d 1243 (10th Cir. 2000). ............................................. 31

United States v. Peden, 961 F.2d 517 (5th Cir. 1992). ........................................ 55

United States v. Peneaux, 432 F.3d 882 (8th Cir. 2005). ................................................ 77

United States v. Perez, 940 F. Supp. 540 (S.D.N.Y. 1996). ................................... *Passim*

United States v. Phillips, 239 F.3d 829 (7th Cir. 2001)........................................... *Passim*

United States v. Pimentel, 346 F.3d 285 (2d Cir. 2003)......................................... *Passim*

United States v. Plummer, 221 F.3d 1298 (11th Cir. 2000). ........................................ 121

United States v. Polanco, 145 F.3d 536 (2d Cir. 1998). ........................................ *Passim*

United States v. Pungitore, 910 F.2d 1084 (3d Cir. 1990). ........................................ 125

United States v. Quintanilla, 2 F.3d 1469 (7th Cir. 1993). ........................................ 112

United States v. Rahman, 189 F.3d 188 (2d Cir. 1999). ........................................ 106, 107

United States v. Rahman, 189 F.3d 88 (2d Cir. 1999). ........................................ *Passim*

United States v. Reavis, 48 F.3d 763 (4th Cir. 1995). ........................................ 65

United States v. Redmond, 803 F.2d 438 (9th Cir. 1986). ........................................ 50

United States v. Reyes, 157 F.3d 949 (2d Cir. 1998). ........................................ 93, 105

United States v. Reyes-Castro, 13 F.3d 377 (10th Cir. 1993). ........................................ 89

United States v. Richardson, 167 F.3d 621 (D.C. Cir. 1999). ........................................ 139

United States v. Riddle, 249 F.3d 529 (6th Cir. 2001). ........................................ 13, 14

United States v. Riley, 985 F. Supp. 405 (S.D.N.Y. 1997). ........................................ 13

United States v. Roberts, 185 F.3d 1125 (10th Cir. 1999). ........................................ 38

United States v. Rodriguez-Guzman, 56 F.3d 18 (5th Cir. 1995). ........................................ 86, 89

United States v. Rogers, 89 F.3d 1326 (7th Cir. 1996). ........................................ 5, 6, 10, 12

United States v. Rolett, 151 F.3d 787 (8th Cir. 1998). ........................................ 10, 12, 93, 103

United States v. Rosa, 11 F.3d 315 (2d Cir. 1993). ........................................ 93, 134

United States v. Saavedra, 223 F.3d 85 (2d Cir. 2000). ........................................ 117, 118

United States v. Salamanca, 990 F.2d 629 (D.C. Cir. 1993). ........................................ 57

United States v. Salerno, 108 F.3d 730 (7th Cir. 1997). ........................................ 10, 138

United States v. Sans, 731 F.2d 1521 (11th Cir. 1984). ........................................ 112

United States v. Santiago, 207 F. Supp. 2d 129 (S.D.N.Y. 2002). ................................ 74

United States v. Satterfield, 743 F.2d 827 (11th Cir. 1984). ........................................ 52

United State v. Scalzritti, 578 F.2d 507 (3d Cir. 1978). ............................................. 131

Untied States v. Schmucker-Bula, 609 F.2d 399 (7th Cir. 1980). ............................... 121

United States v. Scroggins, 27 F. Cas. 999 (Circuit Court D. Ark. 1847). ..................... 57

United States v. Seegers, 445 F.2d 232 (D.C. Cir. 1971). .......................................... 101

United States v. Shaw, 701 F.2d 367 (5th Cir. 1983). ........................................... *Passim*

United States v. Shepard, 231 F.3d 56 (1st Cir. 2000). ................................................ 22

United States v. Sides, 944 F.2d 1554 (10th Cir. 1991). .............................................. 33

United States v. Smith, 13 F.3d 380 (10th Cir. 1993). ............................................... 101

United States v. Smith, 413 F.3d 1253 (10th Cir. 2005). ...................................... *Passim*

United States v. Spinelli, 352 F.3d 48 (2d Cir. 2003). ......................................... 93, 134

United States v. Stands, 105 F.3d 1565 (8th Cir. 1997). ........................................ 38, 50

United States v. Stantini, 85 F.3d 9 (2d Cir. 1996). ..................................................... 43

United States v. Stone, 472 F.2d 909 (5th Cir. 1973). ................................................. 58

United States v. Sturgis, 48 F.3d 784 (4th Cir. 1995). ................................................. 67

United States v. Thai, 29 F.3d 785 (2d Cir. 1994). ............................... 74, 102, 106, 111

United States v. Thomas, 34 F.3d 44 (2d Cir. 1994). ............................... 29, 33, 34, 35

United States v. Tipton, 90 F.3d 861 (4th Cir. 1996). ............................ 10, 102, 106, 139

United States v. Tokars, 95 F.3d 1520 (11th Cir. 1996). .............................................. 55

United States v. Tolliver, 61 F.3d 1189 (5th Cir. 1995). ........................... 18, 25, 46, 136

United States v. Torcasio, 959 F.2d 503 (4th Cir. 1992). ........................................... 112

United States v. Torres, 129 F.3d 710 (2d Cir. 1997). ................................................. 13

United States v. Torres, 162 F.3d 6 (1st Cir. 1998). ................................................ 65

United States v. Turcks, 41 F.3d 893 (3d Cir. 1994). .............................................. 114

United States v. Turkette, 452 U.S. 576 (1981). ........................................ 10, 12, 17, 117

United States v. Turley, 352 U.S. 407 (1957). ........................................................ 68

United States v. Two Eagle, 318 F.3d 785 (8th Cir. 2003). ...................................... 77

United States v. Uselton, 927 F.2d 905 (6th Cir. 1991). ......................................... 129

United States v. Vargas-Duran, 356 F.3d 598 (5th Cir. 2004). .......................... 86, 87

United States v. Vasquez, 267 F.3d 79 (2d Cir. 2001). ...................................... *Passim*

United States v. Vasquez-Velasco, 15 F.3d 833 (9th Cir. 1994). ....................... *Passim*

United States v. Velazquez, 100 F.3d 418 (5th Cir. 1996). ...................................... 86

United State v. Velazquez-Overa, 100 F.3d 418 (5th Cir. 1996). ............................ 89

United States v. Vickers, 578 F.2d 1057 (5th Cir. 1978). ........................................ 52

United States v. Viola, 35 F.3d 34 (2d Cir. 1994). ................................................. 112

United States v. Walker, 137 F.3d 1217 (10th Cir. 1998). ....................................... 48

United States v. Walker, 524 F.2d 1125 (10th Cir. 1975). ....................................... 52

United States v. Warren, 984 F.2d 325 (9th Cir. 1993). .......................................... 38

United States v. Webster, 620 F.2d 640 (7th Cir. 1980). ......................................... 75

United States v. Wei, 862 F. Supp. 1129 (S.D.N.Y. 1994). ....................... 18, 126, 141

United States v. Welch, 10 F.3d 573 (8th Cir. 1993). .............................................. 50

United States v. Williams, 155 F.3d 418 (4th Cir. 1998). ...................................... 127

United States v. Williams, 181 F. Supp. 2d 267 (S.D.N.Y. 2001). ............. 117, 128, 134

United States v. Williams, 342 F.3d 350 (4th Cir. 2003). ............................. 33, 34, 36

United States v. Williams, 342 U.S. 350 (4th Cir. 2003). ................................................. 30

United States v. Williams, 998 F.2d 258 (5th Cir. 1993). .................................................. 51

United States v. Wills, 346 F.3d 476 (4th Cir. 2003). ........................................................ 51

United States v. Wilson, 116 F.3d 1066 (5th Cir. 1997). ........................................... *Passim*

United States v. Wolford, 444 F.2d 876 (D.C. Cir. 1971). ................................................ 51

United States v. Wong, 40 F.3d 1347 (2d Cir. 1994). ........................................................ 43

United States v. Wright-Barker, 784 F.2d 161 (3rd Cir. 1986). ...................................... 121

United States v. Yeaman, 194 F.3d 442 (3d Cir. 1999). ................................................... 131

United States v. Young, 248 F.3d 260 (4th Cir. 2001). ..................................................... 50

United States v. Young, 512 F.2d 321 (4th Cir. 1975). ..................................................... 52

United States v. Yousef, 327 F.3d 56 (2d Cir. 2003). ............................................... 120, 121

Zaidi v. Ashcroft, 374 F.3d 357 (5th Cir. 2004). .......................................................... 86, 88

## STATE CASES

Commonwealth v. Farrell, 78 N.E.2d 697 (Mass. 1948). ................................................. 60

Commonwealth v. Hogan, 387 N.E.2d 158 (Mass. App. Ct. 1979). ........................... 60, 61

Commonwealth v. Slaney, 185 N.E.2d 919 (1962). .......................................................... 69

Commonwealth v. Tucceri, 399 N.E.2d 1110 (Mass. App. Ct. 1980). ............................. 60

Dahlin v. Fraser, 288 N.W. 851 (Minn. 1939). ................................................................. 69

Goodman v. Superior Court, 148 Cal. Rptr. 799 (Cal. Ct. App. 1978). ........................... 59

Halligan v. State, 375 N.E.2d 1151 (Ind. App. 1978). ...................................................... 69

Kirby v. State, 272 N.W.2d 113 (Wisc. Ct. App. 1979). ................................................... 61

Matter of Andre O, 182 A.D.2d 1108 (4th Dept. 1992). ................................................... 80

People v. Askerneese, 93 N.Y.2d 884 (1999). ................................................................... 79

People v. Bouldin, 40 A.D.2d 1045 (3d Dept. 1972)..................................................... 71

People v. Carter, 53 N.Y.2d 113 (1981). ..................................................................... 70

People v. Castillo, 199 A.D.2d 276 (2d Dept. 1993). ................................................... 80

People v. Cwikla, 46 N.Y.2d 434 (1979)...................................................................... 70

People v. Foster, 278 A.D.2d 241 (2d Dept. 2000)................................................. 79, 80

People v. Galvin, 65 N.Y.2d 761 (1985). ..................................................................... 70

People v. Gill, 228 A.D.2d 240 (1st Dept. 1996).......................................................... 80

People v. Green, 111 A.D.2d 183 (2d Dept. 1985)....................................................... 80

People v. Jason, 75 N.Y.2d 638 (1990). ....................................................................... 79

People v. Johnson, 284 N.W.2d 718 (Mich. 1979)................................................. 68, 69

People v. Mack, 268 A.D.2d 599 (2d Dept. 2000). ...................................................... 80

People v. Martinez, 257 A.D.2d 667 (2d Dept. 1999).................................................. 80

People v. Newble, 174 Cal. Rptr. 637 (Cal. Ct. App. 1981)......................................... 59

People v. Nunes, 190 P. 486 (Cal. App. 1920). ............................................................ 59

People v. Ozarowski, 38 N.Y.2d 481 (1976)................................................................ 70

People v. Page, 163 Cal. Rptr. 839 (Cal. Ct. App. 1980). ............................................ 59

People v. Robles, 173 A.D.2d 337 (1st Dept. 1991)..................................................... 80

People v. Rojas, 61 N.Y.2d 726.................................................................................... 81

People v. Rumaner, 45 A.D.2d 290 (3d Dept. 1974).............................................. 70, 71

People v. Su, 239 A.D.2d 703 (3d Dept. 1997). ........................................................... 80

State v. Collins, 311 S.E.2d 350 (N.C. App. 1984). ..................................................... 68

State v. Smith, 309 N.W.2d 454 (Iowa 1981)............................................................... 68

State v. Williams, 484 A.2d 331 (N.J. Super. Ct. App. Div. 1984).................................. 64

I.  **INTRODUCTION AND OVERVIEW**

A.  **Introduction**

In 1984, Congress enacted the Comprehensive Crime Control Act of 1984, Pub. L. No. 98-473, Ch. X, Part A (Oct. 12, 1984), which added, inter alia, a new offense, Violent Crimes in Aid of Racketeering Activity.[1] This offense, initially codified as 18 U.S.C. § 1952B, was renumbered in 1988 as 18 U.S.C. § 1959, without any substantive change.[2]

Section 1959 makes it a crime to commit any of a list of violent crimes in return for anything of pecuniary value from an enterprise engaged in racketeering activity, or for the purpose of joining, remaining with, or increasing a position in such an enterprise. The listed violent crimes are murder, kidnapping, maiming, assault with a dangerous weapon, assault resulting in serious bodily injury, and threatening to commit a "crime of violence," as defined in 18 U.S.C. § 16. The listed crimes may be violations of State or Federal law. In addition, attempts and conspiracies to commit the listed crimes are covered. The maximum penalty varies with the particular violent crime involved, ranging from a fine and/or three years imprisonment up to a fine and/or life imprisonment, except for any murder occurring on or after September 13, 1994, which murder would be subject to the death penalty.

---

[1] See S. Rep. No. 225, 98th Cong., 1st Sess. 304-307 (1983) (hereinafter "S. Rep. No. 98-225"), reprinted in 1984 U.S. Code Cong. & Admin. News (U.S. C.C.A.N.) 3182, 3483-3487, and excerpts of this report are included at Appendix A. At the same time, Congress enacted the Murder-for-Hire statute codified at 18 U.S.C. § 1952A and later renumbered as 18 U.S.C. § 1958. Id. Section 1958 makes it a crime to travel or use facilities in interstate or foreign commerce with intent that a murder in violation of state or federal law be committed for money or other pecuniary compensation. This Manual does not address Section 1958. Questions regarding the Murder-for-Hire statute should be directed to the Domestic Security Section of the Criminal Division.

[2] See Stantini v. United States, 268 F. Supp. 2d 168, 180 (E.D.N.Y. 2003); Pub. L. 100-690, Title VII, § 7053(b), Nov. 18, 1988, 102 Stat. 4402.

For any murder occurring on or after September 13, 1994, the prosecutor must comply with the Department's death penalty protocol. See USAM 9-10.000.

**B.      Prior Approval by the Organized Crime and Racketeering Section Is Required**

**1.      Approval Authority**

The Code of Federal Regulations, 28 C.F.R. § 0.55 provides that the "coordination of enforcement activities directed against organized crime and racketeering" "are assigned to and shall be conducted, handled, or supervised by the Assistant Attorney General, Criminal Division." Pursuant to that grant of authority, the authority to approve prosecutions under 18 U.S.C. § 1959 has been delegated to the Organized Crime and Racketeering Section. See USAM 9-110.800 through 816, which are included at Appendix B.

Accordingly, no criminal prosecution under Section 1959, including a charge of Accessory After the Fact to a Section 1959 violation, shall be initiated by indictment, complaint or information without the prior approval of the Organized Crime and Racketeering Section (OCRS). All requests for approval must be submitted at least 15 business days in advance and must be accompanied by a detailed prosecution memorandum and final proposed indictment. See USAM 9-110.801.

Because Section 1959 reaches conduct within state and local jurisdictions, there is, absent compelling circumstances, a need to avoid encroaching on state and local law enforcement authority. Moreover, Section 1959 complements the Racketeering Influenced and Corrupt Organizations Act ("RICO"), 18 U.S.C. §§ 1961-1968, and adopts RICO provisions, such as the existence of an "enterprise" and the definition of "racketeering activity." It is important to maintain consistent applications and interpretations of the elements of RICO. All proposed prosecutions under Section 1959 therefore must be submitted to OCRS for approval in accordance with the following guidelines.

The review process for authorization of prosecutions under Section 1959 is similar to that for RICO prosecutions under 18 U.S.C. §§ 1961 to 1968.  See USAM 9-110.200, et seq.  To commence the formal review process, submit a final draft of the proposed indictment and a detailed prosecution memorandum to OCRS.  The prosecution memorandum should be similar, in organization and types of information provided, to a RICO prosecution memorandum, which is described in the Criminal Resource Manual at section 2071 et seq.  Before the formal review process begins, prosecuting attorneys are encouraged to consult with OCRS in order to obtain preliminary guidance and suggestions.

The review process can be time-consuming, especially in cases where the death penalty may apply, because of the likelihood that modifications will be made to the indictment and because of the heavy workload of the reviewing attorneys.  Therefore, unless extraordinary circumstances justify a shorter time frame, a period of at least 15 working days must be allowed for the review process.

**2.     Guidelines for Section 1959 Prosecutions**

In deciding whether to approve a prosecution under Section 1959, OCRS will analyze the prosecution memorandum and proposed indictment to determine whether there is a legitimate reason the offense cannot or should not be prosecuted by state or local authorities.  For example, federal prosecution may be appropriate where local authorities do not have the resources to prosecute, where local authorities are reasonably believed to be corrupt, where local authorities have requested federal participation, or where the offense involves an enterprise operating in more than one state or is closely related to a federal investigation or prosecution.  A prosecution will not be authorized over the objection of local authorities in the absence of a compelling reason.  Accordingly, every prosecution memorandum must state the views of local authorities with respect to the proposed prosecution, or the reasons for not soliciting their views.

Section 1959 was enacted to combat "contract murders and other violent crimes by organized crime figures." See S.Rep. No. 98-225 at 304-307. The statutory language is extremely broad in that it covers not only murder, but also conduct such as a threat to commit an assault, or other crime of violence, and other relatively minor conduct normally prosecuted by local authorities. Thus, although the involvement of traditional organized crime will not be a requirement for approval of proposed prosecutions, a prosecution will not be authorized unless the violent crimes involved are substantial because of the seriousness of injuries, the number of incidents, or other aggravating factors.

The statutory definition of "enterprise" also is very broad; it is essentially the same as the definition of "enterprise" in the RICO statute, 18 U.S.C. § 1961(4). No prosecution under section 1959 will be approved unless the enterprise has some degree of ongoing organization and either involves, or poses a reasonable threat of, ongoing unlawful conduct and otherwise meets the standards for a RICO enterprise.

### 3. Prosecution Memorandum

As noted above, every request for approval of a proposed prosecution under section 1959 must be accompanied by a final draft of a proposed indictment and by a thorough prosecution memorandum. The prosecution memorandum should generally conform to the standards outlined for RICO prosecutions. See USAM 9-110.400. The memorandum must contain a concise summary of the facts and a statement of the admissible evidentiary basis for each count against each defendant, a statement of the applicable law, a discussion of anticipated defenses and unusual legal issues (federal, and where applicable, state), and a statement of justification for using Section 1959. It is especially important that the memorandum include a discussion of the nexus between the enterprise and the crime of violence, the defendant's relationship to the enterprise, and the evidentiary basis for each Section 1959 count. Submission of a thorough memorandum is particularly important because of the complexity of the issues involved and the statute's similarity to RICO.

### 4. Post-Indictment Duties

Once the indictment or information has been approved and filed, it is the duty of the prosecuting attorney to submit to OCRS a copy of the indictment or information bearing the seal of the clerk of the court. In addition, the prosecuting attorney should keep OCRS informed of any adverse decision regarding Section 1959 and unusual legal problems that arise in the course of the case, so those problems can be considered in providing guidance to prosecutors.

### C. Legislative History Of Section 1959 and Its Relationship To RICO

Congress designed Section 1959 to supplement RICO and hence Section 1959 may be used in addition to RICO.[3] In that respect, the Senate Report to Section 1959 states, in relevant part:

> With respect to [Section 1959], the Committee concluded that the need for Federal jurisdiction is clear, in view of the Federal Government's strong interest, as recognized in existing statutes, in suppressing the activities of organized criminal enterprises, and the fact that the FBI's experience and network of informants and intelligence with respect to such enterprises will often facilitate a successful Federal investigation where local authorities might be stymied. Here again, however, the Committee does not intend that all such offenses should be prosecuted federally. Murder, kidnapping, and assault also violate State law and the States will still have an important role to play in many such cases that are committed as an integral part of an organized crime operation.

---

[3] See, e.g., United State v. Kehoe, 310 F.3d 579, 588 (8th Cir. 2002); United States v. Mapp, 170 F.3d 328, 335 (2d Cir. 1999); United States v. Rogers, 89 F.3d 1326, 1335 (7th Cir. 1996); United States v. Concepcion, 983 F.2d 369, 380 (2d Cir. 1992); United States v. Perez, 940 F. Supp. 540, 544 (S.D.N.Y. 1996); United States v. Morales, 881 F. Supp. 769, 770 (D. Conn. 1995). Frequently, RICO and Section 1959 charges are brought in the same indictment regarding the same or overlapping conduct.

S. Rep. No. 98-225 at 305.

There are substantial similarities between RICO and Section 1959. For example, Section 1959 defines "enterprise" essentially the same as "enterprise" is defined under RICO, 18 U.S.C. § 1961(4).[4] The only differences are that Section 1959's definition of enterprise includes a required nexus to interstate commerce (see supra n. 4), whereas RICO requires the same nexus to interstate commerce in its definition of the proscribed unlawful conduct, and RICO's definition of enterprise includes "an individual," whereas Section 1959's does not. See 18 U.S.C. § 1962(b) and (c). However, these differences are immaterial. The Senate Report to Section 1959 states that "[t]he Committee intends that the term enterprise here have the same scope" as the term enterprise under RICO. S. Rep. No. 98-225 at 307. Moreover, courts have repeatedly held that the elements of "enterprise" and the interstate nexus requirement under RICO have the same meaning as these elements under Section 1959 and that, therefore, the body of law under RICO regarding "enterprise" and the interstate nexus requirement also applies to determining the scope of those elements under Section 1959.[5]

Similarly, Section 1959(b) provides:

"As used in this section - (1) 'racketeering activity' has the meaning set forth in section 1961 of this title [i.e., RICO]."

Therefore, the body of law under RICO regarding "racketeering activity" may be used to determine

---

[4] 18 U.S.C. § 1959(b)(2) provides: "'Enterprise' includes any partnership, corporation, association, or other legal entity, and any union or group of individuals associated in fact although not a legal entity, which is engaged in, or the activities of which affect, interstate or foreign commerce."

[5] See, e.g., United States v. Phillips, 239 F.3d 829, 843 (7th Cir. 2001); United States v. Morales, 185 F.3d 74, 80 (2d Cir. 1999); Rogers, 89 F.3d at 1335; United States v. Fiel, 35 F.3d 997, 1003 (4th Cir. 1994); Concepcion, 983 F.2d at 380-81; Perez, 940 F. Supp. at 544-45; Morales, 881 F. Supp. at 770-71 and n. 3; United States v. King, 850 F. Supp. 750, 751 (C.D. Ill. 1994).

the meaning of racketeering activity under Section 1959.[6]  However, unlike RICO, Section 1959 does not require proof of a pattern of racketeering activity.  See infra Section II (D).

### D. Liberal Construction Rule

As is the case with RICO, courts have ruled that Section 1959 should "be construed liberally in order to effectuate its remedial purposes." Mapp, 170 F.3d at 335; Concepcion, 983 F.2d at 381; Morales, 881 F. Supp. at 771.

## II. ELEMENTS OF SECTION 1959 OFFENSES

### A. Overview of Elements and Mens Rea

Section 1959 provides, in relevant part, as follows:

§ 1959. Violent crimes in aid of racketeering activity

(a) Whoever, as consideration for the receipt of, or as consideration for a promise or agreement to pay, anything of pecuniary value from an enterprise engaged in racketeering activity, or for the purpose of gaining entrance to or maintaining or increasing position in an enterprise engaged in racketeering activity, murders, kidnaps, maims, assaults with a dangerous weapon, commits assault resulting in serious bodily injury upon, or threatens to commit a crime of violence against any individual in violation of the laws of any State or the United States, or attempts or conspires so to do, shall be punished --

\* \* \*

(b) As used in this section --

>(1) "racketeering activity" has the meaning set forth in section 1961 of this title; and

>(2) "enterprise" includes any partnership, corporation, association, or other legal entity, and any union or group of individuals associated in fact although not a legal entity, which is engaged in, or the activities of which affect, interstate or foreign commerce.

To establish a completed substantive violation of Section 1959, the United States must prove

---

[6] See, e.g., Kehoe, 310 F.3d at 588; United States v. Feliciano, 223 F.3d 102, 113 (2d Cir. 2000); United States v. Mapp, 170 F.3d 328, 335 (2d Cir. 1999).

all of the following elements beyond a reasonable doubt.

1. The existence of an "enterprise" as defined in 18 U.S.C. § 1959(b)(2).

2. The charged enterprise engaged in, or its activities affected, interstate or foreign commerce.

3. The charged enterprise engaged in "racketeering activity" as defined in 18 U.S.C. §§ 1959(b)(1) and 1961(1).

4. The defendant committed one of the following crimes:

    a. murder
    b. kidnapping
    c. maiming
    d. assault with a dangerous weapon
    e. assault resulting in serious bodily injury upon any individual, **or**
    f. threatens to commit a crime of violence against any individual[7],

    which offense was in violation of the laws of any state[8], or the United States.

5. Such underlying crime of violence was committed either:

    a. as consideration for the receipt of, or as consideration for a promise or agreement to pay, anything of pecuniary value from the charged enterprise, **or**,
    b. for the purpose of gaining entrance to or maintaining or increasing position in the charged enterprise.[9]

---

[7] Hereinafter, these offenses will be referred to as a Section 1959 predicate offense, or underlying crime of violence.

[8] By a 1990 amendment to the Murder-for-Hire statute, 18 U.S.C. § 1958, Congress defined "State" for purposes of Sections 1958 and 1959 to include a state of the United States, the District of Columbia, and any commonwealth, territory, or possession of the United States. 18 U.S.C. § 1958 (b)(3).

[9] For cases setting forth these elements, see United States v. Smith, 413 F.3d 1253, 1277 (10th Cir. 2005); United States v. Frampton, 382 F.3d 213, 220 (2d Cir. 2004); United States v. Crenshaw, 359 F.3d 977, 991 (8th Cir. 2004); United States v. Phillips, 239 F.3d 829, 845 (7th Cir. 2001); United States v. Rahman, 189 F.3d 88, 126 (2d Cir. 1999); United States v. Polanco, 145 F.3d 536, 539-40 (2d Cir. 1998); United States v. Wilson, 116 F.3d 1066, 1075 (5th Cir. 1997); United States v. Houlihan, 92 F.3d 1271, 1293 (1st Cir. 1996); United States v. Bracy, 67 F.3d 1421, 1429 (9th Cir. 1995); United States v. Vasquez-Velasco, 15 F.3d 833, 842 (9th Cir. 1994); United States
(continued...)

Attempts and conspiracies to commit any of the Section 1959 predicate offenses are also proscribed by Section 1959. See infra Section II (L). Moreover, in addition to liability as a principal, liability may be based upon aiding and abetting, accessory after the fact and Pinkerton. See infra Section III.

The mens rea element of Section 1959 is commonly referred to as the purpose element; that is, that the Section 1959 predicate crime was committed for the purpose of **either** the receipt of, or as consideration for a promise or an agreement to pay, anything of pecuniary value, **or** "for the purpose of gaining entrance to or maintaining or increasing position in an enterprise."[10] The defendant must also act with the intent required by the Section 1959 predicate offense.[11]

It is particularly significant that Section 1959 does not enumerate violations of specific federal or state statutes that constitute the underlying crimes of violence. Rather, Section 1959 identifies "generically" the types of proscribed underlying predicate offenses. Section II (E) below explains how to determine whether a particular state or federal offense falls within the "generic" definition of the crimes of violence referenced in Section 1959. Likewise, Sections II (B) through (M) below explain all the elements of Section 1959 offenses.

**B.     The Existence of An Enterprise**

Unquestionably, proving the existence of an "enterprise" is central to proving a Section 1959 charge. As stated above in Section I (C), the term "enterprise" under Section 1959 has the same

---

[9](...continued)
v. Concepcion, 983 F.2d 369, 380-81 (2d Cir. 1992); United States v. Cuong Gia Le, 310 F. Supp. 2d 763, 778 (E.D.Va. 2004).

[10] See, e.g., Frampton, 382 F.3d at 220-21; Concepcion, 983 F.2d at 381.

[11] See, e.g., Mapp, 170 F.3d at 335-36; Houlihan, 92 F.3d at 1293; Concepcion, 983 F.2d at 381-82.

meaning as the term "enterprise" under RICO. Therefore, consult the body of law regarding "enterprise" under RICO, including Chapters II (D) and III (C) of OCRS' Racketeer Influenced and Corrupt Organizations: A Manual for Federal Prosecutors (4th ed. July 2000), (hereinafter "RICO Manual").[12]

Thus far, all the Section 1959 charges brought by the United States involve an enterprise consisting of a group of individuals associated in fact. The existence of such an association-in-fact enterprise is proven "by evidence of an ongoing organization, formal or informal, and by evidence that the various associates function as a continuing unit." United States v. Turkette, 452 U.S. 576, 583 (1981). The federal circuit courts have adopted somewhat different approaches on the proof required to establish such an association in fact enterprise. See OCRS' RICO Manual at pp. 47-61. Therefore, a prosecutor needs to carefully follow the law on this issue in his/her particular circuit and consult with the RICO Unit of OCRS.[13]

The Eighth Circuit employs the strictest test for determining the existence of an enterprise under Section 1959, as it does under RICO. For example, in Crenshaw, the Eighth Circuit followed its RICO precedent in United States v. Bledsoe, 674 F. 2d 647, 664 (8th Cir. 1982), and "identified three characteristics which an enterprise must have: a common purpose shared by the individual

---

[12] Available at www.usdoj.gov/usao/eousa/foia_reading_room/usam/title9/rico.pdf. OCRS plans to issue its fifth revised edition of its RICO Manual in 2007.

[13] For cases discussing the enterprise element under Section 1959, see Crenshaw, 359 F.3d at 991-92; United States v. Patrick, 248 F. 3d 11, 17-19 (1st Cir. 2000); Phillips, 239 F. 3d at 842-44; United States v. Morales 185 F. 3d 74, 80-82 (2d Cir. 1999); United States v. Rolett, 151 F. 3d 787, 790-91 (8th Cir. 1998); United States v. Gray, 137 F. 3d 765, 772-73 (4th Cir. 1998); United States v. Salerno, 108 F. 3d 730, 738-740 (7th Cir. 1997); United States v. Tipton, 90 F. 3d 861, 887-88 (4th Cir. 1996); United States v. Rogers, 89 F. 3d 1326, 1335-38 (7th Cir. 1996); United States v. Bracy, 67 F. 3d 1421, 1429-30 (9th Cir. 1995); United States v. Fiel, 35 F. 3d 997, 1003-04 (4th Cir. 1994).

associates; some continuity of structure and personnel; and [ascertainable] structure distinct and separate from that inherent in the racketeering activity alleged." Crenshaw, 359 F.3d at 991. In Crenshaw, the Eighth Circuit concluded that a "gang," known as the Rolling 60's Crips, satisfied these requirements for an enterprise, noting that "[t]here was a hierarchy of members, ranging from the senior 'OG's' or 'Inner Circle,' down through the 'little homeys' or 'shorties'. . . . . Members were subject to rules" they held regular meetings to discuss business and members had coded gang names. 359 F.3d at 991. The court added that:

> There is overwhelming evidence that the Rolling 60's Crips had continuity of leadership and membership, that the members shared a common purpose of selling drugs, and that they engaged in mutual defense and in collateral instructional, organizational, and social activities to support the gang's business and its continued existence. There was abundant proof that there was an "enterprise" in this case.

Crenshaw, 359 F. 3d at 992.[14]

Other courts continue to criticize the Eighth Circuit's enterprise test as being too stringent. See, e.g., Rogers, 89 F. 3d at 1337 ("[I]t would be nonsensical to require proof that an enterprise had purposes or goals separate and apart from the pattern of racketeering activity. . . . . The continuity of an informal enterprise and the differentiation among roles can provide the requisite 'structure'

---

[14] Other courts have likewise held that similar "gangs" constitute an enterprise under Section 1959. See, e.g., Phillips, 239 F. 3d at 843-44 ("Dawg Life", a street gang engaged in drug trafficking); Fiel, 35 F. 3d at 1003-04 (Fates Northern Virginia Chapter of a motorcycle club). Cf. Gray, 137 F. 3d at 772 (a drug distribution ring). But see United States v. Morales, 185 F. 3d 74, 80-82 (2d Cir. 1999), where the court found insufficient evidence to prove the existence of an ongoing organization ("the Park Avenue Boys") allegedly lasting from 1987 to 1996 when there was a seven-year hiatus in criminal activity during the defendants' incarceration from 1988 to 1995. The government argued that the defendants' rapid resumption of armed robberies after their release from prison, that were very similar to their armed robberies before their incarcerations, "showed that they had a continuing understanding during their incarceration that they would resume their criminal activities after leaving prison." 185 F. 3d at 80. The court rejected these arguments, stating that "[t]he government did not present sufficient evidence to show that the enterprise continued during the seven-year period that the defendants were incarcerated." 185 F. 3d at 81.

to prove the element of 'enterprise.'"); Patrick, 248 F. 3d at 17-18 (rejecting an instruction based on Bledsoe that the enterprise must have an "ascertainable structure" separate from the pattern of racketeering activity, stating that "[w]e today explicitly reject the Bledsoe test as an additional requirement beyond the Turkette instruction. Indeed, we think the defendants' proposed Bledsoe instruction could be misleading").[15]

It is particularly significant to note that it is not necessary to prove that the defendant is a member of the charged enterprise. See Rolett, 151 F. 3d at 790. Rather, a defendant may be a complete outsider who was hired by the enterprise to commit an underlying crime of violence, or who committed an underlying crime of violence for the purpose of assisting another person to gain entrance to or maintain or increase his position in the charged enterprise. See infra Sections II (M) and III (A).

**C. The Enterprise Engaged in, or Its Activities Affected, Interstate or Foreign Commerce**

As stated above in Section I (C), the body of law regarding the requisite interstate commerce nexus under RICO may be used to determine the required interstate commerce nexus under Section 1959.[16] As is the case under RICO, it is not required to prove that each racketeering act or all the

---

[15] OCRS agrees with the criticism that the Eighth Circuit's requirement that the enterprise must have an ascertainable structure distinct from that inherent in the conduct of a pattern of racketeering is too restrictive and exceeds the requirements for proving an enterprise imposed by the Supreme Court in United States v. Turkette, 452 U.S. 576, 583 (1981). See OCRS' RICO Manual at pp. 59-60.

[16] Therefore, consult OCRS' RICO Manual at pp. 126-131 regarding the requisite interstate nexus under RICO.

racketeering activity affects interstate or foreign commerce. Rather, it is the "enterprise" that must be "engaged in, or the activities of which affect, interstate or foreign commerce." 18 U.S.C. § 1959(b)(2). However, the underlying racketeering activity **may** supply the requisite interstate commerce nexus since such activity constitutes "the activities" of the enterprise within the meaning of 18 U.S.C. § 1959(b)(2).[17]

Moreover, consistent with RICO case law, courts have held that only a de minimis effect on interstate or foreign commerce is required in each particular case, and have rejected challenges that Section 1959 exceeds Congress' authority under the Commerce Clause.[18] Accordingly, courts have found the requisite effect on interstate or foreign commerce in a wide variety of circumstances.[19]

---

[17] See, e.g., United States v. Fernandez, 388 F. 3d 1199, 1249-50 (9th Cir. 2004); Crenshaw, 359 F. 3d at 992; United States v. Riddle, 249 F. 3d 529, 537-38 (6th Cir. 2001); United States v. Gray, 137 F. 3d 765, 772-73 (4th Cir. 1998); United States v. Garcia, 68 F. Supp. 2d 802, 809 (E.D. Mich. 1999).

[18] See e.g., Crenshaw, 359 F. 3d at 983-87; Tse v. United States, 290 F. 3d 462, 465-66 (1st Cir. 2002); United States v. Marino, 277 F. 3d 11, 34-35 (1st Cir. 2002); United States v. Vasquez, 267 F. 3d 79, 86-89 (2d Cir. 2001); Riddle, 249 F. 3d at 535-38; United States v. Feliciano, 223 F. 3d 102, 117-19 (2d Cir. 2000); United States v. Torres, 129 F. 3d 710, 713, 717 (2d Cir. 1997). But cf. United States v. Riley, 985 F. Supp. 405, 406-410 (S.D.N.Y. 1997) (rejecting Commerce Clause challenge to Section 1959 because Section 1959 regulates activity that substantially affects interstate commerce); United States v. Perez, 940 F. Supp. 540, 543-46 (S.D.N.Y. 1996) (same).

[19] See, e.g., Crenshaw, 359 F. 3d at 992 ("evidence that the cocaine the Rolling 60's [the enterprise] sold in St. Paul [Minnesota], up to ten kilos per month, came from Louisiana and California"); Vasquez, 267 F. 3d at 86-89 ("either heroin or cocaine trafficking necessarily involves foreign commerce, because the raw materials for these substances originate outside the United States"); Riddle, 249 F. 3d at 537 ("The Ohio-based enterprise [the Strollo] branch of the LCN in Youngstown, Ohio here purchased Pennsylvania lottery tickets to protect against losses in the illegal gambling business; the members sold in Pennsylvania a ring taken from the Youngstown murder victim Biondillo; the enterprise extorted money from a victim who sold fireworks in New York; and the government alleged that the Pittsburgh Mafia family was involved in the enterprise (although all of those charged were Ohio residents)"); Feliciano, 223 F. 3d at 117-19 (the enterprise sold cocaine, crack cocaine and heroin); Gray, 137 F. 3d at 772-73 (evidence that **either** the enterprise
(continued...)

However, in United States v. Garcia, 68 F. Supp. 2d 802, 809-13 (E.D.Mich. 1999), the district court held pre-trial that the application of Section 1959 to a local murder committed by an enterprise, a street gang known as the Cash Flow Posse, that did not substantially affect interstate commerce exceeded Congress' power under the Commerce Clause. In that respect, the district court stated:

> In this case, the enterprise's connection to interstate commerce is weak. The Government merely alleges that some of its members drove within the state on an interstate highway in order to commit acts of murder. It also alleges that the gun used in connection with [the § 1959 murder] may have crossed state lines. Members of the gang are alleged to have purchased a gun at a trade center with out-of-state customers. There is evidence that one gang member heard from a cellmate that a law enforcement officer had alluded to the possibility of Cash Flow Posse "cells" existing in other states. Finally, two gang members, in their plea colloquies, acknowledged discussing with outside parties law enforcement initiatives against the Cash Flow Posse, while on a trip to Mexico. There is no evidence that the activities of the Cash Flow Posse, brutish and tyrannical as they may have been, substantially affected interstate commerce, nor that the aggregate of these tenuous commerce connections can be defined in any meaningful way as substantial.

Garcia, 68 F. Supp. 2d at 811-12.

Garcia graphically illustrates the difficulty in satisfying the requisite effect on interstate commerce when the enterprise is a local street gang that is not directly involved in economic activities. In similar cases, it is essential for prosecutors to develop stronger evidence that the charged enterprise was either engaged in, or its activities affected, interstate or foreign commerce. Although OCRS disagrees with much of the district court's legal analysis regarding Congress' Commerce Clause power, OCRS will examine more closely the interstate commerce nexus in

---

[19](...continued)
dealt in heroin **or** the murder victim was a heroin user who had robbed one of the enterprise's stash houses that contained heroin was sufficient ); Tse v. United States, 112 F. Supp. 2d 189, 195 (D.Mass. 2000), (the Ping On Gang, the enterprise, "was an international organization involved in extortion, prostitution, illegal interstate gambling and the smuggling of illegal aliens into the United States"), aff'd in part and vacated in part on other grounds, 290 F. 3d 462 (1st Cir. 2002).

proposed Section 1959 and RICO prosecutions where the enterprise is a street gang or similar association-in-fact enterprise that mainly engages in local, violent conduct, with little, if any, nexus to interstate commercial/economic activities.[20]

### D. The Enterprise Engaged in Racketeering Activity

Section 1959 explicitly requires proof that the "enterprise engaged in racketeering activity" and provides that "racketeering activity" has the same meaning as set forth under RICO. See supra Section I (C). Significantly, Section 1959, unlike RICO, does not by its explicit terms require that a defendant commit a "pattern of racketeering activity." Compare 18 U.S.C. § 1959(b) with 18 U.S.C. §§ 1961(5) and 1962. Therefore, courts have held that to establish a Section 1959 violation, it is not necessary to prove that any defendant committed a pattern of racketeering activity or that any alleged racketeering activity satisfies the "continuity plus relationship" test set forth in Sedima, S.P.R.L. v. Imrex Co., 473 U.S. 479 n. 14 (1985) and its progeny.[21] Rather, Section 1959 requires evidence that "the enterprise" "engaged in racketeering activity." Therefore, there must be some nexus between the enterprise and the racketeering activity to conclude that the charged enterprise "engaged in racketeering activity." That an enterprise consisting of a group of individuals associated in fact "engaged in racketeering activity" may be established by evidence that individual members committed racketeering activity "for the group and/or in concert with other members, or acted in ways that contributed to [or furthered] the purposes of the group, or that were facilitated or

---

[20] Upon request, OCRS will supply prosecutors with extensive memoranda regarding Congress' Commerce Clause authority that demonstrate that the district court in Garcia misapplied the Supreme Court's Commerce Clause jurisprudence. Nevertheless, the factual basis for the effect on interstate commerce in Garcia was very weak, and the trial court may have reached the correct result, albeit under erroneous legal reasoning.

[21] See, e.g., Bracy, 67 F.3d at 1430; United States v. Garfinkle, 842 F. Supp. 1284, 1291-92 & n. 1 (D. Nev. 1993).

made possible by the group." United States v. Feliciano, 223 F.3d 102, 116-117 (2d Cir. 2000). Accord United States v. Pimentel, 346 F.3d 285, 297 (2d Cir. 2003) (same); United States v. Phillips, 239 F.3d 829, 845 (7th Cir. 2001) (sufficient that "the shooting was the type of behavior encouraged and demanded of members of [the enterprise]"); Gray, 137 F.3d at 773 ("[T]he evidence that the enterprise dealt in drugs would likewise be sufficient to support a jury finding that the enterprise engaged in racketeering"); Fiel, 35 F. 3d at 1004 (sufficient that the enterprise, a group of individuals who were members of a motorcycle club, facilitated drug dealing).[22]

Moreover, it is not settled whether a substantive violation of Section 1959 requires proof of more than one racketeering act. Some courts have held that at least one of the charged racketeering activities is sufficient.[23] Whereas the court in United States v. Cutolo, 861 F. Supp. 1142, 1146 (E.D.N.Y. 1994), stated:

> Presumably § 1959 does not apply where such persons committed only a single crime. The word "engaged" implies more than that. But this court need not decide [pre-trial] how extensive the criminal activity must be before the enterprise may be said to "engage" in racketeering.

OCRS likewise does not think that it is necessary to delineate precisely how extensive the

---

[22] See also Garfinkle, 842 F. Supp. at 1292, where the court stated:

> For an "enterprise" to be "engaged in" racketeering activity we think it is enough to show that the "enterprise" is currently involved in the commission of an act of racketeering activity. By this we don't mean that the enterprise must be committing an act of racketeering activity at the same exact instant as the underlying crime of violence. We only mean that the enterprise must have committed or is planning to commit some racketeering activity within a period of time short enough under the circumstances so that it is fair to deem the enterprise as "engaged in racketeering activity."

[23] See, e.g., Pimentel, 346 F.3d at 297; Bracy, 67 F.3d at 1430; Garfinkle, 842 F. Supp. at 1292.

charged racketeering activity must be. However, several factors lead OCRS to conclude that, at least as a matter of sound policy, to obtain approval for a proposed Section 1959 charge, the enterprise must engage in activity that either constitutes, or poses a reasonable threat of some degree of, ongoing racketeering activity. First, proof of an association-in-fact enterprise is proven "by evidence of an ongoing organization, formal or informal, and by evidence that the various associates functions as a continuing unit." Turkette, 452 U.S. at 583. This at least suggests that the enterprise must function "as a continuing unit" to achieve its shared unlawful objectives over some period of time. Moreover, if an enterprise is not engaged in, or does not pose a reasonable threat of, ongoing racketeering activity, the enterprise may not pose a sufficient threat or problem to warrant federal prosecution. Hence, it may be more appropriate for local authorities to prosecute the alleged underlying crime of violence. Furthermore, adherence to OCRS' policy will minimize the likelihood of adverse decisions, at least until the case law on this issue becomes more settled.

### E. Generic Offenses - Determining Whether A Particular Statutory Offense Qualifies as A Section 1959 Predicate Offense

1.  Section 1959 does not enumerate violations of specific statutes that constitute the underlying crimes of violence. Rather, the Committee responsible for Section 1959 stated that:

> While Section [1959] proscribes murder, kidnapping, maiming, assault with a dangerous weapon, and assault resulting in serious bodily injury in violation of federal or State law, it is intended to apply to these crimes in **a generic sense**, whether or not a particular State has chosen those precise terms for such crimes.

129 Cong. Rec. 22, 906 (98$^{th}$ Cong. 1$^{st}$ Sess. Aug 4, 1983) (emphasis added).[24]

---

[24] For discussions of generic offenses under Section 1959, see United States v. Crenshaw, 359 F.3d 977, 988-89 n. 4 (8$^{th}$ Cir. 2004); United States v. Pimentel, 346 F.3d 285, 301-05 (2d Cir. 2003); United States v. Kehoe, 310 F.3d 579, 588 (8$^{th}$ Cir. 2002); United States v. Marino, 277 F.3d
(continued...)

To determine whether a particular predicate violation incorporated into a federal statute, such as RICO or Section 1959, falls within the "generic definition" of a particular type of offense, the Supreme Court has examined analogous provisions of the Model Penal Code and state and federal statutes existing at the time Congress enacted the federal statute at issue to determine the prevailing definition of the offense at that time. For example, RICO's definition of "racketeering activity" (18 U.S.C. § 1961(1)) includes "any act or threat involving murder, kidnapping, gambling, arson, robbery, bribery, extortion, dealing in obscene matter, or dealing in a controlled substance . . . which is chargeable under state law." Scheidler v. National Organization for Women, Inc., et al., 537 U.S. 393 (2003) presented an issue whether a state extortion statute could constitute a RICO predicate offense. The Supreme Court ruled that Congress intended RICO's definition of racketeering activity to encompass violations under state law that fall within "generic" definitions of these types of offenses. Scheidler, 537 U.S. at 409-410.

The Supreme Court determined the generic definition of the predicate crime "extortion" as follows:

> [W]here as here the Model Penal Code and a majority of States recognize the crime of extortion as requiring a party to obtain or to seek to obtain property, as the Hobbs Act requires, the state extortion offense for purposes of RICO must have a similar requirement.
>
> Because [the defendants] did not obtain or attempt to obtain [plaintiffs'] property, both the state extortion claims and the claim of attempting or conspiring to commit

---

[24](...continued)
11, 29-30 (1st Cir. 2002); United States v. Carrillo, 229 F.3d 177, 182-86 (2d Cir. 2000); United States v. Diaz, 176 F. 3d 52, 96 (2d Cir. 1999); United States v. Tolliver, 61 F.3d 1189, 1208-09 (5th Cir. 1995); United States v. Orena, 32 F.3d 704, 714 (2d Cir. 1994); United States v. Cuong Gia Le, 316 F. Supp. 2d 355, 359-64 (E.D.Va. 2004); United States v. Cuong Gia Le, 310 F. Supp. 2d 763, 782-84 (E.D.Va. 2004); United States v. Morales, 881 F. Supp. 769, 770-72 (D. Conn. 1995); United States v. Wei, 862 F. Supp. 1129, 1138-39 (S.D.N.Y. 1994); United States v. Cutolo, 861 F. Supp. 1142, 1146-47 (E.D.N.Y. 1994).

state extortion were fatally flawed.

Scheidler, 537 U.S. at 410.

The Scheidler Court stated, 537 U.S. at 409-410, that its analysis in that regard was consistent with its decision in Nardello v. United States, 393 U.S. 286 (1969), where the Court determined the meaning of generic "extortion" under state law incorporated into the federal Travel Act,

18 U.S.C. § 1952, by examining analogous provisions in the Model Penal Code and state statutes in existence at about the time Congress enacted the Travel Act. In Nardello, 393 U.S. at 290, 295-96, the Court concluded that generic "extortion" meant "obtaining something of value from another with his consent induced by the wrongful use of force, fear or threats", and that a statutory offense that included these elements fell within the generic definition of extortion regardless of the state's classification of the statute or its labels. Similarly, in Perrin v. United States, 444 U.S. 37, 42 (1979), the Supreme Court ruled that "we look to the ordinary meaning of the term [bribery] at the time Congress enacted the [Travel Act] in 1961" to determine whether a particular state offense involving commercial bribery was encompassed by the "generic" definition of "bribery."

Moreover, Taylor v. United States, 495 U.S. 575, 595, 602 (1990), presented the issue whether the defendant's prior conviction for second degree burglary under Missouri law fell within the generic definition of burglary, and therefore could be used as a prior "burglary" conviction to enhance the defendant's sentence pursuant to 18 U.S.C. §§ 922(g)(1) and 924(e). The Supreme Court ruled that the generic definition of an offense is determined by examining the prevailing definition at the time the federal statute at issue was enacted, and that a statutory offense involving burglary constitutes "generic" burglary if "its statutory definition substantially corresponds to 'generic' burglary." 495 U.S. at 602. The Supreme Court explained that Congress intended a "categorical approach" to determine whether a statutory offense falls within a generic definition, which focuses on the statute's "specific elements," and not on the underlying factual circumstances or whether the state statute used the same label as the generic definition. Taylor, 495 U.S. at 588-90.

The Supreme Court found that **generic** burglary "contains at least the following elements: an unlawful or unprivileged entry into, or remaining in, a building or other structure, with intent to commit a crime." 495 U.S. at 598. However, the Supreme Court could not determine whether the elements of the state burglary offense upon which the defendant was convicted substantially conformed to generic burglary because the Missouri burglary offense at issue was broader than generic burglary. Therefore, the Supreme Court remanded the matter to determine whether the defendant's prior conviction was for an offense that fell within generic burglary. Id. at 602.

The Supreme Court explained the framework for making that determination, stating:

> If the state statute is **narrower** than the generic view, *e.g.*, in cases of burglary convictions in common-law States or convictions of first-degree or aggravated burglary, there is no problem, because the conviction necessarily implies that the defendant has been found guilty of all the elements of generic burglary. And if the defendant was convicted of burglary in a State where the generic definition has been adopted, with minor variations in terminology, then the trial court need find only that the state statute corresponds in substance to the generic meaning of burglary.

Id. at 599 (emphasis added). But, in Taylor, the state statute that underlay the defendant's conviction was broader than generic burglary, which raised the specter that the defendant may have been convicted of an offense based on elements that did not substantially correspond to generic burglary. In such cases, the Supreme Court stated that the reviewing court must determine whether "the charging paper and jury instructions actually required the jury to find all the elements of generic burglary in order to convict the defendant." Id. at 602.

Similarly, Shepard v. United States, 544 U.S. 13 (2005), involved the issue whether the defendant's prior convictions, based on his guilty pleas to state "burglary" offenses in violation of Massachusetts law, constituted generic burglary, which could provide the basis for an enhanced sentence. Because Massachusetts law defines "burglary" more broadly than generic burglary as construed in Taylor, supra, by extending it to entries into boats and cars, the courts had to determine how the federal sentencing court might tell whether a prior burglary conviction was for the "generic" burglary offense.

The district court had rejected the government's argument that the sentencing court could examine police reports submitted by the police with applications for issuance of the complaints to determine whether the defendant's guilty plea was to an offense that constitutes generic burglary. Therefore, the district court refused to enhance the defendant's sentence based upon his prior burglary conviction. On appeal, the First Circuit vacated the sentence and ruled that the complaint applications and police reports may count as "sufficiently reliable evidence for determining whether a defendant's plea of guilty constitutes an admission to generically violent crime." United States v. Shepard, 231 F.3d 56, 67 (1st Cir. 2000).

The Supreme Court reversed and remanded for further proceedings in light of its holding. The Supreme Court stated that "[i]n this case, the offenses charged in state complaints were broader than generic burglary, and there were of course no jury instructions that might have narrowed the charges to the generic limit" since the defendant had pled guilty. Shepard, 544 U.S. at 17. The Supreme Court rejected the government's argument that "a sentencing court can look to police reports or complaint applications to determine whether an earlier guilty plea necessarily admitted, and supported a conviction for, generic burglary." Id. at 16. Rather, the Court explicitly held that "a later court determining the character of an admitted burglary is generally limited to examining the statutory definition, charging document, written plea agreement, transcript of plea colloquy, and any explicit factual finding by the trial judge to which the defendant assented." Id. at 15.

The foregoing authority makes clear that the determination of whether a statutory offense falls within the generic definition of a particular crime involves a pure issue of statutory construction that can be resolved prior to indictment and turns on whether the **statutory elements** of the offense, and not the factual circumstances of the specific case, substantially corresponds to the generic definition of the crime. Once it has been determined that a statutory offense falls within the generic definition of a crime of violence under Section 1959, and hence the **statutory** offense qualifies as a Section 1959 predicate offense, a second distinct issue may arise: that is, whether the defendant's conviction rested on an offense that fell within the generic definition of the particular crime at issue. This second issue, which does not involve a pure issue of statutory construction, cannot be resolved prior to indictment since it involves examination of the circumstances at trial. However, this issue may be anticipated when drafting the indictment. The prosecutor should ensure that the Section 1959 count alleges a violation of a statutory offense that falls within the generic definition of the offense, and allege the requisite elements of that generic offense.

Thus, when the statutory offense that served as the basis for the defendant's conviction is **broader** than the generic definition of a particular offense, it may be necessary to examine the particular circumstances of the case, such as the charging documents and the jury instructions, to determine whether the particular offense upon which the defendant was convicted fell within the generic definition of the crime. For example, suppose a defendant were convicted of a statutory violation, "theft by extortion and other means," that satisfied the generic definition of "extortion" in that its elements included obtaining property from another by the wrongful use of force, fear or threats, but was broader than the generic definition of extortion and also included "theft by false statements," which fell outside the ambit of generic extortion. If there were a general verdict, the defendant might argue that he was convicted of theft by false statements and not theft by extortion. In such circumstances, the reviewing court must examine the charging documents and jury instructions to determine whether the defendant was convicted of "theft by extortion."

In Sections II (F) through (J) below, OCRS applies the foregoing principles to determine the generic definitions of murder, kidnapping, maiming, assault with a dangerous weapon and assault resulting in serious bodily injury. First, we examine the analogous provisions of the Model Penal Code and federal and state statutes existing in 1984 when Section 1959 was enacted to determine the prevailing definitions in 1984 of murder, kidnapping, maiming, assault with a dangerous weapon, and assault resulting in serious bodily injury. We conclude that any statute that contains elements that substantially correspond to the generic definitions in 1984 of murder, kidnapping, maiming, assault with a dangerous weapon and assault resulting in serious bodily injury may constitute predicate crimes of violence under Section 1959.

It is especially significant to bear in mind that it is immaterial whether the statute at issue uses the same labels or terms as the list of violent crimes under Section 1959. Conversely, it is not dispositive that the statute at issue uses the same labels as the Section 1959 underlying crimes of violence. Likewise, it is not dispositive that the defendant's underlying misconduct violated the generic definition of the particular crime at issue. Rather, the dispositive issue is whether required elements of the statute at issue substantially conform to the generic definitions in 1984 of murder, kidnapping, maiming, assault with a dangerous weapon, and assault resulting in serious bodily injury. See cases cited supra, n. 24 and infra, n. 87, and especially Cuong Gia Le, 316 F. Supp. 2d at 359-364.

2. Once it has been concluded that the particular state or federal statute at issue may properly be used as a predicate crime of violence under Section 1959, a highly significant issue

arises: whether it is necessary to instruct the jury that to convict the defendant on the Section 1959 charge, the government must prove the requisite elements of the underlying state or federal law that underlies the charge.

Initially, the Second Circuit had ruled that because RICO and Section 1959 incorporate "generic definitions" of the covered state predicate offenses, it was not necessary to allege in the indictment, or instruct the jury on, all the requisite elements of the state predicate offense.[25] However, the Second Circuit has retreated from that position and has pointedly warned that the failure to prove, and instruct the jury on, all the requisite elements of the state law violation used for the basis of a RICO or Section 1959 charge may lead to reversible error.[26] As the Second Circuit explained in United States v. Carrillo, 229 F.3d 177 (2d Cir. 2000):

> If the conduct proved at trial did not satisfy the elements of the offense as defined by state law, a jury could not find that the defendant had committed the state law offense charged as a predicate act of racketeering. Likewise, even assuming

---

[25] See, e.g., United States v. Bagaric, 706 F.2d 42, 62-63 (2d Cir. 1983), cert. denied, 464 U.S. 840 (1983) (trial court not required to instruct the jury on the elements of the alleged state law violations involving murder, arson, and extortion); United States v. Orena, 32 F.3d 704, 714 (2d Cir. 1994) (not required to allege in the indictment an overt act as required under the predicate state law murder violations); United States v. Miller, 116 F.3d 641, 675 (2d Cir. 1997) (holding that RICO's reference to state crimes was not intended to incorporate elements of state crimes, but only to provide a general substantive frame of reference); United States v. Diaz, 176 F.3d 52, 96 (2d Cir. 1999) (same rule for Section 1959 and therefore government was not required to prove an overt act as required under Connecticut law to establish a conspiracy to assault resulting in serious bodily injury). See also, Tolliver, 61 F.3d at 1208-09 (finding any error in failing to instruct the jury on the elements of murder under Louisiana law to be harmless).

[26] See, e.g., United State v. Pimentel, 346 F.3d 285, 301-305 (2d Cir. 2003); United States v. Carrillo, 229 F.3d 177, 182-86 (2d Cir. 2000); United States v. Feliciano, 223 F.3d 102, 115 (2d Cir. 2000). On the particular facts of these cases, the Second Circuit found any error in failing to instruct the jury on the elements of the underlying state violations was harmless error. But see United States v. Dhinsa, 243 F.3d 635, 672-74 (2d Cir. 2001) (defendant's Section 1959 conviction based on alleged threat to murder his victim in violation of state law (N.Y. Penal Law § 135.65) reversed for failure to prove all the requisite elements of New York State Penal Law § 135.65 "coercion in the first degree.").

evidence from which a jury *could* find a violation of state law, if the defendant's acts as found by the jury did not include all the essential elements of the state law offense, by definition, no state offense would have been found. It is difficult to see (notwithstanding the statements in Diaz) how the defendant could be properly convicted if the conduct found by the jury did not include all the elements of the state offense since RICO requires that the defendant have committed predicate acts "chargeable under state law." If a district judge failed to charge a jury on the state law elements of the crime constituting a racketeering act, neither we nor the district judge could know what were the factual determinations on which the jury based its verdict. Thus, we would be unable to determine what the jury decided the defendant actually did, and whether, under the jury's findings, the defendant committed the state law offense charged as a racketeering act.

Carrillo, 229 F.3d at 183-184.

OCRS agrees with the Second Circuit's analysis in Carrillo. The same rationale applies to Section 1959 predicate offenses that must be in violation of state or federal law. Therefore, when a Section 1959 charge is based upon a violation of state or federal law that satisfies the generic definition of the predicate violent crimes listed in Section 1959, the government must prove, and the jury must be instructed on, all the requisite elements of that state or federal offense.[27] However, it remains good law under Section 1959 and RICO that references in the indictment to the state law predicate violations do not incorporate state procedural and evidentiary rules, such as requiring corroboration for witness accomplices, discovery, statute of limitations, etc.[28] See also infra, Section

---

[27] Moreover, as noted in Section II (E)(1) above, to avoid the problems noted in Taylor, 495 U.S. 575 and Shepard, 544 U.S. 13, whenever a statutory violation used as a Section 1959 predicate is broader than the generic definition of the predicate Section 1959 crime of violence at issue, the jury should be specifically instructed that to convict it must find all the elements that are necessary to satisfy the generic definition of the crime of violence at issue. For example, if a state violation "assault with a dangerous weapon" covers dangerous weapons that satisfy the generic definition of "assault with a dangerous weapon," but also more broadly covers weapons that do not satisfy the generic definition, the jury should be given adequate instructions to ensure that a reviewing court is able to determine that the jury found that the defendant used a weapon that satisfies the generic definition.

[28] See, e.g., United States v. Crenshaw, 359 F.3d at 988-89; Morales, 881 F. Supp. at 771-72;
(continued...)

II (L), demonstrating that Section 1959 does not incorporate state law of attempts and conspiracies.

**F.     Murder**

The Senate Report regarding Section 1959 indicates that Congress intended Section 1959's reference to murder to include violations of the then-principal federal murder statute, 18 U.S.C. § 1111, but also to expand the scope of covered murders to include "generic murder" because, in part, Congress viewed Section 1111 as too restrictive. See S. Rep. No. 98-225 at 305-06, 311. Therefore, OCRS will first address the elements of murder under 18 U.S.C. § 1111 since a violation of this provision may constitute an underlying crime of violence under Section 1959.

**1.     The Federal Murder Statute -- 18 U.S.C. § 1111**

Title 18, United States Code Section 1111, first enacted in 1948, provides that:

(a) Murder is the unlawful killing of a human being with malice aforethought. Every murder perpetrated by poison, lying in wait, or any other kind of willful, deliberate, malicious, and premeditated killing; or committed in the perpetration of, or attempt to perpetrate, any arson,[29] escape, murder, kidnapping, treason, espionage, sabotage, aggravated sexual abuse or sexual abuse,[30] child abuse,[31] burglary, or robbery; or perpetrated as part of a pattern or practice of assault or torture against a child or children; or perpetrated from a premeditated design unlawfully and maliciously to effect the death of any human being other than him who is killed, is murder in the first degree.

Any other murder is murder in the second degree.

---

[28](...continued)
Wei, 862 F. Supp. at 1138; Cutolo, 861 F. Supp. at 1147.

[29] In 1984, Section 1004 of Pub.L. 98-473 amended Section 1111 by adding after the word "arson" the words "escape, murder, kidnaping, treason, espionage, sabotage." In 1988, Pub.L. 100-690 inserted a comma after "arson."

[30] In 1986, Pub.L. 99-646 substituted "aggravated sexual abuse or sexual abuse" for rape.

[31] In 2003, Pub.L. 108-21, § 102(1)(A), (B), inserted "child abuse," after "sexual abuse," and inserted "or perpetrated as part of a pattern or practice of assault or torture against a child or children;" after "robbery."

(b) Within the special maritime and territorial jurisdiction of the United States,

Whoever is guilty of murder in the first degree shall be punished by death or by imprisonment for life;[32]

Whoever is guilty of murder in the second degree, shall be imprisoned for any term of years or for life.

(c)[33] For purposes of this section–

(1) the term "assault" has the same meaning as given that term in section 113;

(2) the term "child" means a person who has not attained the age of 18 years and is--

(A) under the perpetrator's care or control; or

(B) at least six years younger than the perpetrator;

(3) the term "child abuse" means intentionally or knowingly causing death or serious bodily injury to a child;

(4) the term "pattern or practice of assault or torture" means assault or torture engaged in on at least two occasions;

(5) the term "serious bodily injury" has the meaning set forth in section 1365; and

(6) the term "torture" means conduct, whether or not committed under the color of law, that otherwise satisfies the definition set forth in section 2340(1).

**(a)　　Elements**

The principal federal murder statute criminalizes several types of homicides: (1) first-degree, i.e., traditional "premeditated" homicide; (2) first-degree felony murder; and (3) second-degree murder, which requires malice aforethought but not premeditation. Of course, in addition to the element of causing the death of another, the government must prove federal jurisdiction–for

---

[32] In 1994, Pub.L. 103-322, § 60003(a)(4), substituted "shall be punished by death or imprisonment for life" for "shall suffer death unless the jury qualifies its verdict by adding thereto 'without capital punishment,' in which event he shall be sentenced to imprisonment for life."

[33] In 2003, Section (c) was added pursuant to Pub. L. 108-21 § 102(2).

purposes of this statute, that the act occurred within the special or maritime jurisdiction of the United States.

For the crime of murder in the **first degree (premeditation)**, the elements of a § 1111 violation are:

1. The defendant unlawfully killed the victim;
2. The defendant acted with malice aforethought;
3. The killing was premeditated; and
4. The killing occurred within the special maritime or territorial jurisdiction of the United States.[34]

For the crime of murder in the **first degree (felony murder)**, the elements are:

1. The defendant unlawfully killed the victim;
2. The death of the victim occurred as a consequence of, and during the commission of, or attempted commission of, one of the enumerated felonies in the statute (arson, escape, murder, kidnapping, treason, espionage, sabotage, aggravated sexual abuse or sexual abuse, child abuse, burglary, or robbery; or perpetrated as part of a pattern or practice of assault or torture against a child or children; or perpetrated from a premeditated design unlawfully and maliciously to effect the death of any human being other than him who is killed); and
3. The killing occurred within the special maritime or territorial jurisdiction of the United States.[35]

---

[34] See, e.g., United States v. Shaw, 701 F.2d 367, 392-93 (5th Cir. 1983); 8th Circuit Model Crim. Jury Instructions § 6.18.1111A (2003); 5th Circuit Model Crim. Jury Instructions § 2.55 (2001); 10th Circuit Model Crim. Jury Instructions § 2.52 (2006); 11th Circuit Model Crim. Jury Instructions § 45.1 (2003).

[35] See, e.g., United States v. Thomas, 34 F.3d 44, 48-49 (2d Cir. 1994); United States v. (continued...)

For the crime of murder in the **second degree**, there are four essential elements:

1. The defendant unlawfully killed the victim;
2. The defendant did so with malice aforethought; and
3. The killing occurred within the special maritime or territorial jurisdiction of the United States. [36]

**(b)   "Unlawful" killing**

Section 1111 defines murder as the "unlawful" killing of another person with malice aforethought. The issue of whether a killing is "unlawful" typically arises in cases in which the defendant claims self-defense or another form of legal justification. Self-defense is an affirmative defense, with the burden of production on the defendant. However, once properly raised, it is the government's burden to disprove the defense beyond a reasonable doubt. See, e.g., United States v. Alvarez, 755 F.2d 830, 842 (11th Cir. 1985); United States v. Corrigan, 548 F.2d 879 (10th Cir. 1977).

**(c)   Malice Aforethought**

For both first and second degree murder, the government must prove "malice aforethought." To establish malice, "the government must prove that the defendant killed intentionally **or** recklessly

---

[35](...continued)
Chischilly, 30 F.3d 1144, 1159-60 (9th Cir. 1994); United States v. Miguel, 338 F.3d 995, 1005 (9th Cir. 2003); 10th Circuit Model Crim. Jury Instructions § 2.52.1 (2006); 11th Circuit Model Crim. Jury Instructions § 45.2 (2003).

[36] See, e.g., United States v. Shaw, 701 F.2d 367, 392-93 (5th Cir. 1983); United States v. Miguel, 338 F.3d 995, 1005 (9th Cir. 2003); Beardslee v. United States, 387 F.2d 280 (8th Cir. 1967); 18 U.S.C. § 1111(a) ("Any other murder [other than first degree premeditated or felony murder] is murder in the second degree."); 8th Circuit Model Crim. Jury Instructions § 6.18.1111B (2003); 5th Circuit Model Crim. Jury Instructions § 2.56 (2001); 10th Circuit Model Crim. Jury Instructions § 2.53 (2006); 11th Circuit Model Crim. Jury Instructions § 45.3 (2003).

with extreme disregard for human life." United States v. Paul, 37 F.3d 496, 499 (9th Cir. 1994) (emphasis added). The government need not show a subjective intent to kill, but rather malice "may be established by conduct which is a 'reckless and wanton and a gross deviation from a reasonable standard of care, of such a nature that a jury is warranted in inferring that defendant was aware of a serious risk of death or serious bodily harm.'" United States v. Shaw, 701 F.2d 367, 392 n.20 (5th Cir. 1983) (quoting United States v. Black Elk, 579 F.2d 49, 51 (8th Cir. 1978)); accord United States v. Williams, 342 U.S. 350, 356 (4th Cir. 2003). See also United States v. Celestine, 510 F.2d 457, 459 (9th Cir. 1975) (malice aforethought includes "the state of mind with which one intentionally commits a wrongful act without legal justification or excuse," and "may be inferred from circumstances which show 'a wanton and depraved spirit, a mind bent on evil mischief without regard to its consequences.'").[37]

The Supreme Court has held that the prosecution must prove beyond a reasonable doubt the absence of the heat of passion on sudden provocation when the issue is properly presented. See Mullaney v. Wilbur, 421 U.S. 684, 697-98, 704 (1975).[38]

**(d)    Premeditation**

---

[37] Other circuits employ slightly different formulations. See, e.g., United States v. Hicks, 389 F.3d 514, 529 (5th Cir. 2004) ("Malice aforethought 'encompasses three distinct mental states: (1) intent to kill; (2) intent to do serious bodily injury; and (3) extreme recklessness and wanton disregard for human life ('depraved heart').'" (citation omitted)); United States v. Pearson, 203 F.3d 1243, 1271 (10th Cir. 2000) ("Second-degree murder's malice aforethought element is satisfied by: (1) intent-to-kill without the added ingredients of premeditation and deliberation; (2) intent to do serious bodily injury; (3) a depraved-heart; or (4) commission of a felony when the crime does not fall under the first-degree murder paragraph of § 1111(a).").

[38] If the requisite element is not proven–in other words, if there is no malice or the killing is during the commission of a nonfelonious act–the killing may be chargeable under the federal manslaughter statute, 18 U.S.C. § 1112. This statute, however, is not a predicate for a § 1959 violation, as it is not a "murder." See infra pp. 42, 44 and n. 50.

To establish traditional first degree murder, the government must prove premeditation, that is, something that "involve[s] a prior design to commit murder." United States v. Brown, 518 F.2d 821, 826 (7th Cir. 1975).[39] However, although a prior design to commit murder must be proven, no particular period of time is necessary for such deliberation and premeditation. See, e.g., United States v. Shaw, 701 F.2d 367 (5th Cir. 1983); United States v. Brown, 518 F.2d 821, 826 (7th Cir. 1975); United States v. Blue Thunder, 604 F.3d 550, 553 (8th Cir. 1979). "There must be some appreciable time for reflection and consideration before execution of the act, although the period of time 'does not require the lapse of days or hours or even minutes." Shaw, 701 F.2d at 393 (quoting Bostic v. United States, 94 F.2d 636, 638 (D.C. Cir. 1937)); Brown, 518 F.2d at 828 (in affirming conviction, "the evidence showed an interval for reflection and that this killing was not a mere persistence of an initial impulse or passion. There was time for second thought."). The jury may be entitled to infer the existence of premeditation from various evidentiary factors:

> (1) facts about how and what the defendant did prior to the actual killing which show he was engaged in activity directed toward the killing, that is, Planning activity; (2) facts about the defendant's prior relationship and conduct with the victim from which Motive may be inferred; and (3) facts about the Nature of the killing from which it may be inferred that the manner of killing was so particular and exacting that the defendant must have intentionally killed according to a preconceived design.

Blue Thunder, 604 F.2d at 553 (quoting W. LaFave & A. Scott, Jr., Criminal Law § 73 at p. 564 (1972)).

Premeditation is a distinct element from malice aforethought, as the two terms are not synonymous. See Ornelas v. United States, 236 F.2d 392, 394 (9th Cir. 1956); Shaw, 701 F.2d at 393 (noting that both first and second degree murder require malice, and that "[a] conviction for first

---

[39] Alternatively, the government may prove poisoning, or lying in wait for the victim, which is typically "watching and waiting in a concealed position with an intent to kill or do serious bodily harm to another." Shaw, 701 F.2d at 393.

degree murder require the additional proof of premeditation, poisoning, or lying in wait."); see also United States v. Garcia-Meza, 403 F.3d 364, 372 (6th Cir. 2005) (in trial for first-degree and second-degree murder, although trial court instructed jury to consider all facts and circumstances that bore upon question of malice aforethought and premeditation, rather than question of malice aforethought and question of premeditation, no error warranting reversal of first-degree murder conviction given that court distinguished the two elements of malice aforethought and premeditation).

### (e) Felony Murder

As an alternative to proving malice aforethought, the government may establish that the killing was committed "in the perpetration of, or attempt to perpetrate," one of the felonies enumerated in the statute.

The government need not establish some proof of a state of mind other than the intent required for commission of the underlying felony. United States v. Nguyen, 155 F.3d 1219, 1225 (10th Cir. 1998).[40] In a first degree felony murder case, "to prove the 'malice aforethought' element . . . , the prosecution only need show commission of the specified felony." United States v. Pearson, 159 F.3d 480, 485 (10th Cir. 1998). "Because malice aforethought is proved by commission of the felony, there is no actual intent requirement with respect to the homicide." United States v. Chanthadara, 230 F.3d 1237, 1258 (10th Cir. 2000). On the other hand, the intent required of the

---

[40] The only intent required for felony murder is the intent to commit the underlying felony. See, e.g., United States v. Chischilly, 30 F.3d 1144, 1159-60 (9th Cir. 1994); United States v. Nguyen, 155 F.3d 1219, 1229 (10th Cir. 1998); United States v. Flores, 63 F.3d 1342, 1371 (5th Cir. 1995); United States v. Thomas, 34 F.3d 44, 48-9 (2d Cir. 1994); United States v. Williams, 342 F.3d 350, 355 (4th Cir. 2003).

underlying felony must be proven. See, e.g., United States v. Lilly, 512 F.2d 1259 (9th Cir. 1975) (specific intent was required element of robbery used as basis for Section 1111 felony murder prosecution).

There is occasionally some confusion in the case law and in the commentary as to whether a conviction for felony murder requires a separate "malice aforethought" distinct from the commission of the felony. See, e.g., Lilly, 512 F.2d at 1261 n.4 ("We note in passing that under § 1111 all murder, including second-degree murder and felony murder, requires 'malice aforethought'."); United States v. Sides, 944 F.2d 1554, 1557 (10th Cir. 1991) ("first degree murder thus requires proof of: either a premeditated, malicious, and unlawful killing of a human being, or a malicious and unlawful killing of a human being committed in the perpetration of a robbery"); United States v. Williams, 342 F.3d 350, 356-57 (4th Cir. 2003).[41]

However, the law is well established that the perpetration of the felony constitutes, or substitutes for, the requisite malice. The Tenth Circuit, in Chanthadara, 230 F.3d at 1258, explained the rationale:

---

[41] For another example of this confusion, see also Henry S. Noyes, Felony-Murder Doctrine Through the Federal Looking Glass, 69 Indiana Law Journal 533, 539-540 (1994) (emphasis added):

"Malice aforethought" remains a remains a necessary element of every murder, be it murder in the first degree, murder in the second degree, or felony murder. . . . The language of 18 U.S.C. § 1111(a) requires that the government first establish that "murder" was committed with "malice aforethought" before it can address whether the "murder" is of the first or the second degree. The fact that the "murder" occurred during the commission of a felony simply supplies the predicate to make the "murder" a murder of the first degree. In addition, because the Due Process Clause requires the government to prove every element of an offense beyond a reasonable doubt, the prosecution may not shift the burden of proof to the defendant by presuming a necessary element upon proof of the other elements of an offense. **The federal felony-murder statute does not "presume" the existence of "malice aforethought" from the commission of a felony, because "malice aforethought" is an element of the offense.**

Under a literal reading of the federal statute, "malice aforethought" is an element of every type of murder. See 18 U.S.C. § 1111(a) (stating generally that "murder is the unlawful killing of a human being with malice aforethought"). However, the meaning of "malice aforethought" differs with respect to each kind of murder.

*****

As to first degree felony murder, "to prove the 'malice aforethought' element . . . , the prosecution only need show commission of the specified felony." [Citing cases] **Because malice aforethought is proved by commission of the felony, there is no actual intent requirement with respect to the homicide**.

Id. at 1258. (emphasis added). See also United States v. Browner, 889 F.2d 549, 552 n.2 (5th Cir. 1989) ("The common law also recognized a fourth variety of malice, known as the 'felony murder' rule. Some aspects of this traditional rule survive in the provisions of [Section 1111(a)] elevating the seriousness of murder committed in the course of certain felonies."); United States v. Thomas, 34 F.3d 44, 48 (2d Cir. 1994) (rejecting defendants' argument that malice aforethought must be proven in addition to perpetration of enumerated felony: "Under the statute, which largely follows the common law's definition of murder, there are several ways in which the element of malice aforethought can be satisfied. One way the government can demonstrate malice aforethought is by showing that the killing was committed in the commission of a robbery; under the traditional common law felony murder rule, the malice of the robbery satisfies murder's malice requirement.'"); United States v. Pearson, 159 F.3d 480, 485 (10th Cir. 1998) ("In the typical case of felony murder, there is no malice 'in fact' with respect to the homicide; the malice is supplied by the 'law'."); United States v. Chischilly, 30 F.3d 1144, 1159-60 (9th Cir. 1994) ("[U]nder a felony murder charge the commission of the underlying offense substitutes for malice aforethought."); United States v. Miguel, 338 F.3d 995, 1005 (9th Cir. 2003) ("Second-degree murder includes an element that felony murder does not include: 'proof that the defendant acted with malice aforethought.'" (quoting Chischilly)).

In other words, Section 1111 does not require both the finding of "malice aforethought" and that the killing was committed during the perpetration of the felony. United States v. Thomas, 34 F.3d 44 (2d Cir. 1994). In Schad v. Arizona, 501 U.S. 624, 639-40 (1991), the Supreme Court construed a statute similar to Section 1111, and pointed out that at common law, "[t]he intent to kill and the intent to commit a felony were alternative aspects of the single concept of 'malice aforethought.'"

One common issue that often arises is whether the killing actually was "committed in perpetration of," or attempted perpetration of, the enumerated felony. See, e.g., Brackett v. Peters, 11 F.3d 78, 80 (7th Cir. 1993) (for purposes of felony murder rule, act is cause of event if two conditions satisfied: event would not have occurred without the act, and act made the event more likely to occur); United States v. Miguel, 338 F.3d 995, 1003 (9th Cir. 2003) (for conviction under § 1111 for felony murder, government must show that a participant in the underlying felony committed the killing during the course of the felony); United States v. Williams, 342 F.3d 350, 357 (4th Cir. 2003) (robbery and killing so closely related that they could fairly be called part of same criminal enterprise). The purpose of this rule is to confine felony murder liability to deaths that occur during the course of a felony. United States v. Martinez, 16 F.3d 202, 208 (7th Cir. 1994). Importantly, this does not require that the death itself was in furtherance of the felony, but simply that the act that caused the death was in furtherance of the felony. Id.

### (f) Jurisdiction

For purposes of Section 1111 homicides, federal jurisdiction attaches if the killing occurs "[w]ithin the special maritime and territorial jurisdiction of the United States." § 1111(b). This term is defined in 18 U.S.C. § 7 to include the high seas, federal lands and buildings, guano islands designated as appertaining to the United States, aircraft and spacecraft, places outside the jurisdiction of any nation, and foreign vessels to or from the United States. In 2001, after some conflicting case law, Congress amended Section 7 to explicitly attach federal jurisdiction to premises of United States diplomatic, consular, military, and other government missions located overseas with respect to offenses committed by or against United States nationals. See 18 U.S.C. § 7(9).[42]

For purposes of Section 1111, the location of a murder is governed by 18 U.S.C. § 3236, which provides that "[i]n all cases of murder or manslaughter, the offense shall be deemed to have been committed at the place where the injury was inflicted, or the poison administered or other means employed which caused the death, without regard to the place where the death occurs." See, e.g., United States v. Parker, 622 F.2d 298, 301, 307-08 (8th Cir. 1980) (victim left on military base in freezing weather after being hit on the head: if blow to the head alone, which occurred off base, killed the victim, no federal offense was committed; however, if exposure to freezing weather on

---

[42] There are, of course, other statutes which attach federal jurisdiction to homicides, including killing of certain federal officers and employees while they are engaged in, or on account of, the performance of their official duties, see 18 U.S.C. § 1114, presidential assassinations, see 18 U.S.C. § 1751, killing of foreign officials, official guests, or internationally protected persons, see 18 U.S.C. § 1116, killing of Members of Congress, Cabinet members, presidential candidates, and Supreme Court Justices, see 18 U.S.C. § 351, foreign murders of U.S. nationals, see 18 U.S.C. § 1119, murders by federal prisoners, see 18 U.S.C. § 1118, and by escaped federal prisoners, see 18 U.S.C. § 1120, murder of state or local officials assisting federal officials, see 18 U.S.C. § 1121; killing of witnesses, see 18 U.S.C. § 1512, interstate travel or use of an interstate facility for murder-for-hire, see 18 U.S.C. § 1958, and influencing a federal official by murdering a family member, see 18 U.S.C. § 115. See also 7 U.S.C. § 2146(b) (murder of any person while engaged in or on account of performance of handling official duties with respect to handling of certain animals); 8 U.S.C. § 1324(a) (murder with death resulting from smuggling aliens); 15 U.S.C. § 1825(a) (killing of official while engaged in or on account of performance of official duties relating to protection of horses in shows, exhibitions, etc.); 18 U.S.C. §§ 32, 34 (willful destruction of aircraft within special aircraft jurisdiction where death results); 18 U.S.C. §§ 33, 34 (willful destruction of motor vehicles engaged in interstate commerce, where death results); 18 U.S.C. § 36 (drive-by shooting in furtherance of or to escape detection of major drug offense).

base contributed to death, federal jurisdiction attaches).

The issue of where the killing occurred is a question of fact to be determined by the jury but the issue of federal jurisdiction is a question of law to be decided by the court. See, e.g., United States v. Hernandez-Fundora, 58 F.3d 802, 812 (2d Cir. 1995) (district court may determine a federal prison falls within special maritime and territorial jurisdiction of the United States and remove that matter from jury); United States v. Warren, 984 F.2d 325, 327 (9th Cir. 1993) (district court may determine a military base satisfies federal jurisdictional requirements); see also United States v. Stands, 105 F.3d 1565, 1575 (8th Cir. 1997) (location of crime is a factual issue for the jury, but it is for the court, not the jury, to determine whether that land is in Indian country and thus within federal jurisdiction); United States v. Levesque, 681 F.2d 75, 78 (1st Cir. 1982) (same); United States v. Roberts, 185 F.3d 1125, 1140 (10th Cir. 1999) ("We agree with our sister circuits the district court can find, as a matter of law, a geographic area or particular location is Indian Country, and then instruct the jury to determine factually whether the offense occurred there.").

Pursuant to 18 U.S.C. § 3236, venue for a federal murder prosecution lies "at the place where the injury was inflicted, or the poison administered or other means employed which caused the death, without regard to the place where the death occurs." However, unlike Section 1111, Section 1959 is a continuing offense, see infra Section IV (A). Accordingly, Section 1959 is governed by 18 U.S.C. § 3237(a). See, e.g., United States v. Saavedra, 223 F.3d 85, 91 (2d Cir. 2000); United States v. Perez, 940 F. Supp. 540, 548 (S.D.N.Y. 1996) (because Section 1959 offense is continuing offense, venue appropriate in any district in which offense was begun, continued, or completed).

**2.    Generic Murder**

a.    To determine the definition of generic murder, OCRS will first examine the relevant provisions of the Model Penal Code (hereinafter "MPC") in 1984 when Congress enacted Section

1959.[43] The MPC provided three classifications of "criminal homicide": (1) murder; (2) manslaughter; (3) negligent homicide. MPC § 210.1. The MPC § 210.2 defined "murder" as follows:

> (1) Except as provided in Section 210.3 (1)(b), [see infra n. 45] criminal homicide constitutes murder when:
>
> > (a) it is committed purposely or knowingly; or
> > (b) it is committed recklessly under circumstances manifesting extreme indifference to the value of human life. Such recklessness and indifference are presumed if the actor is engaged or is an accomplice in the commission of, or an attempt to commit, or flight after committing or attempting to commit robbery, rape or deviate sexual intercourse by force or threat of force, arson, burglary, kidnapping or felonious escape.

This definition of murder includes three forms of murder: that is, when the act of causing the death of another person is done: (1) purposely or knowingly,[44] (2) with reckless indifference to the value of human life, **or** (3) during the commission of various serious felonies -- i.e., felony murder.

Regarding the meaning of purposeful or intentional, knowingly and recklessly, the MPC provided that:

> (a) **Purposely**.
> A person acts purposely with respect to a material element of an offense when:
> > (i) if the element involves the nature of his conduct or a result thereof, it is his conscious object to engage in conduct of that nature or to cause such a result; and
> > (ii) if the element involves the attendant circumstances, he is aware

---

[43] The Proposed Official Draft of the MPC was completed in 1962. See Herbert Wechsler, Foreword to Model Penal Code (U.L.A.), at 5 (1985). In 1980, a final version of Part II of the MPC (definitions of specific crimes) with comments was published. Id. at 6. A final version of Part I of the MPC (general provisions) with comments was completed in 1984 and published in 1985. Id.

[44] The term "purposely" means the same as "intentionally" or "with intent." MPC § 1.13(12).

of the existence of such circumstances or he believes or hopes that they exist.

(b) **Knowingly**.
A person acts knowingly with respect to a material element of an offense when:
(i) if the element involves the nature of his conduct or the attendant circumstances, he is aware that his conduct is of that nature or that such circumstances exist; and
(ii) if the element involves a result of his conduct, he is aware that it is practically certain that his conduct will cause such a result.

(c) **Recklessly**.
A person acts recklessly with respect to a material element of an offense when he consciously disregards a substantial and unjustifiable risk that the material element exists or will result from his conduct. The risk must be of such a nature and degree that, considering the nature and purpose of the actor's conduct and the circumstances known to him, its disregard involves a gross deviation from the standard conduct that a law-abiding person would observe in the actor's situation.

MPC §§ 2.02(2)(a)(b) and (c).

Thus, the MPC's definition of murder includes: (1) intentional, knowingly or purposeful murder, (2) murder committed recklessly with extreme indifference to the value of human life and (3) felony murder. Significantly, this definition of murder does not include manslaughter[45] or negligent homicide.[46]

---

[45] The MPC provided that:
(1) Criminal homicide constitutes manslaughter when:
 (a) it is committed recklessly; or
 (b) a homicide which would otherwise be murder is committed under the influence of extreme mental or emotional disturbance for which there is reasonable explanation or excuse. The reasonableness of such explanation or excuse shall be determined from the viewpoint of a person in the actor's situation under the circumstances as he believes them to be.
MPC § 210.3 (1).

[46] "Criminal homicide constitutes negligent homicide when it is committed negligently." MPC § 210.4. The MPC § 2.02(2)(d) defined "negligently" as follows:

(continued...)

b. The above-referenced MPC's definition of murder reflects the development and clarification of the common law definition of murder and the prevailing definition of murder under state law at the time the MPC was drafted in 1980. See MPC § 210.2 Cmt. at 16-41 (Official Draft and Revised Comments 1980) (hereinafter "MPC § ____ Cmt."). "At common law, murder was defined as the unlawful killing of another human being with 'malice aforethought.'" MPC § 210.2 Cmt. at 13-14; see also Schad v. Arizona, 501 U.S. 624, 640 (1991). Over time, "malice aforethought" was interpreted to include four states of mind sufficient to constitute knowing or purposeful murder: (1) intent to kill, (2) intent to cause grievous bodily harm if death resulted, (3) homicide under circumstances evincing a "depraved mind" or "extreme recklessness" regarding homicidal risk, and (4) felony murder. See MPC § 210.2 Cmt. at 14-15; see also S. Rep. No. 98-225 at 311 ("Under the common law, a murder committed during any felony was held to be committed with a sufficient degree of malice to warrant punishment as first degree murder.").

"Prior to the recodification effort begun by the Model Penal Code, most American jurisdictions maintained a law of murder built around these common-law classifications." MPC § 210.2 Cmt. at 16. "[T]herefore, it was the pattern in this country prior to the Model Penal Code to incorporate the common-law in some jurisdictions and to build upon it in others. Murder was generally defined to include intentional homicides, unintentional homicides committed with callous

---

[46](...continued)
    A person acts negligently with respect to a material element of an offense when he should be aware of a substantial and unjustifiable risk that the material element exists or will result from his conduct. The risk must be of such a nature and degree that the actor's failure to perceive it, considering the nature and purpose of his conduct and the circumstances known to him, involves a gross deviation from the standard of care that a reasonable person would observe in the actor's situation.

disregard of human life, and some variant of felony murder. However, fewer statutes explicitly specified 'intent to injure' as a sufficient *mens rea* for murder." Id. at 19.[47]

In summary, OCRS concludes that, based upon the MPC's definition of murder and the prevailing definition of murder under state law in 1984 when Section 1959 was enacted, the generic definition of murder within the scope of Section 1959 consists of three alternative classifications of murder: (1) intentional, knowingly or purposeful murder, (2) murder committed recklessly under circumstances manifesting extreme indifference to the value of human life or (3) felony-murder. Therefore, any statutory offense that includes elements that substantially conform to any one (or more) of these three classifications of murder falls within the generic definition of murder prevailing in 1984 and may constitute a crime of "murder" within the ambit of Section 1959. However, this generic definition of murder does **not** include manslaughter as commonly defined, or negligent homicide. To be sure, all fifty states have enacted statutory offenses that substantially conform with the generic definition of murder prevailing in 1984 and hence may constitute a predicate crime for murder under Section 1959.

---

[47] See, e.g., N.Y. PENAL LAW §§ 125.25(1)(2) and (3) (McKinney 1984) (which proscribed as "murder," respectively: (1) intentional murder, (2) under circumstances evincing a depraved indifference to human life, [a defendant] recklessly engages in conduct which creates a grave risk of death to another person, and thereby causes the death of another person or (3) felony murder); N.J. STAT. ANN. §§ 2C: 11-3(a)(1)-(3) (West 1982) (which proscribed, respectively, purposeful murder, knowing murder and felony murder); 18 PA. CONS. STAT. ANN. §§ 2502(a), (b) and (c) (West 1978) (which proscribed, respectively, intentional murder, felony murder and reckless murder); CAL. PENAL CODE § 189 (West 1982) (which proscribed any kind of willful, deliberate and premeditated killing and felony murder); TEXAS PENAL CODE ANN. §§ 19.02 (a)(1) and (3) (Vernon 1973) (proscribing, respectively, intentional or knowing murder and felony murder).

### 3. Section 1959 Cases Charging Murder

Murder in violation of state law is the most common underlying crime of violence charged in Section 1959 prosecutions.[48] As previously discussed above in Section II (E), in such cases the United States must prove all the essential elements of the predicate state law violation to prove the charged underlying murder violation. Therefore, the prosecution memorandum accompanying the proposed Section 1959 charge must demonstrate that the admissible evidence establishes all the requisite elements of the alleged state murder violations.

It is important to bear in mind that as long as the charged conduct falls within any of the three classifications of the generic definition of murder and violates the charged state law, it is immaterial what degree of murder the defendant has committed. For example, in Owens v. United States, 236 F. Supp. 2d 122, 137-40 (D. Mass. 2002), the Section 1959 count alleged that the defendant had committed first degree murder in that the defendant "willfully and knowingly, and with deliberately premeditated malice aforethought and extreme atrocity and cruelty, murdered Rodney Belle." Id. at 138. The defendant argued that the indictment was constructively amended to permit conviction

---

[48] See, e.g., United States v. Bruno, 383 F.3d 65, 84-85 (2d Cir. 2004) (N.Y. Penal Law); Crenshaw, 359 F.3d at 993-95 (Minnesota Law); Pimentel, 346 F.3d at 292, 295-300 (N.Y. and Pennsylvania Law); United States v. Kehoe, 310 F.3d 579, 583 (8th Cir. 2002) (Arkansas Law); United States v. Vasquez, 267 F.3d 79, 82-86 (2d Cir. 2001) (N.Y. Law); United States v. Dhinsa, 243 F.3d 635, 660-64, 670-72 (2d Cir. 2001) (N.Y. Law); United States v. Johnson, 219 F.3d 349, 355-56 (4th Cir. 2000) (Maryland, New York, Pennsylvania and Virginia Law); United States v. Rahman, 189 F.3d 88, 140-142 (2d Cir. 1999) ( New York Law); United States v. Diaz, 176 F.3d 52, 81-82, 99-101 (2d Cir. 1999) (Connecticut Law); Mapp, 170 F.3d at 335-36 (N.Y. Penal Law § 125.25(3)); United States v. Polanco, 145 F.3d 536, 539 (2d Cir. 1998) (New York Law); United States v. Stantini, 85 F.3d 9, 11-12 (2d Cir. 1996) (N.Y. Penal Law § 125.25); United States v. Tolliver, 61 F.3d 1189, 1208-09 (5th Cir. 1995) (Louisiana Law); United States v. Wong, 40 F.3d 1347, 1379-81 (2d Cir. 1994) (N.Y. Law); Locascio, 6 F.3d 924, 929, 940-42 (2d Cir. 1993) (N.Y. Law); United States v. Concepcion, 983 F.2d 369, 380-82 (2d Cir. 1992) (N.Y. Law).

for second degree murder by the court's jury instruction that omitted the premeditation requirement necessary to establish first degree murder. The district court rejected this argument, stating in relevant part:

> The charge at issue, violation of 18 U.S.C. § 1959(a)(1), imposes liability for murder in aid of racketeering. The statute is not restricted to first or second degree murder. Accordingly, inasmuch as the charged offense's elements are concerned, whether the jury found him guilty of second or first degree murder, [the defendant] violated 18 U.S.C. § 1959(a)(1).

Id. at 138.

Moreover, in accordance with OCRS' analysis of the definition of generic murder within the scope of Section 1959, courts have held that felony murder in violation of state law falls within the ambit of Section 1959,[49] and that manslaughter does not.[50]

### G. Kidnapping

#### 1. Federal Kidnapping Statute, 18 U.S.C. § 1201

Section 1959(a) plainly states that it includes a predicate crime of violence for anyone who "kidnaps. . . . in violation of the laws of . . . the United States." In 1984, when Section 1959 was enacted, 18 U.S.C. § 1201 was the principal federal kidnapping statute. Section 1201 provides as follows:

> **(a)** Whoever unlawfully seizes, confines, inveigles, decoys, kidnaps, abducts, or carries away and holds for ransom or reward or otherwise any person, except in the case of a minor by the parent thereof, when–

---

[49] See, e.g., Mapp, 170 F.3d at 335-36.

[50] See, e.g., Diaz, 176 F.3d at 100-01 (holding that manslaughter is not a lesser included offense of RICO or Section 1959 murder and therefore the trial court's refusal to instruct the jury that manslaughter was a lesser included offense was not error); United States v. Colon, 2005 WL 2764820 at 3 (D. Conn. Oct. 21, 2005) ("Manslaughter is not a lesser included offense of VCAR murder" and hence "the court properly refused to give that instruction to the jury.").

**(1)** the person is willfully transported in interstate or foreign commerce, regardless of whether the person was alive when transported across a State boundary if the person was alive when the transportation began;

**(2)** any such act against the person is done within the special maritime and territorial jurisdiction of the United States;
**(3)** any such act against the person is done within the special aircraft jurisdiction of the United States as defined in section 46501 of title 49;
**(4)** the person is a foreign official, an internationally protected person, or an official guest as those terms are defined in section 1116(b) of this title; or
**(5)** the person is among those officers and employees described in section 1114 of this title and any such act against the person is done while the person is engaged in, or on account of, the performance of official duties, shall be punished by imprisonment for any term of years or for life and, if the death of any person results, shall be punished by death or life imprisonment.
**(b)** With respect to subsection (a)(1), above, the failure to release the victim within twenty-four hours after he shall have been unlawfully seized, confined, inveigled, decoyed, kidnapped, abducted, or carried away shall create a rebuttable presumption that such person has been transported to interstate or foreign commerce. Notwithstanding the preceding sentence, the fact that the presumption under this section has not yet taken effect does not preclude a Federal investigation of a possible violation of this section before the 24- hour period has ended.
**(c)** If two or more persons conspire to violate this section and one or more of such persons do any overt act to effect the object of the conspiracy, each shall be punished by imprisonment for any term of years or for life.
**(d)** Whoever attempts to violate subsection (a) shall be punished by imprisonment for not more than twenty years.
**(e)** If the victim of an offense under subsection (a) is an internationally protected person outside the United States, the United States may exercise jurisdiction over the offense if (1) the victim is a representative, officer, employee, or agent of the United States, (2) an offender is a national of the United States, or (3) an offender is afterwards found in the United States. As used in this subsection, the United States includes all areas under the jurisdiction of the United States including any of the places within the provisions of sections 5 and 7 of this title and section 46501(2) of title 49. For purposes of this subsection, the term "national of the United States" has the

meaning prescribed in section 101(a)(22) of the Immigration and Nationality Act (8 U.S.C. 1101(a)(22)).

**(f)** In the course of enforcement of subsection (a)(4) and any other sections prohibiting a conspiracy or attempt to violate subsection (a)(4), the Attorney General may request assistance from any Federal, State, or local agency, including the Army, Navy, and Air Force, any statute, rule, or regulation to the contrary notwithstanding.

**(g) Special rule for certain offenses involving children.--**

>**(1) To whom applicable.--**If--
>>**(A)** the victim of an offense under this section has not attained the age of eighteen years; and
>>**(B)** the offender--
>>>**(i)** has attained such age; and
>>>**(ii)** is not--
>>>>**(I)** a parent;
>>>>**(II)** a grandparent;
>>>>**(III)** a brother;
>>>>**(IV)** a sister;
>>>>**(V)** an aunt;
>>>>**(VI)** an uncle; or
>>>>**(VII)** an individual having legal custody of the victim;

the sentence under this section for such offense shall include imprisonment for not less than 20 years.

>**[(2) Repealed.** Pub.L. 108-21, Title I, § 104(b), Apr. 30, 2003, 117 Stat. 653]
>
>**(h)** As used in this section, the term "parent" does not include a person whose parental rights with respect to the victim of an offense under this section have been terminated by a final court order.[51]

---

[51] History and Amendments (since 1980):

2003 Amendments. Subsec. (g)(1).

Pub.L. 108-21, § 104(b), in the undesignated paragraph at the end of par. (1), substituted "the sentence under this section for such offense shall include imprisonment for not less than 20 years." for "the sentence under this section for such offense shall be subject to paragraph (2) of this subsection."

(continued...)

[51](...continued)

Subsec. (g)(2). Pub.L. 108-21, § 104(b), struck out par. (2), which read:

**"(2) Guidelines.**--The United States Sentencing Commission is directed to amend the existing guidelines for the offense of 'kidnapping, abduction, or unlawful restraint,' by including the following additional specific offense characteristics: If the victim was intentionally maltreated (i.e., denied either food or medical care) to a life-threatening degree, increase by 4 levels; if the victim was sexually exploited (i.e., abused, used involuntarily for pornographic purposes) increase by 3 levels; if the victim was placed in the care or custody of another person who does not have a legal right to such care or custody of the child either in exchange for money or other consideration, increase by 3 levels; if the defendant allowed the child to be subjected to any of the conduct specified in this section by another person, then increase by 2 levels."

1998 Amendments. Subsec. (a)(1). Pub.L. 105-314, § 702(a), inserted ", regardless of whether the person was alive when transported across a State boundary if the person was alive when the transportation began", before the semicolon.

Subsec. (a)(5). Pub.L. 105-314, § 702(b), struck "designated" and inserted "described".

Subsec. (b). Pub.L. 105-314, § 702(c), added "Notwithstanding the preceding sentence, the fact that the presumption under this section has not yet taken effect does not preclude a Federal investigation of a possible violation of this section before the 24-hour period has ended.".

1996 Amendments. Subsec. (e). Pub.L. 104-132, § 721(f), added "For purposes of this subsection, the term 'national of the United States' has the meaning prescribed in section 101(a)(22) of the Immigration and Nationality Act (8 U.S.C. 1101(a)(22))." following "section 46501(2) of title 49.", and substituted "If the victim of an offense under subsection (a) is an internationally protected person outside the United States, the United States may exercise jurisdiction over the offense if (1) the victim is a representative, officer, employee, or agent of the United States, (2) an offender is a national of the United States, or (3) an offender is afterwards found in the United States." for "If the victim of an offense under subsection (a) is an internationally protected person, the United States may exercise jurisdiction over the offense if the alleged offender is present within the United States, irrespective of the place where the offense was committed or the nationality of the victim or the alleged offender."

1994 Amendments. Heading. Pub.L. 103-322, § 330021(1), substituted "Kidnapping" for "Kidnaping" as the section heading.

Subsec. (a)(3). Pub.L. 103-272, § 5(e)(8), substituted "section 46501 of title 49" for "section 101(38) of the Federal Aviation Act of 1958".

Subsec. (a). Pub.L. 103-322, § 60003(a)(6), inserted in the provisions following par. (5) the phrase
(continued...)

**(a) Elements**

To establish a substantive violation of Section 1201, the government must prove four elements: (1) the transportation in interstate commerce; (2) of an unconsenting person who is; (3) held for ransom or reward or otherwise; and (4) such acts being done knowingly and willfully. See, e.g., United States v. Barton, 257 F.3d 433, 439 (5th Cir. 2001); United States v. Walker, 137 F.3d 1217, 1220 (10th Cir. 1998); United States v. Jackson, 978 F.2d 903 (5th Cir. 1992); United States v. McCabe, 812 F.2d 1060 (8th Cir. 1987); United States v. Chancery, 715 F.2d 543 (11th Cir. 1983).

Section 1201 also criminalizes conspiracies, 18 U.S.C. § 1201(c), and attempts.

---

[51](...continued)
"and, if the eath of any person results, shall be punished by death or life imprisonment".

Subsec. (b). Pub.L. 103-322, § 330021(2), substituted "kidnapped" for "kidnaped".

Subsec. (d). Pub.L. 103-322, § 320903(b), substituted "subsection (a)" for "subsection (a)(4) or (a)(5)".

Subsec. (c). Pub.L. 103-272, § 5(e)(2), substituted "section 46501(2) of title 49" for "section 101(38) of the Federal Aviation Act of 1958, as amended (49 U.S.C. 1301(38))".

Subsec. (h). Pub.L. 103-322, § 320924, added subsec. (h).

1990 Amendments. Subsec. (a)(3). Pub.L. 101-647, § 3538(1), (2), substituted "101(38)" for "101(36)" and struck ", as amended (49 U.S.C. 1301(36))" following "Federal Aviation Act of 1958".

Subsec. (g). Pub.L. 101-647 added subsec. (g).

1986 Amendments. Subsec. (a). Pub.L. 99-646, § 36, in provision preceding par. (1) substituted "when--" for "when:", in par. (5) substituted "the person" for "The person" and "official duties" for "his official duties", and aligned the margin of par. (5) with the margins of pars. (1) to (4).

Subsec. (d). Pub.L. 99-646, § 37(b), inserted "or (a)(5)" after "subsection (a)(4)".

1984 Amendments. Subsec. (a)(5). Pub.L. 98-473 added par. (5).

18 U.S.C. § 1201(d).[52]

### (b) Kidnapping by force (seizure, confinement, kidnapping, abduction, or carrying away) or seduction (decoying and inveigling)

The government must prove that the defendant seized, confined, inveigled, decoyed, kidnaped, abducted, or carried away the victim. Thus, "the statute specifies seven methods by which a victim may be 'taken.' Five of these terms–seizing, confining, kidnapping, abducting, and carrying away–involve an actual physical or bodily carrying away or restriction of the victim. The remaining two methods–inveigling or decoying–involve nonphysical takings by which the kidnapper, through deception or some other means, lures the victim into accompanying him." United States v. Macklin, 671 F.2d 60, 65-66 (2d Cir. 1982).

To prove that the defendant seized, confined, kidnaped, abducted, or carried away a victim, the government must show that the defendant used, or threatened to use, some form of physical or mental force. See Chatwin v. United States, 326 U.S. 455, 460 (1946) (statutory language "necessarily implies an unlawful physical or mental restraint for an appreciable period against the person's will and with a willful intent so to confine the victim."); see also United States v. Macklin, 671 F.2d at 64; United States v. Lentz, 383 F.3d 191, 201 (4th Cir. 2004); United States v. Adams, 83 F.3d 1371, 1374 (11th Cir. 1996).

Even if a victim originally accompanies another consensually, this does not prevent kidnapping where force is later used to seize or confine the victim. See, e.g., United States v.

---

[52] Portions of this section were derived from Chapter 10 of the Civil Rights Manual of the United States Department of Justice, which is available on USABook at http://10.173.2.12/usao/eousa/ole/usabook/civr/10civr.htm. OCRS expresses its appreciation to Barbara Kay Bosserman and Lorna Grenadier, the authors of that section.

Redmond, 803 F.2d 438, 439 (9th Cir. 1986); United States v. Bordeaux, 84 F.3d 1544 (8th Cir. 1996).

Alternatively, the government may prove that the defendant kidnapped by inveiglement or decoy. See Macklin, 671 F.2d at 65-66. For instance, a kidnapping may occur where a defendant lies to his victim, and the victim wilfully accompanies the defendant, so long as the victim did not consent to the nature of the trip that actually occurred. See, e.g., United States v. Boone, 959 F.2d 1550, 1556 (11th Cir. 1992) ("Where an alleged kidnapper successfully inveigles or decoys his victim, transports that person in interstate or foreign commerce, and holds the victim for ransom, reward, or otherwise, the mere fact that the kidnapper was not required to physically hold his victim prior to the crossing of state lines, thereby sparing himself the effort of using forcible action to accomplish the kidnapping, does not take his conduct outside of the statute."); United States v. Hoog, 504 F.2d 45 (8th Cir. 1974); United States v. Young, 248 F.3d 260, 273 (4th Cir. 2001); United States v. Stands, 105 F.3d 1565, 1576 (8th Cir. 1997); United States v. Peden, 961 F.2d 517, 523 (5th Cir. 1992); United States v. Hughes, 716 F.2d 234, 239 (4th Cir. 1983).

**(c) Transportation in interstate commerce**

The proof of transportation in interstate (and/or foreign) commerce is relatively straightforward. Importantly, however, the government need only prove that the defendant crossed state lines, not that he knew that state (or national) boundaries were being crossed. See, e.g., United States v. Lewis, 115 F.3d 1531, 1535 (11th Cir. 1997); United States v. Welch, 10 F.3d 573, 574 (8th Cir. 1993) ("The language of the statute, however, does not require that an offender know that he is crossing state lines. So long as he 'wilfully transports' his victim and, in doing so, travels in interstate commerce, he need not do so knowingly.").

Apart from the "interstate commerce" jurisdictional predicate, Section 1201 also prohibits kidnaping within the special maritime, territorial, or aircraft jurisdiction of the United States, if the person is a foreign official or other internationally-protected person, or federal employees. See 18 U.S.C. § 1201(a)(2)-(5).

**(d)     For "Ransom or Reward or Otherwise" Requirement**

A typical problematic issue in Section 1201 prosecutions is whether the victim was "held for ransom or reward or otherwise" as required by the statute. This element requires that the purpose must be for some benefit to the defendant. United States v. Wills, 346 F.3d 476 (4th Cir. 2003); United States v. Eagle Thunder, 893 F.2d 950, 953 (8th Cir. 1990) (defendant need only hold purpose for "some purpose of his own." (quoting United States v. Melton, 883 F.2d 336, 338 (5th Cir. 1989)); United States v. Dixon, 273 F.3d 636, 638 (5th Cir. 2001) ("The phrase 'or otherwise' has been interpreted 'to encompass any benefit a captor might attempt to receive.'"); United States v. Wolford, 444 F.2d 876, 881 (D.C. Cir. 1971) ("We think that Congress by the phrase 'or otherwise' intended to include any object of a kidnaping which the perpetrator might consider of sufficient benefit to himself to induce him to undertake it." (quoting United States v. Parker, 103 F.2d 857 (3d Cir. 1939)). See also Gawne v. United States, 409 F.2d 1399 (9th Cir. 1969) (kidnapping undesirable in itself, regardless of purpose). Thus, the purpose need not be illegal, see, e.g., United States v. Healy, 376 U.S. 75, 82 (1964); United States v. Adams, 83 F.3d 1371, 1373 (11th Cir. 1996); United States v. Williams, 998 F.2d 258, 267-68 (5th Cir. 1993), nor financial in nature, see, e.g., Gooch v. United States, 297 U.S. 124 (1936); Healy, 376 U.S. at 81; United States v. Crosby, 713 F.2d 1066 (5th Cir. 1983), nor immoral, see United States v. Jones, 808 F.2d 561, 565-66 (7th Cir. 1986) (contrasting kidnapping statute with the Mann Act, which requires an immoral purpose).

Accordingly, courts have upheld convictions where the purpose was to assault, see United States v. Bordeaux, 84 F.3d 1544, 1548 (8th Cir. 1996); to commit theft or robbery, see United States

v. Martell, 335 F.2d 764 (4th Cir. 1964); United States v. Young, 512 F.2d 321 (4th Cir. 1975); United States v. De La Motte, 434 F.2d 289 (2d Cir. 1970) (truck hijacking); sexual assault, see United States v. Brown, 330 F.3d 1073 (8th Cir. 2003); De Herrera v. United States, 339 F.2d 587 (10th Cir. 1964); United States v. Lutz, 420 F.2d 414 (3rd Cir. 1970); sexual gratification see United States v. Lowe, 145 F.3d 45, 52 (1st Cir. 1998); United States v. McBryar, 553 F.2d 433 (5th Cir. 1997); to silence a witness see United States v. Satterfield, 743 F.2d 827 (11th Cir. 1984); to escape from police, see Gooch v. United States, 297 U.S. 124 (1936); Hess v. United States, 254 F.2d 578 (8th Cir. 1958); United States v. Walker, 524 F.2d 1125 (10th Cir. 1975) (prison escape); to have the defendant's estranged wife discuss their marital affairs, see United States v. Vickers, 578 F.2d 1057 (5th Cir. 1978); for revenge, see United States v. McCabe, 812 F.2d 1060, 1062 (8th Cir. 1987); or to take a child in the belief that she was being mistreated by her parents, see United States v. Atchinson, 524 F.2d 367 (7th Cir. 1975).

As the Supreme Court stated in Healy, "[a] murder committed to accelerate the accrual of one's rightful inheritance is hardly less heinous than one committed to facilitate a theft; by the same token, we find no compelling correlation between the propriety of the ultimate purpose sought to be furthered by a kidnaping and the undesirability of the act of kidnaping itself." 376 U.S. at 81.

### 2.  Generic Kidnapping

The Model Penal Code defined kidnapping as follows:

A person is guilty of kidnapping if he unlawfully removes another from his place of residence or business, or a substantial distance from the vicinity where he is found, or if he unlawfully confines another for a substantial period in a place of isolation, with any of the following purposes:

> (a) to hold for ransom or reward, or as a shield or hostage; or
> (b) to facilitate commission of any felony or flight thereafter; or
> (c) to inflict bodily injury on or to terrorize the victim or another; or
> (d) to interfere with the performance of any governmental or political function.
>
> ... A removal or confinement is unlawful within the meaning of this Section if it is accomplished by force, threat or deception, or in the case of a person who is under the age of 14 or incompetent, if it is accomplished without the consent of a parent, guardian or other person responsible for general supervision of his welfare.

MPC § 212.1. This definition provides that the crux of kidnapping is an "unlawful" removal of the victim from his residence or place of business, or other substantial removal or confinement for any of four purposes. Under each of the four purposes, the definition of kidnapping is confined "to instances of substantial removal or confinement. . . . The removal or confinement must be accompanied by force, threat, or deception, or in the case of underage children or incompetents, without the consent of a parent or other appropriate person." MPC § 212.1 Cmt. at 208.

At common law, "kidnapping" was defined "as the unlawful confinement and transportation of another out of the country." Id. at 210. The MPC's definition of kidnapping is far broader than its common law definition and reflects the development of state kidnapping statutory provisions. Id. at 210. For example, the MPC's definition requires substantial unlawful removal or confinement, but not "asportation out of the country." Id. at 210-211. The MPC's drafters explained that the requisite removal or confinement must involve something more substantial than confinement or restraint that is incidental to most crimes of violence. In that regard, the drafters stated:

> This phrasing of the asportation requirement eliminates the absurdity of liability for kidnapping where a robber forces his victim into his own home or into the back of a store in order to retrieve valuables located there. For situations in which the victim is seized elsewhere than in his residence or place of business, the section requires removal "a substantial distance from the vicinity where he is found." By using the word "vicinity" rather than "place" and by speaking only of "substantial" removal, the provision precludes kidnapping convictions based on trivial changes of location having no bearing on the evil at hand. Thus, for example, the rapist who forces his

victim into a parked car or dark alley may be punished quite severely for the crime of rape, but he does not thereby also become liable for kidnapping.

Id. at 223-24. Moreover, the MPC's definition of kidnapping expands its scope beyond ransom, to include four broad purposes.

As of 1984, at least twenty-two states adopted the four enumerated purposes found in the Model Penal Code,[53] and another five had adopted the first three, omitting the purpose of interference with governmental functions.[54]

Therefore, OCRS concludes that MPC's widely adopted definition of kidnapping sets forth the prevailing definition of kidnapping as of 1984 and constitutes the generic definition of kidnapping within the scope of Section 1959. Accordingly, a statutory offense may constitute a predicate offense involving "kidnapping" under Section 1959 when its elements substantially conform to the MPC's elements for kidnapping, involving unlawful removal or restraint, and one or more of the four stated purposes set forth in MPC § 212.1.

### 3. Section 1959 Cases Charging Kidnapping

---

[53] For those twenty-two states statutes which had adopted all four, see ALA. CODE § 13A-6-43 (1977) (four purposes); ALASKA STAT. (1989); ARIZ. REV. STAT. ANN. § 13-1304 (West 1977); ARK. CODE ANN. § 41-1702 (Michie 1977); CONN. GEN. STAT. ANN. § 53a-92 (West 1977); FLA. STAT. ANN. § 787.01 (West 1976); HAW. REV. STAT. ANN. § 707-720 (Michie 1976); KAN. CRIM. CODE ANN. § 21-3420 (West 1974); KY. REV. STAT. ANN. § 509.040 (Michie 1975); N.J. STAT. ANN. § 2C:13-1 (Rev. 1982); ME. REV. STAT. ANN. tit. 17A, § 301 (West 1978); MO. ANN. STAT. § 565.110 (West 1978); MONT. REV. CODE ANN. § 94-5-303 (Smith 1977); NEB. REV. CODE ANN. § 28-313 (Michie 1978); N.Y. PENAL LAW § 135.25 (McKinney 1975); N.D. CENT. CODE § 12.1-18-01 (1976); OHIO REV. CODE. ANN § 2905.01 (West 1974); 18 PA. CONS. STAT. ANN. § 2901 (West 1973); S.D. CODIFIED LAWS § 22-19-1 (Michie 1977); TEX. PENAL CODE ANN. § 20.04 (Vernon 1974); UTAH CODE ANN. § 76-5-302 (1975); WASH. REV. CODE ANN. § 9A.40.020 (West 1977).

[54] For those five state statutes which had adopted the three purposes (excluding interference with governmental/political functions), see DEL. CODE ANN. tit. 11, § 783A (1974); MINN. STAT. ANN. § 609.25 (West 1964); N.C. GEN. STAT. § 14-39 (1969); N.H. REV. STAT. ANN. § 633:1 (1974); WYO. STAT ANN. § 6-2-201 (1977).

In United States v. Tokars, 95 F.3d 1520, 1539-40 (11th Cir. 1996), the court rejected the defendant's argument that even if there was sufficient evidence to link the defendant to a plot to murder his wife, Sara, there was insufficient evidence to convict him of participation in her kidnapping. The evidence showed that the defendant Tokars asked Lawrence, a co-conspirator in his money laundering business, to kill his wife because she wanted to divorce him and obtain a large monetary settlement. Id. at 1528. The plan was to kill the defendant's wife in her home and make it look like a burglary. Lawrence, in turn, hired Rower to kill the defendant's wife. Id. at 1528. However, Rower forced the defendant's wife into a vehicle and they left for Atlanta, and she was shot and killed en route. Id. at 1528-29.

The Court held that the evidence was sufficient to support the defendant's conviction for kidnapping his wife in violation of Section 1959 because:

> Sara's kidnapping was a reasonably foreseeable consequence of placing a contract "hit" on Sara's life. Tokars and Lawrence were co-conspirators in a cocaine conspiracy; therefore, it was reasonably foreseeable that originally unintended acts of violence might occur.

Id. at 1540.

United States v. Matta-Ballesteros, 71 F.3d 754, 765 (9th Cir. 1995) and United States v. Lopez-Alvarez, 970 F.2d 583, 589-93 (9th Cir. 1992), upheld the convictions of several defendants, who were members of a drug trafficking cartel, for their participation in the kidnapping, torture and murders in Mexico of DEA Agent Enrique Camarena-Salazar and an informant, Alfredo Zavala. In Lopez-Alvarez, 970 F.2d at 593, the court ruled that the evidence was sufficient to support defendant Lopez-Alvarez's admission that he helped kidnap and torture agent Camarena.[55] In,

---

[55] However, the court held that there was insufficient evidence to support defendant Lopez-Alvarez's convictions for participation in the kidnapping and murder of Zavala, and for being an (continued...)

Matta-Ballesteros, 71 F.3d at 765, the court upheld defendant Matta-Ballesteros' conviction for conspiring to kidnap Agent Camarena in violation of Section 1959, stating:

> The evidence showed that Matta-Ballesteros was a member of the Guadalajara [drug] cartel and that he participated in some of the meetings with other members of the cartel where Camarena's kidnapping was planned. The evidence also showed members of the Cartel abducted, tortured and murdered Camarena. . . . Thus, the evidence was sufficient to show that Matta-Ballesteros was involved in a conspiracy targeted at Camarena. Furthermore, because a conspirator is liable for all foreseeable substantive offenses committed in furtherance of the conspiracy. . . there was also sufficient evidence to support his conviction on the substantive charges.

Id. at 765 (footnote and citations omitted).

### H. Maiming

#### 1. Generic Maiming

a. "'Maim' is the modern equivalent of the old word 'mayhem'. . . . Mayhem, according to the English Common Law is maliciously depriving another of the use of such as of his members as may render him less able, in fighting, either to defend himself or to annoy his adversary." ROLLIN M. PERKINS & RONALD N. BOYCE, CRIMINAL LAW, § 8, at 237-38 (3d Ed. 1982) (hereinafter "PERKINS"). Under English Common Law, therefore, "[t]o cut off, or permanently to cripple, a man's hand or finger, or to strike out his eye or fore tooth, were all mayhems. . . if done maliciously, because any such harm rendered the person less efficient as a fighting man." PERKINS at 239; see also WAYNE R. LAFAVE, SUBSTANTIVE CRIMINAL LAW § 16.5 at 599 (2d Ed. 2006) (hereinafter "LAFAVE"). Thus, the essence of "mayhem" or "maiming" at common law was "malicious maiming or maliciously and intentionally disfiguring another." PERKINS at 240.

---

[55](...continued)
accessory after the fact regarding the kidnapping and murder of Camarena and Zavala. Lopez-Alvarez, 970 F.3d at 593-94.

As the law developed in the United States up to 1984, "mayhem" or "maiming" encompassed "malicious maiming or disfigurement" that resulted in permanent or protracted disfigurement, dismemberment or disabling. Some statutes also required specific intent to maim or disfigure. See MPC § 211.1 Cmt. at 175; PERKINS at 241; LAFAVE at 599-600. For example, in 1984, 18 U.S.C. § 114, proscribed "maiming within maritime and territorial jurisdiction," and provided as follows:

> Whoever, within the special maritime and territorial jurisdiction of the United States, and with intent to maim, or disfigure, cuts, bites, or slits the nose, ear, or lip, or cuts out or disables the tongue, or puts out or destroys an eye, or cuts off or disables a limb or any member of another person; or
>
> Whoever, within the special maritime and territorial jurisdiction of the United States, and with like intent, throws or pours upon another person, any scalding water, corrosive acid, or caustic substance--
>
> Shall be fined not more than $1,000 or imprisoned not more than seven years, or both.[56]

In United States v. Salamanca, 990 F.2d 629, 635-36 (D.C. Cir. 1993), the defendant was convicted of assault with intent to commit murder, assault with intent to kill a federal officer in performance of his duties, and maiming. The convictions stemmed from the defendant's striking a police officer multiple times with a club that split open the officer's skull, shattered his eye socket, knocked out three of his teeth, and broke his jaw. Id. at 635. The court held that the jury could have properly concluded that Salamanca possessed both the specific intent to murder and the specific

---

[56] Section 114 was enacted in 1948. 62 Stat. 683, 689 (1948). However, maiming was initially made a federal offense under the Act of 1790. See 1 Stat. 15; United States v. Scroggins, 27 F. Cas. 999 (Circuit Court D. Ark. 1847) ("If any person should purposely and maliciously disable the tongue of another by biting, or put out an eye by shooting, striking, gouging, or such like means, or should disable any limb or member of another, by cutting, shooting, or any other means, with intent to maim or disfigure, such person would, undoubtedly, be liable to conviction on this statute.").

intent to maim under two scenarios: (1) they "might have concluded that [the defendant] began the attack with the specific intent to maim, and at some point during the attack altered his intent, seeking to finish the job by killing" him; or (2) they might have found that "[the defendant] held alternative intents, thinking: 'Either I'll kill him, or at least put his eye out.'" Id.[57]

Moreover, in 1984 at least fourteen states (California, Maryland, Massachusetts, Michigan, Mississippi, Nevada, North Carolina, Oklahoma, Rhode Island, Tennessee, Utah, Vermont, Virginia and Wisconsin) had statutes that specifically proscribed "mayhem" or "maiming."[58] For example, the California offense of "mayhem" provided that:

> Every person who unlawfully and maliciously deprives a human being of a member of his body, or disables, disfigures, or renders it useless, or cuts or disables the tongue, or puts out an eye, or slits the nose, ear, or lip, is guilty of mayhem.

---

[57] But see United States v. Stone, 472 F.2d 909 (5th Cir. 1973), where the court held that the evidence introduced in a rape case did not support the charge of maiming under § 114:

> Evidence was introduced at trial that Mrs. Doe's assailant cut off part of the hair on her head and her pubic hair, hit and kicked her, whipped her with a branch, cut her wrist with a knife, and burned her with his lighted cigarette and the car's cigarette lighter. No evidence was introduced regarding damage to Mrs. Doe's nose, ears, lips, tongue, or eyes, or that her assailant threw or poured damaging substance upon her. Nor does the language "cuts off or disables a limb or any member" cover the physical abuse Mrs. Doe suffered here. We conclude that this charge should not have been submitted to the jury.

Stone, 472 F.2d at 915.

[58] See CAL PENAL CODE § 203 (1955); MD. CODE ANN., CRIMES AND PUNISHMENT, § 35; MASS. GEN. LAWS ANN. Ch. 265, § 14 (1970); MICH. COMP. LAWS ANN. § 750.397 (1970); MISS. CODE ANN. § 97-3-59 (1942); NEV. REV. STAT. ANN § 200.280 (1979); N.C. GEN. STAT. § 14-30 (1979); OKLA. STAT. ANN. tit. 21. § 751-752; R.I. GEN. LAWS § 11-29-1 (1956); TENN. CODE ANN. § 392-111 (1922); UTAH CODE ANN. § 76-5-105 (1973); VT. STAT. ANN. tit. 13, § 2701 (1971); VA. CODE ANN. § 18.2-51 (1950); WIS. STAT ANN. § 940.21 (1982). Ten of these states' maiming statutes (Maryland, Massachusetts, Michigan, Mississippi, North Carolina, Oklahoma, Vermont, Virginia, Utah and Wisconsin) require proof of specific intent to maim or disfigure; the remaining four states' maiming statutes require general criminal intent.

CAL PENAL CODE § 203 (1955). Under this provision, specific intent to commit mayhem is not an element of the offense: "If a person unlawfully strikes another, not with the specific intent to commit the crime of mayhem, and the blow so delivered results in the loss or disfigurement of a member of the body of the assaulted party or in putting out his eye, the crime is nevertheless mayhem." People v. Nunes, 190 P. 486, 487 (Cal. App. 1920); see also Goodman v. Superior Court, 148 Cal. Rptr. 799, 800-01 (Cal. Ct. App. 1978) (finding that as a matter of law, a trier of fact could reasonably find mayhem where the victim's face was permanently disfigured though not functionally impaired, and noting that the common law definition of mayhem was gradually expanded "to include mere disfigurement without an attendant reduction in fighting ability").

Courts in California have relied on the stated rationale of the crime to include serious injuries to body parts in addition to those specifically listed in the statute: "The fact that various parts of the head are mentioned in section 203 is probably attributable more to historical happenstance than to a current legislative intent to exclude from the purview of mayhem areas of the head not specifically mentioned." People v. Newble, 174 Cal.Rptr. 637, 640 (Cal. Ct. App. 1981) (holding that the head is a "member" of the body under § 203); see also People v. Page, 163 Cal. Rptr. 839, 843-44 (Cal. Ct. App. 1980) (finding that "tatooing" a victim's breasts and abdomen against her will it could constitute mayhem regardless of whether the injury could be corrected by modern plastic surgery).

The crime of "mayhem" under Massachusetts law includes the intent to maim or disfigure found in the federal offense of maiming:

> Whoever, with **malicious intent to maim or disfigure**, cuts out or maims the tongue, puts out or destroys an eye, cuts or tears off an ear, cuts, slits or mutilates the nose or lip, or cuts off or disables a limb or member, of another person, and whoever is privy to such intent, or is present and aids in the commission of such crime, or whoever, with **intent to maim or disfigure, assaults another person with** a dangerous weapon, substance or chemical, and by such assault disfigures, cripples or inflicts serious or permanent physical injury upon such person, and whoever is

> privy to such intent, or is present and aids in the commission of such crime, shall be punished by imprisonment in the state prison for not more than twenty years or by a fine of not more than one thousand dollars and imprisonment in jail for not more than two and one half years.

MASS. GEN. LAWS ANN. Ch. 265, § 14 (1970) (emphasis added). Unlike the California mayhem provisions, Massachusetts law requires a specific intent to maim or disfigure. See, e.g., Commonwealth v. Hogan, 387 N.E.2d 158, 163-64 (Mass. App. Ct. 1979). The specific intent to maim or disfigure can be inferred from the nature and results of the attack. Commonwealth v. Tucceri, 399 N.E.2d 1110, 1111-12 (Mass. App. Ct. 1980) (holding that the specific intent to maim or disfigure was supported by "the sustained nature of the assault on the eyes; and, as applied to so delicate an organ as an eye, dirt can be found to be a dangerous substance within the meaning of the statute").

Furthermore, courts have interpreted "maiming" to have its ordinary and plain meaning and that the specific intent to maim is synonymous with an intent to inflict "some serious bodily injury." Commonwealth v. Farrell, 78 N.E.2d 697, 704 (Mass. 1948) (defining maim "as meaning to disable, wound, cause bodily hurt or disfigurement to the body"). Therefore, courts have held that under some circumstances the resulting injury need not be permanent. See, e.g., Farrell, 78 N.E. 2d at 704-05 ("a crippling may be found... even though there may be complete recovery in time"); Hogan, 387 N.E. 2d at 165 (defendant's "participation in the vicious beating which resulted in the disablement of Condon's limbs due to the multiple fractures was sufficient...even though there may be complete recovery in time"). Wisconsin's "mayhem" offense also requires specific intent, and provides:

> Whoever, with intent to disable or disfigure another, cuts or mutilates the tongue, eye, ear, nose, lip, limb or other bodily member of another, is guilty of a Class B felony.

WIS. STAT. ANN. § 940.21 (1982). See Kirby v. State, 272 N.W.2d 113, 116 (Wisc. Ct. App. 1979).

("A conviction for mayhem thus requires proof of specific intent to disable or disfigure as distinguished from a general intent to do the acts and consciousness of the nature of the acts and possible results.").[59]

---

[59] See also, MD CODE ANN., Crimes and Punishments § 385. (1957) ("Every person, his aiders, abettors and counsellors, who shall be convicted of the crime of cutting out or disabling the tongue, putting out an eye, slitting the nose, cutting or biting off the nose, ear or lip, or cutting or biting off or disabling any limb or member of any person, of malice aforethought, **with intention in so doing to mark or disfigure such person**, shall be guilty of a felony. . . .") (emphasis added); MICH. COMP. LAWS ANN. § 750.397 (1970) ("Any person who, **with malicious intent to maim or disfigure**, shall cut out or maim the tongue, put out or destroy an eye, cut or tear off an ear, cut or slit or mutilate the nose or lip, or cut off or disable a limb, organ or member, of any other person, and every person privy to such intent, who shall be present, aiding in the commission of such offense, shall be guilty of a felony, punishable by imprisonment in the state prison not more than 10 years, or by fine of not more than 5,000 dollars.") (emphasis added); MISS. CODE ANN. § 97-3-59 (1972) ("Every person who, **from premeditated design or with intent to kill or commit any felony**, shall mutilate, disfigure, disable or destroy the tongue, eye, lip, nose, or any other limb or member of any person, shall be guilty of mayhem, and, on conviction thereof, shall be punished by imprisonment in the penitentiary not more than seven years or in the county jail not less than six months.") (emphasis added); NEV. REV. STAT. ANN. § 200.280 (1979) ("Mayhem consists of unlawfully depriving a human being of a member of his body, or disfiguring or rendering it useless. If a person cuts out or disables the tongue, puts out an eye, slits the nose, ear or lip, or disables any limb or member of another, or voluntarily, or of purpose, puts out an eye or eyes, that person is guilty of mayhem. . . ."); N.C. GEN. STAT. § 14-30 (1970) ("'Malicious maiming'. If any person shall, of malice aforethought, unlawfully cut out or disable the tongue or put out an eye of any other person, **with intent to murder, maim or disfigure**, the person so offending, his counselors, abettors and aiders, knowing of and privy to the offense, shall be punished as a Class H felon.") (emphasis added); OKLA. STAT. ANN. tit. 21, § 751. ("Every person who, **with premeditated design to injure another**, inflicts upon his person any injury which disfigures his personal appearance or disables any member or organ of his body or seriously diminishes his physical vigor, is guilty of maiming.") (emphasis added); R.I. GEN. LAWS § 11-29-1 (1956) ("Every person who shall voluntarily, maliciously or of purpose put out an eye, slit the nose, ear, or lip, or cut off, bite off, or disable any limb or member of another, shall be imprisoned not exceeding ten (10) years nor less than one year."); TENN. CODE ANN. § 39-2-111 (1982) ("No person shall unlawfully and maliciously cut off or disable the tongue of another, by clipping, biting, or wounding; put out an eye, slit, cut off, or bite off the nose, ear, or lip of another, or any part of either of them, whereby the person is maimed or disfigured; cut off or disable the hand, arm, leg, or foot of another, or any part of either of them, whereby the person injured shall lose the proper use of any of those members; or, by cutting or otherwise, disable the organs of generation of another, or any part thereof. For the purposes of this section "put out an eye" shall mean to so severely damage an eye that there is a partial or total loss of sight. Whoever shall commit any of these offenses, shall, on conviction, be imprisoned in the
(continued...)

In sum, the crux of these federal and state offenses for "mayhem" or "maiming" is unlawful conduct with intent to disfigure or maim another person that results in either permanent or protracted disfigurement, dismemberment or disability.

b. The Model Penal Code did not propose an offense specifically limited to "mayhem" or "maiming". Rather, Model Penal Code § 211.1 provides for several gradations of "assault" offenses in an integrated provision, as follows:

§ 211.1 Assault

(1) Simple Assault. A person is guilty of assault if he:
    (a) attempts to cause or purposely, knowingly or recklessly causes bodily injury to another; or
    (b) negligently causes bodily injury to another with a deadly weapon; or
    (c) attempts by physical menace to put another in fear of imminent serious bodily injury.

Simple assault is a misdemeanor unless committed in a fight or scuffle entered into by mutual consent, in which case it is a petty misdemeanor.

(2) Aggravated Assault. A person is guilty of aggravated assault if he:
    (a) attempts to cause serious bodily injury to another, or causes such

---

[59](...continued)
penitentiary not less than two (2) years nor more than ten (10) years."); UTAH CODE ANN. § 76-5-105 (1975) ("Every person who unlawfully and **intentionally deprives a human** being of a member of his body, or disables or renders it useless, or who cuts out or disables the tongue, puts out an eye, or slits the nose, ear, or lip, is guilty of mayhem.") (emphasis added); VT. STAT. ANN. tit. 13, § 2701 (1971) ("Any person **with malicious intent to maim or disfigure**, who shall cut out or maim the tongue, put out or destroy an eye, cut or tear off an ear, cut, slit or mutilate the nose or lip, or cut or disable a limb or member of another person, and any person privy to such intent who shall be present aiding in the commission of such offense shall be imprisoned for life or for not less than seven years.") (emphasis added); VA. CODE ANN. § 18-2-51 (1950) ("If any person maliciously shoot, stab, cut or wound any person or by any means cause him bodily injury, **with intent to maim**, disfigure, disable, or kill, he shall [be punished]") (emphasis added).

> injury purposely, knowingly or recklessly under circumstances manifesting extreme indifference to the value of human life; or
> (b) attempts to cause or purposely or knowingly causes bodily injury to another with a deadly weapon.
>
> Aggravated assault under paragraph (a) is a felony on the second degree; aggravated assault under paragraph (b) is a felony of the third degree.

MPC § 210.00 (3) provides that:

> "Serious bodily injury" means bodily injury which creates a substantial risk of death or which causes serious, permanent disfigurement, or protracted loss or impairment of the function of any bodily member or organ.

The MPC drafters stated that MPC § 211.1 "effects a consolidation of the common-law crimes of mayhem, battery, and assault and also consolidates into a single offense what the antecedent statutes in this country normally treated as a series of aggravated assaults or batteries." MPC § 211.1 Cmt. at 172; see also id. at 188 ("This definition encompasses the drastic harms covered under the common-law felony of mayhem and adds a residual category of harm creating substantial risk of death."). Thus, in effect, the Model Penal Code integrates the offense of "mayhem" or "maiming" into "Aggravated Assault."

The Model Penal Code approach for assault reflects the modern practice among the states. Most states have adopted assault offenses resulting in "serious" or "great bodily" harm that encompass unlawful conduct that would constitute "mayhem" or "maiming." See MPC § 211.1 Cmt. at 180-87; PERKINS at 243; LAFAVE at 599-601 (2d Ed. 2003).[60] Indeed, the Senate Report regarding

---

[60] In 1984, at least thirty-seven states had an assault or battery offense that proscribed conduct that typically is covered by the generic offense of maiming/mayhem: Alabama, Alaska, Arizona, Arkansas, California, Colorado, Connecticut, Delaware, Florida, Hawaii, Indiana, Iowa, Kentucky, Louisiana, Maine, Minnesota, Missouri, Montana, Nebraska, Nevada, New Hampshire, New Jersey, New Mexico, New York, North Dakota, Ohio, Oklahoma, Oregon, Pennsylvania, Rhode Island, South Dakota, Tennessee, Texas, Utah, Vermont, Wisconsin and Wyoming. See Assault statutes cited in Appendix C. For example, New York Penal Law § 120.10(2) provides as
(continued...)

Section 1959 recognized that "an offense constituting maiming could usually be prosecuted . . . as an 'assault resulting in serious bodily injury.'" S. Rep. No. 98-225 at 323.

Based on the foregoing analysis of the development of the common law offense of mayhem, OCRS concludes that the generic definition of "maiming" within the scope of Section 1959 encompasses conduct with intent to maim or disfigure that results in permanent or protracted disfigurement, disablement or dismemberment of a body part of another person. Moreover, in most circumstances, such conduct may be prosecuted under "maiming" statutes proscribing such conduct or offenses for assault resulting in serious bodily injury, as discussed infra Section II (J).

### 2. Section 1959 Prosecutions Charging Maiming

---

[60](...continued)
follows:

> A person is guilty of assault in the first degree when:
>
> 2. With intent to disfigure another person seriously and permanently, or to destroy, amputate or disable permanently a member or organ of his body, he causes such injury to such person or to a third person.

This "provision in effect retains the 'maiming' offense - as first degree assault." N.Y PENAL LAW § 120.10, Practice Commentaries (1975).

Similarly, Section 2 (C) 12-1(b)(1) of the New Jersey Code of Criminal Justice defines the offense of aggravated assault:

> A person is guilty of aggravated assault if he: (1) Attempts to cause serious bodily injury to another, or causes such injury purposely or knowingly or under circumstances manifesting extreme indifference to the value of human life recklessly causes such injury.

"The definitions of bodily injury and serious bodily injury are taken from the Model Penal Code. . . . The definition of serious bodily injury encompasses the drastic harms covered under the common-law felony of mayhem and adds a residual category of harm creating substantial risk of death." State v. Williams, 484 A.2d 331, 333 (N.J. Super. Ct. App. Div. 1984) (internal citations and quotations omitted).

Although the United States has brought Section 1959 prosecutions charging "maiming"[61], as of this writing there are no published decisions discussing maiming under Section 1959.

## I. Assault With A Dangerous Weapon

### 1. Federal Definition Under 18 U.S.C. § 113

Section 1959 includes a predicate crime of violence for "assaults with a dangerous weapon," but does not define "assault" or "dangerous weapon." In 1984, when Section 1959 was enacted, 18 U.S.C. § 113(c) was the principal analogous federal assault offense and provided as follows:

> Whoever, within the special maritime and territorial jurisdiction of the United States, is guilty of an assault shall be punished as follows . . .
>
> (c) Assault with a dangerous weapon, with intent to do bodily harm, and without just cause or excuse, by fine of not more than $1,000 or imprisonment for not more than five years, or both.

June 15, 1948, ch. 645, 62 Stat. 689.[62]

To sustain a conviction under 18 U.S.C. § 113(a)(3)(formerly § 113(c)), "the government is required to prove: (1) that the victim was assaulted, (2) with the use of a dangerous weapon, and (3) with the intent to inflict bodily harm." United States v. LeCompte, 108 F.3d 948, 952 (8th Cir. 1997); see also United States v. Guilbert, 692 F.2d 1340, 1343 (11th Cir. 1982); cases cited infra, n. 63. An "assault" within the meaning of Section 113 "is any intentional and voluntary attempt or threat to do injury to the person of another, when coupled with the apparent present ability to do so sufficient to put the person against whom the attempt is made in fear of immediate bodily harm" (LeCompte,

---

[61] See, e.g., United States v. Torres, 162 F.3d 6, 9 (1st Cir. 1998); United States v. Reavis, 48 F.3d 763 (4th Cir. 1995).

[62] Assault with a dangerous weapon is currently codified under 18 U.S.C. § 113(a)(3).

108 F.3d at 952), as well as any attempt to intentionally use unlawful force against another person, regardless of whether the victim "experienced reasonable apprehension of immediate bodily harm." Guilbert, 692 F.2d at 1343. See also United States v. Dupree, 544 F.2d 1050, 1051-52 (9th Cir. 1976) cases and cited infra n. 69. An "injury" to the victim is not required. See Guilbert, 692 F.2d at 1343.

The term "dangerous weapon" under Section 113 has been expansively construed to include "almost any object 'which as used or attempted to be used may endanger life or inflict great bodily harm,'" or which "'is likely to produce death.'" United States v. Johnson, 324 F.2d 264, 266 (4th Cir. 1963). For example, in Johnson, 324 F.2d at 266, the court held that a "metal and plastic chair" that the defendant used to bring "down upon the victim's head" constituted assault with a dangerous weapon. The court explained that the dipositive issue is not whether the object at issue is a "dangerous weapon per se," but rather it is whether the object, under the circumstances in which it is used, is likely to cause great bodily harm or death. Id. at 266. The court added that cases have held that a wide variety of objects constituted a "dangerous weapon" when used in certain circumstances, including a wine bottle, shoes, a rake, a thrown club, a brick and a chair leg. Id. at 266 (citing cases).[63]

---

[63] See, e.g., United States v. LeCompte, 108 F.3d 948, 952-53 (8th Cir. 1997) (holding, under one count, sufficient evidence of assault with a dangerous weapon, a rock, when the defendant punched and kicked the victim, knocking her into a ditch whereupon he held a "rock" as he stood over the victim and continued to kick her; and holding sufficient another charge of assault with a dangerous weapon, when the defendant struck the victim in the head with a "telephone"); United States v. Sturgis, 48 F.3d 784, 785-88 (4th Cir. 1995) (defendant's teeth qualified as a dangerous weapon when the defendant, who knew he was HIV positive, bit a prison guard on his thumb, holding the bite for several seconds and inflicting a serious wound that bled heavily); United States v. Gibson, 896 F.2d 206, 209-211 (6th Cir. 1990) (defendant intentionally struck a police officer with his "motor vehicle"); United States v. Moore, 846 F.2d 1163, 1165-69 (8th Cir. 1988) (holding that defendant's mouth and teeth, when used to bite his victim, constitutes a dangerous weapon regardless of the presence or absence of AIDS); United States v. Hollow, 747 F.2d 481, 482-83 (8th Cir. 1984) (defendant's pushing of victim with both hands while holding a knife in one hand
(continued...)

The meaning of "assault with a dangerous weapon" under 18 U.S.C. § 113 may be used as a guide to determine the meaning of "assault with a dangerous weapon" under Section 1959 because Section 113 was the principal analogous federal offense at the time Section 1959 was adopted.

**2.     Generic Assault With A Dangerous Weapon**

a.      As noted above, Section 1959 includes a predicate crime of violence for "assault with a dangerous weapon," in violation of state or federal law, but does not define "assault" or "dangerous weapon." The first issue to be decided, therefore, is what constitutes the generic definition of "assault." It is well established that, as a general rule, where "a federal criminal statute uses a common law term [such as assault] without defining it, the term is given its common law meaning." United States v. Bell, 505 F.2d 539, 540 (7th Cir. 1974).[64] "At common law, 'assault' had two meanings, one being criminal assault, which is an attempt to commit a battery[65], and the other being tortious assault, which is an act that puts another in reasonable apprehension of immediate bodily harm. Furthermore, where the assault is of the first type, i.e., an attempted battery, the victim need not have experienced reasonable apprehension of immediate bodily harm, and the fact that the battery is actually committed does not result in a merger therein of the assault; proof of a battery supports

---

[63](...continued)
constituted using the knife as a dangerous weapon, even though the defendant did not swing at his victim with the knife); United States v. Guilbert, 692 F.2d 1340, 1342-45 (11th Cir. 1982) (broken beer bottle and pool stick constitute dangerous weapons when the defendant hit the victim with the pool stick and swung a broken beer bottle at his victim); United States v. Bey, 667 F.2d 7 (5th Cir. 1982) (prisoners struck prison guard with "mop handles").

[64] Accord Guilbert, 692 F.2d at 1343; United States v. Dupree, 544 F.2d 1050, 1051 (9th Cir. 1976); Brundage v. United States, 365 F.2d 616, 618-19 (10th Cir. 1966). See generally United States v. Turley, 352 U.S. 407, 411 (1957); Morissette v. United States, 342 U.S. 246, 263 (1952).

[65] At common law, a battery "covered any unlawful application of force to the person of another willfully or in anger." MPC § 211.1 Cmt. at 175-76.

a conviction for assault." Guilbert, 692 F.2d at 1343.[66]

It is particularly significant that both meanings of "assault" are embraced within 18 U.S.C. § 113,[67] the MPC's definition of assault[68] and various state assault offenses.[69] Therefore, OCRS concludes that the generic definition of "assault" within the scope of Section 1959 includes the above-referenced two meanings of "assault:" that is, any intentional act or threat that puts another person in reasonable apprehension of immediate bodily harm, or any attempt to intentionally use unlawful force against another person, regardless of whether the victim experienced reasonable apprehension of bodily harm.[70] Accordingly, to establish generic assault it is not necessary to prove

---

[66] Accord Dupree, 544 F.2d at 1052; Bell, 505 F.2d at 540-41; Brundage, 365 F.2d at 619-20; see also, infra, n. 69.

[67] See Guilbert, 692 F.2d at 1343.

[68] See MPC § 211.1 Cmt. at 172, 177-78 and 188.

[69] [In] [t]he majority of jurisdictions at the time the Model Code was drafted. . . assault thus consisted either of an actual attempt to commit a battery or of an intentional subjection of another to reasonable apprehension of receiving a battery. The assault offense was thus expanded to include menacing as well as actual attempts to do physical harm to another. It also generally included so-called conditional assaults, i.e., situations where the actor threatened violence without justification or excuse if the victim did not engage in conduct demanded by the actor.

MPC § 211.1 Cmt. at 177-78 (footnotes omitted). See, e.g., State v. Collins, 311 S.E.2d 350 (N.C. App. 1984); State v. Smith, 309 N.W.2d 454 (Iowa 1981); People v. Johnson, 284 N.W.2d 718 (Mich. 1979); Halligan v. State, 375 N.E.2d 1151 (Ind. App. 1978); Dahlin v. Fraser, 288 N.W. 851 (Minn. 1939); Commonwealth v. Slaney, 185 N.E.2d 919 (1962).

[70] As the Drafters of the Model Penal Code explained:

This evolution of the concept of assault has led to serious confusion about its relation to the law of attempt. Under the ancient definition of assault as an attempt to commit a battery, the notion of attempted assault was perceived as a logical absurdity and

(continued...)

that the victim of the assault was injured or was put in fear of injury, although such evidence may establish an "assault."

b. Turning to the generic definition of a "dangerous weapon," the MPC did not define a dangerous weapon, but the prevailing definitions in 1984 under state law were substantially similar to the meaning of "dangerous weapon" under 18 U.S.C. § 113. For example, New York Penal Law § 120.10(1), adopted in 1965, provides as follows:

> A person is guilty of assault in the first degree when:
>
> 1. With intent to cause serious physical injury to another person, he causes such injury to such person or to a third person by means of a deadly weapon or a dangerous instrument.

In turn, N.Y. Penal Law § 10.00(13) provides as follows:

> "Dangerous instrument" means any instrument, article or substance, including a "vehicle" as that term is defined in this section, which, under the circumstances in which it is used, attempted to be used or threatened to be used, is readily capable of causing death or other serious physical injury.[71]

---

[70](...continued)
often condemned as such. Yet there is plainly nothing wrong with invoking the law of attempt in states that have incorporated the civil notion of assault as physical menacing. The law may punish the unsuccessful effort to frighten another by physical menace on the same terms as it deals with any other inchoate offense. Thus, many jurisdictions that have made the assimilation of civil assault into the criminal offense have also recognized the possibility of liability for an attempt to assault. Even in jurisdictions that adhere to the older definition requiring an attempted battery and a present ability, an attempted assault prosecution might be appropriate where the actor actually induces fear but lacks the required present ability to inflict injury.

MPC § 211.1 Cmt. at 179 (footnotes omitted).

[71] N.Y. Penal Law § 10.00(12) provides:

> "Deadly weapon" means any loaded weapon from which a shot, readily capable of producing death or other serious physical injury, may be discharged, or a switchblade

(continued...)

Because this definition is substantially similar to the definition of "dangerous weapon" under 18 U.S.C. § 113,[72] it is not surprising that New York courts interpreted the scope of the term "dangerous instrument," as did federal courts under 18 U.S.C. § 113 for a dangerous weapon, very broadly to include any object, under the circumstances in which it is used, that is likely to cause serious physical or bodily injury or death.[73] New York's definition of a dangerous instrument as applied to N.Y. Penal Law § 120.10(1) is especially significant because Congress cited to New York Penal Law § 120.10(1) as an example of the assault offenses covered by Section 1959. See 129 Congressional Record at 22906 (98th Cong. 1st Sess., August 4, 1983).

Moreover, in 1984, at least forty-two other states in 1984 had offenses for assault with a "dangerous weapon" or "deadly weapon" that had substantially the same meaning as that offense

---

[71](...continued)
knife, gravity knife, pilum ballistic knife, metal knuckle knife, dagger, billy, blackjack, or metal knuckles.

[72] New York's definition of a dangerous instrument refers to any instrument capable of causing "serious physical injury," whereas the judicial interpretation of a "dangerous weapon" under 18 U.S.C. § 113 refers to any instrument that is likely to cause "great bodily harm." This slight difference in terminology is immaterial; state statutes define both terms to mean essentially the same thing. See infra Section II( J) and Appendix C.

[73] See, e.g., People v. Galvin, 65 N.Y. 2d 761 (1985) (holding that concrete sidewalk was a dangerous instrument when the defendant inflicted serious physical injury on his victim by pounding his head against the pavement); People v. Carter, 53 N.Y. 2d 113, 117 (1981) (holding that a pair of rubber boots constituted a dangerous instrument when "the defendant used the rubber boots to stomp the head and face of his victim, causing her head to contact the pavement below with tremendous force."); People v. Cwikla, 46 N.Y. 2d 434, 442 (1979) ("the handkerchief with which the victim was gagged and which led to his death by asphyxiation was a dangerous instrument"); People v. Ozarowski, 38 N.Y. 2d 481, 491 (1976) (defendant used a "baseball bat" to hit his victim); People v. Rumaner, 45 A.D. 2d 290 (3d Dept. 1974) (heavy leather boots used to kick a victim in the face 10 to 12 times); People v. Bouldin, 40 A.D. 2d 1045 (3d Dept. 1972) (a spatula used to inflict a two-inch cut in the left abdomen area).

under 18 U.S.C. § 113 and N.Y. Penal Law §§ 120.10(1) and 10(13).[74] Therefore, OCRS concludes that the generic definition of assault with a dangerous weapon in 1984 was an "assault," as defined at common law (see supra, pp. 68-69), committed with any object that, under the circumstances in which it is used, attempted to be used or threatened to be used, is capable of causing death or other serious physical injury.

### 3. Section 1959 Cases Charging Assault With A Dangerous Weapon

In United States v. Cuong Gia Le, 316 F. Supp. 2d 355, 358-61 (E.D.Va. 2004), the defendant was charged under Section 1959's provision "assault with a dangerous weapon" with shooting and

---

[74] See, e.g., ALA. CRIMINAL CODE §§ 13-A-1-2, 13A-6-20 (1977); ALASKA STAT. §§ 11.41.200, 11.41.210, 11.81.900 (11) (1984); ARIZ. REV. STAT. §§ 13-105 (7) AND 13-1204 (1984); ARK. CODE ANN. §§ 16-90-121, 5-1-102 (4) (1977); CAL. PENAL CODE § 245 (a)(1) (1984); COLO. REV. STAT. ANN §§ 18-3-202 and 18-1-901(3)(e); CONN. GEN. STAT. ANN. §§ 53a-59 and 53a-3(7) (West 1971); DEL. CODE ANN. tit. 11, §§ 222 (4), 612 and 613 (1974); GA. CODE ANN. § 16-5-21(a)(2) (1983); HAW. REV. STAT. (PENAL CODE) §§ 707-700 (4) and 707-711 (1979); IDAHO CODE § 18-905 (1978); IND. CODE ANN. §§ 35-41-12 and 35-42-2-1 (2) (1984); IOWA CODE ANN. §§ 702.7 and 708.1 (3) (1979); KAN. STAT. ANN. § 21-3414 (1984); KY. REV. STAT. ANN. §§ 500.080 (3) and 508.010 (a) (1975); LA. REV. STAT. ANN. §§ 2, 36 and 37 (1974); ME. REV. STAT. ANN. tit., 17-A, § 208 and § 2 (1984); MASS. GEN. LAWS ANN. CH. 265, § 15A (1984); MICH. STAT. ANN. § 750.82 (1984); MINN. STAT. ANN. §§ 609.222 and 609.022 (1964); MISS. CODE ANN. § 97-3-7 (1984); MO. REV. STAT. §§ 556.060 (9) and (10) and 565.050.2 (1979); MONT. CODE ANN. §§ 46-18-221, 45-2-101 (71) (1984); NEB. REV. STAT. 28-1205, 28-109 (7) (1984); N.H. REV. STAT. ANN. § 625:11 (v) and 631:1 (1984); N. J. STAT. ANN. §§ 2c:12-1(b) and 2 (11-1(c) (1982); N. M. STAT. ANN. §§ 30-1-12 (B), 30-3-2 and 30-3-5 (C) (1978); N.D. CENT. CODE §§ 12.1-01-04 (6) and 12.1-17-02 (2) (1984); OHIO REV. CODE ANN. §§ 2903.11(2) and 2923.11(A) (1984); OKLA. STAT. tit. 21, § 645 (1984); OR. REV. STAT. §§ 161.015 (7) and 163.165, 163.175, 163.185 (1984); PA. CONS. STAT. ANN. tit. 18, §§ 2301 and 2702 (4) (1983); R.I. GEN. LAWS §§ 11-5-2 and 11-5-4 (1981); S.C. CODE ANN. § 16-3-610 (1984); S.D. CODIFIED LAWS §§ 22-1-2 (9) and 22-18-1.1 (2) (1984); TENN. CODE ANN. § 39-2-101 (b)(2) (1984); TEX. PENAL CODE ANN. §§ 22.02 (a)(4) and 1.07 (11) (1984); UTAH CODE ANN. § 76-1-601 (10) and 76-5-103 (1)(b) (1973); VT. STAT. ANN. tit. 13, §§ 1024 (a)(2) and 1021 (3) (1984); WASH. REV. CODE §§ 9A.36.010 (1)(a) and 9A.04.110 (6) (1984); WIS. STAT. ANN. § 939.22 (10), 939.63 AND 940.19(1984); WYO. STAT. ANN. §§ 6-1-104 (a)(iv) and 6-2-502 (1984). Therefore, in 1984, seven states (Florida, Illinois, Maryland, Nevada, North Carolina, Virginia and West Virginia) did not have an offense substantially the same as assault with a dangerous weapon under 18 U.S.C. § 113 and New York Penal Law § 120.10(1) and 10(13). See statutes set forth in Appendix C.

wounding his victim, in violation of Va. Code § 18.2-51, which prohibits malicious or unlawful wounding, and Va. Code § 182-282, which prohibits brandishing a firearm.[75]

The defendant argued that these Virginia statutes did not qualify as predicate offenses under Section 1959 because "the elements of these state offenses do not precisely match the elements of assault with a dangerous weapon under federal law." Cuong Gia Le, 316 F. Supp. 2d at 360. The district court rejected this argument, explaining that "it is not necessary that the state law alleged to prohibit an assault with a dangerous weapon under § 1959 carry that precise label" (id. at 360), and that it is sufficient that the state offense "corresponds in substantial part" to the generic definition of the offense at issue. Id. at 363. The district court concluded that the elements of the Virginia statutes correspond in substantial part to the generic definition of assault with a dangerous weapon, and therefore, qualified as a Section 1959 predicate offense. Id. at 363-64.

In several Section 1959 prosecutions, courts have upheld the sufficiency of the evidence of

---

[75] VA. CODE ANN. § 18.2-51, entitled "Shooting, stabbing, etc., with intent to maim, kill, etc.," provides that:

> If any person maliciously shoot, stab, cut or wound any person or by any means cause him bodily injury, with the intent to maim, disfigure, disable, or kill, he shall, except where it is otherwise provided, be guilty of a Class 3 felony. If such act be done unlawfully but not maliciously, with the intent aforesaid, the offender shall be guilty of a Class 6 felony.

VA. CODE ANN. § 18.2-282, entitled "Pointing, holding, or brandishing firearm or object similar in appearance," provides that:

> It shall be unlawful for any person to point, hold, or brandish any firearm, as hereinafter described, or any object similar in appearance to a firearm, whether capable of being fired or not, in such manner as to reasonably induce fear in the mind of another or hold a firearm in a public place in such a manner as to reasonably induce fear in the mind of another being shot or injured.

See Cuong Gia Le, 316 F. Supp. 2d at 360 n. 10.

charges for assault with a dangerous weapon under state law.  For example, in United States v. Desena, 287 F.3d 170, 177-79 (2d Cir. 2002), the court held that the evidence was sufficient to establish that the defendant attempted to commit assault with a dangerous weapon, in violation of N.Y. Penal Law § 120.10(1) (see supra p. 70).  There, the defendant, armed with a loaded gun, directed another to drive him around in pursuit of a band of Hell's Angels so that he could kill a Hell's Angel to avenge an earlier shooting.  Desena, 287 F.3d at 174.  Twice the defendant leaned out of the car and pointed his loaded gun in the direction of a Hell's Angel, but did not shoot because his efforts were thwarted by circumstances beyond his control: in one instance the member quickly left the scene and in another incident a vehicle came between the defendant and his target.  Id. at 178-79.[76]

Similarly, in United States v. Khalil, 279 F.3d 358, 367-69 (6th Cir. 2002), the court held that the evidence was sufficient to establish that the defendant, the National President of the Avengers Motorcycle Club, aided and abetted an attempt to assault members of a rival motorcycle club, the Iron Coffins, with a dangerous weapon, in violation of OHIO REV. CODE ANN. § 2903.11.  There, the evidence showed that the Avengers had engaged in a violent feud with the Iron Coffins and defendant Khalil had encouraged members of the Avengers to take action against members of the Iron Coffins. Consequently, on two occasions members of the Avengers traveled to local bars where they expected to find members of the Iron Coffins and intended to assault them with clubs and beer bottles.[77]

---

[76] Moreover, the court rejected the defendant's affirmative defense of abandonment under New York State law because the defendant did not establish that the renunciation of criminal purpose was "voluntary and complete" as required under New York law.  Rather, the evidence showed that the defendant merely suspended his efforts to shoot a Hell's Angel member due to circumstances beyond his control.  Desena, 287 F.3d at 179-80.

[77] Several other Section 1959 prosecutions charged predicate state offenses involving "assault with a dangerous weapon."  Those opinions, however, did not address the meaning of a "dangerous weapon" or any other issue relating to the elements of such state offenses.  See e.g.,
(continued...)

J.  **Assaults Resulting in Serious Bodily Injury**

1.  **Federal Definitions Under 18 U.S.C. §§ 113 and 1365**

a. Section 1959 includes a predicate crime of violence for "assault resulting in serious bodily injury," but does not define "serious bodily injury." The Senate Report regarding Section 1959, however, cited to 18 U.S.C. § 113, as the principal federal statute applicable to the crimes involving assault. See S. Rep. No. 98-225 at 307, 323. Therefore, the meaning of "assault resulting in serious bodily injury" under 18 U.S.C. § 113(f) may be used as a guide to determining the meaning of the same crime under Section 1959.

Section 113(f) of Title 18 was adopted in 1976,[78] and in 1984 when Section 1959 was enacted, Section 113(f) provided as follows:

> Sec. 113. Assaults within maritime and territorial jurisdiction
>
> Whoever, within the special maritime and territorial jurisdiction of the United States, is guilty of an assault shall be punished as follows: . . .
>
> (f) Assault resulting in serious bodily injury, by fine of not more than $10,000 or imprisonment for not more than ten years, or both.

18 U.S.C. § 113(f) (1976); see also United States v. Webster, 620 F.2d 640, 640 n. 1 (7th Cir. 1980) (stating that although Congress did not define "serious bodily injury," "[t]here is no indication that Congress in adopting such commonly used terms intended to include only the very highest degree of serious bodily injury;" id. at 642).

Because Section 113(f) as originally enacted did not define assault with "serious bodily

---

[77](...continued)
United States v. Phillips, 239 F.3d 829, 845-46 (7th Cir. 2001); United States v. Thai, 29 F.3d 785, 817-18 (2d Cir. 1994); United States v. Santiago, 207 F. Supp. 2d 129, 152-53 (S.D.N.Y. 2002).

[78] See Pub. L. 94-297, 90 Stat. 585 (1976).

injury," courts defined the offense's contours through their decisions. Courts adopted an expansive, flexible definition of assault resulting in serious bodily injury. For example, in United States v. Johnson, 637 F.2d 1224, 1246 (9th Cir. 1980), the court rejected the defendant's argument "that a substantial risk of death **must be present** to constitute 'serious bodily injury.'" (emphasis added). Rather, the court held that the jury should be instructed to use its "common sense" to consider various factors, any one of which may be sufficient, to determine whether serious bodily injury resulted, including:

> whether the victims suffered extreme physical pain, protracted and obvious disfigurement, protracted loss or impairment of the function of a bodily member, organ or mental faculty, protracted unconsciousness, and significant or substantial internal damage (such as important broken bones)[and] a substantial risk of death.

637 F.2d at 1246. In subsequent cases under Section 113(f), courts applied essentially the same definition of serious bodily injury as the Johnson court, and upheld the sufficiency of the evidence of "serious bodily injury."[79]

Moreover, courts have ruled that since "Section 113(f) requires only that the assault shall have resulted in serious bodily harm; the assault need not have been committed with a dangerous weapon, or with intent to do bodily harm." United States v. Knife, 592 F.2d 472, 482 (8th Cir. 1979), quoting

---

[79] See, e.g., United States v. Dennison, 937 F.2d 559, 561-62 (10th Cir. 1991) (finding sufficient evidence that the victim "had seven lacerations on her face, neck and right upper chest, several of them over the major arteries and veins that go to the brain", and that "absent medical treatment, she would have been at risk of infection or aggravating scarring"); United States v. Christopher, 956 F.2d 536, 539-40 (6th Cir. 1991) (finding sufficient evidence of a "gunshot wound to the left temporal area which passed through [victim's] sinus and upper jaw and exited at the front lip" and also "a dislocated left thumb which had to be surgically repaired"); United States v. Demery, 980 F.2d 1187, 1189-90 (8th Cir. 1992) (finding sufficient evidence when the victim's little finger was nearly severed from his hand and he "suffered permanent impairment of movement and sensation in that finger").

United States v. Engle, 586 F.2d 1193 at 1196 (8th Cir. 1978). Furthermore, even though an "assault" at common law need not have caused an injury (see supra Section II (I)(2)), Section 113(f) explicitly requires evidence that the assault **resulted** in serious bodily injury. See, also United States v. Jacobs, 632 F.2d 695, 696-97 (7th Cir. 1980); United States v. Juvenile Male, 930 F.2d 727, 728 (9th Cir. 1991) ("the term 'assault' as used in Section 113(f) must be understood to include battery").[80]

b. In 1994, Congress amended 18 U.S.C. § 113 to distinguish "serious bodily injury" from "substantial bodily injury", and to define both terms as follows:

(b) As used in this subsection –
    (1) the term "substantial bodily injury" means bodily injury which involves –
        (A) a temporary but substantial disfigurement; or
        (B) a temporary but substantial loss or impairment of the function of any bodily member, organ, or mental faculty; and
    (2) the term "serious bodily injury" has the meaning given that term in section 1365 of this title.

Pub. L. 103-322, 108 Stat. 2042, 2043, 2108, 2148 (September 13, 1994). Previously, in 1983 Congress had enacted the following definition of "serious bodily injury" in 18 U.S.C. § 1365(g)(3):

[T]he term "serious bodily injury" means bodily injury which involves -- (A) a substantial risk of death; (B) extreme physical pain; (C) protracted and obvious disfigurement; or (D) protracted loss or impairment of the function of a bodily member, organ, or mental faculty.

---

[80] At common law, "any intentional display of force such as would give the victim reason to fear or expect immediate bodily harm, constitutes an assault." United States v. Jacobs, 632 F.2d 695, 697 n. 4 (7th Cir. 1980). See also surpra pp. 68-69; United States v. Loera, 923 F.2d 727, 728 (9th Cir. 1991) (defining assault at common law); MPC § 211.1 Cmt. at 175-176. ("Originally common-law assault was simply an attempt to commit a battery" and a battery "covered any unlawful application of force to the person of another willfully or in anger"); MPC § 211.1 Cmt. at 180) (at common law, "attacks resulting in injuries that fell short of mayhem were thus necessarily treated as ordinary batteries").

Pub. L. 98-127, 97 Stat. 831 (1983).[81]

Thus, since 1994, 18 U.S.C. § 113 has included a statutory definition of "serious bodily injury" that is essentially the same as set forth in United States v. Johnson, supra, 637 F.2d at 1246 and its progeny. Not surprisingly, therefore, after the 1994 amendment to Section 113, courts' interpretation of the meaning of "serious bodily injury" under both 18 U.S.C. § 113 and § 1365 is consistent with the expansive interpretation of "serious bodily injury" in Johnson and its progeny.[82]

### 2. Generic Assault Resulting in Serious Bodily Injury

As discussed above in Section II (H)(1)(b), Model Penal Code § 211.1 provided for several gradations of "assault" offenses, including for "aggravated assault," as follows:

§ 211.1 Assault. . .

(2) Aggravated Assault. A person is guilty of aggravated assault if he:
(a) attempts to cause serious bodily injury to another, or causes such injury purposely, knowingly or recklessly under circumstances manifesting extreme indifference to the value of human life; or
(b) attempts to cause or purposely or knowingly causes bodily injury to another with a deadly weapon.

Aggravated assault under paragraph (a) is a felony on the second degree; aggravated assault under paragraph (b) is a felony of the third degree.

MPC § 210.00 (3) provides that:

"Serious bodily injury" means bodily injury which creates a substantial risk of death

---

[81] 18 U.S.C. § 1365 criminalized tampering with consumer products.

[82] See, e.g., United States v. Two Eagle, 318 F.3d 785, 791-92 (8th Cir. 2003) (gunshot wounds causing severe pain and broken legs, requiring surgery); United States v. Peneaux, 432 F.3d 882, 890-92 (8th Cir. 2005) (burning a three year old with a lit cigarette, causing scarring and significant pain); United States v. Jourdain, 433 F.3d 652, 657-58 (8th Cir. 2006).

or which causes serious, permanent disfigurement, or protracted loss or impairment of the function of any bodily member or organ.

Significantly, this definition of "serious bodily injury" is substantially similar to the definitions set forth in United States v. Johnson, supra and 18 U.S.C. §§ 113 and 1365.

By 1984, when Section 1959 was enacted, at least forty-three States, including New York, had enacted offenses defining assault causing "serious bodily injury" or "great bodily injury" substantially similar to the definitions of MPC § 211.1 and of 18 U.S.C. §§ 113 and 1365.[83] As noted above supra p.71, New York State's offense, N.Y. Penal Law § 120.10, for assault with intent to cause serious physical injury to another person is particularly significant because Congress cited to that law as an example of the assault offenses covered by Section 1959. See 129 Congressional Record at 22906 (98th Cong. 1st Sess., August 4, 1983). New York Penal Law § 120.10, adopted in 1965, provides as follows:

### § 120.10 Assault in the first degree

A person is guilty of assault in the first degree when:

1. With intent to cause serious physical injury to another person, he causes such injury to such person or to a third person by means of a deadly weapon or a dangerous instrument; or

2. With intent to disfigure another person seriously and permanently, or to destroy, amputate or disable permanently a member or organ of his body, he causes such injury to such person or to a third person; or

3. Under circumstances evincing a depraved indifference to human life, he recklessly engages in conduct which creates a grave risk of death to another person, and thereby causes serious physical injury to another person; or

---

[83] See Appendix C, which sets forth state statutory provisions involving assaults. In 1984, seven states (Maryland, Massachusetts, Michigan, Rhode Island, South Carolina, Virginia and West Virginia), apparently did not have offenses for assault causing serious bodily injury substantially similar to the MPC's definition of that offense.

4. In the course of and in furtherance of the commission or attempted commission of a felony or immediate flight therefrom, he, or another participant if there be any, causes serious physical injury to a person other than one of the participants.

Assault in the first degree is a class B felony.

In turn, New York Penal Law § 10(10) provides that:

"Serious physical injury" means physical injury which creates a substantial risk of death, or which causes death or serious and protracted disfigurement, protracted impairment of health or protracted loss or impairment of the function of any bodily organ.[84]

---

[84] For cases upholding the sufficiency of the evidence for assault resulting in serious bodily injury, in violation of N.Y. Penal L. § 120.10(1), see, e.g., People v. Askerneese, 93 N.Y. 2d 884 (1999) ("the deep puncture wound in [the victim's] upper lip went completely through to the inside of his mouth, causing nerve damage, numbness and sometimes a lack of control over his upper lip"); People v. Jason, 75 N.Y. 2d 638, 658 (1990) (victim "suffered severe injuries to his back and right eye which affected him for nearly a year after the [assault]"); People v. Foster, 278 A.D. 2d 241 (2d Dept. 2000) (victim sustained multiple gunshot wounds); People v. Martinez, 257 A.D. 2d 667 (2d Dept. 1999) (victim sustained "a broken arm, a broken cheekbone, a deviated septum, and severe lacerations of the face requiring stitches, with resulting nerve damage and loss of sensation of the lip"); People v. Su, 239 A.D. 2d 703 (3d Dept. 1997) (beating that resulted in deep cuts, a cerebral contusion, bruises and swelling); People v. Gill, 228 A.D. 2d 240 (1st Dept. 1996) (gunshot wound requiring surgery and multiple returns to the hospital and victim suffered from headaches for one and one-half years showed a protracted impairment of health); People v. Green, 111 A.D. 2d 183 (2d Dept. 1985) (knife wound to the victim's neck requiring 120 stitches and resulting in a "keloid" scar and knife wound to victim's arm requiring 12 to 15 stitches); Tatta v. Mitchell, 962 F. Supp. 21, 24 (E.D.N.Y. 1997) (knife slashes resulting in facial disfigurement requiring plastic surgery and trouble with vision for many months).

For cases finding the evidence insufficient to establish "serious bodily injury" under N.Y. Penal L. § 120.10(1), see, e.g., People v. Mack, 268 A.D. 2d 599, 600 (2d Dept. 2000) ("there was no evidence that the injury to the complaining witness's head, which required four stitches, was life threatening or caused a protracted or serious disfigurement or impairment"); People v. Castillo, 199 A.D. 2d 276, 277 (2d Dept. 1993) (two stab wounds which required suturing, where eighteen months after the assault, the victim said "it hurts once in awhile when the weather changes"); Matter of Andre O, 182 A.D. 2d 1108, 1109 (4th Dept. 1992) (punch in the jaw causing "substantial pain for one week and a slight displacement and clicking of the jaw"); People v. Robles, 173 A.D. 2d 337, 338 (1st Dept. 1991) (The "victim suffered two stab wounds, one at the base of the neck and one on the right shoulder" which "required irrigation and suturing and overnight observation in the hospital, and that thereafter, the victim had trouble eating.").

OCRS concludes that the prevailing definition in 1984 of assault resulting in serious bodily injury, and hence the "generic" definition of this offense, is the nearly identical definitions set forth in United States v. Johnson, supra, p. 75, 18 U.S.C. §§ 113 and 1365, MPC §§ 210(3) and 211.1, and numerous state statutes. Therefore, any state or federal offense whose elements substantially conform to those definitions of assault resulting in serious bodily injury may constitute a predicate offense under Section 1959.

### 3. Section 1959 Cases Charging Assault Resulting in Serious Bodily Injury

In United States v. Muyet, 994 F. Supp. 501 (S.D.N.Y. 1998), the district court ruled that there was sufficient evidence that the defendant assaulted two brothers resulting in serious bodily injury in violation of N.Y. Penal Law §§ 120.10(1) and 10(10) to support the defendant's conviction for violating 18 U.S.C. § 1959, stating:

> The attack left Hermenio Salcedo with six gunshot wounds and Alexis Salcedo with at least one. The brothers required emergency medical treatment and transportation to a hospital for additional treatment. From this testimony, there was sufficient evidence to believe that the injuries posed a substantial risk of death or caused the Salcedos protracted disfigurement, impairment of their health, and impairment of their legs. Feliciano relies upon People v. Rojas, 61 N.Y. 2d 726 . . . (1984), which held that evidence of a gunshot wound, without more, is insufficient to sustain an assault conviction. In this case, the Government presented enough additional evidence to sustain Feliciano's convictions. Feliciano beat, pistol-whipped, and kicked the brothers, who required emergency medical treatment at the scene and transportation to a hospital for more treatment. Thus, the circumstances surrounding the Salcedo shooting provide sufficient evidence for a reasonable jury to conclude that the Salcedo brothers suffered serious physical injury.

994 F. Supp. at 519.

### K. Threats To Commit A Crime of Violence

#### 1. Federal Definition of a Crime of Violence under 18 U.S.C. § 16

Section 1959 proscribes any threat "to commit a crime of violence against any individual in violation of the laws of any state or the United States." Section 1959 does not define a "crime of violence." Rather, the governing definition of a "crime of violence" is contained in 18 U.S.C. § 16, which was enacted as part of the same act (the Comprehensive Crime Control Act of 1984) that enacted 18 U.S.C. § 1959. See 98 Stat. 2136; S. Rep. No. 98-225 at 307. 18 U.S.C. § 16 provides as follows:

> The term "crime of violence" means - (a) an offense that has as an element the use, attempted use, or threatened use of physical force against the person or property of another, or (b) any other offense that is a felony and that, by its nature, involves a substantial risk that physical force against the person or property of another may be used in the course of committing the offense.

The Senate Report regarding 18 U.S.C. §§ 1959 and 16 states, in relevant part:

> Section 1952B [renumbered § 1959] also covers threats to commit a "crime of violence." The term "crime of violence" is defined, for purposes of all of title 18, United States Code, in section 1001 of the bill (the first section of Part A of title X). Although the term is occasionally used in present law, it is not defined, and no body of case law has arisen with respect to it. However, the phrase is commonly used throughout the bill, and **accordingly the Committee has chosen to define it for general application in title 18**.
>
> The definition is taken from S. 1630 as reported in the 97th Congress. The term means an offense -- **either a felony or a misdemeanor** -- that has as an element the use, attempted use, or threatened use of physical force against the person or property of another, or any felony that, by its nature, involves the substantial risk that physical force against another person or property may be used in the course of its commission. The former category would include a threatened or attempted simple assault or battery on another person; offenses such as burglary in violation of a State law and the Assimilative Crime Act would be included in the latter category inasmuch as such an offense would involve the substantial risk of physical force against another person or against the property.

S. Rep. No. 98-225 at 307 (footnotes omitted) (emphasis added).

Moreover, the Senate Report No. 98-225 explains that the term "crimes of violence" as used elsewhere in the Comprehensive Crime Control Act of 1984 was intended to include "essentially the same categories of offenses described in the District of Columbia Code by the terms 'dangerous crime' and 'crime of violence' for which a detention hearing may be held under that statute." S. Rep.

No. 98-225 at 20-21 and n. 60. See also United States v. Lucio-Lucio, 347 F.3d 1202, 1205 (10th Cir. 2003). The referenced D.C. Code provisions defined "crime of violence" to include the following:

> murder, forcible rape, carnal knowledge of a female under the age of sixteen, taking or attempting to take immoral, improper, or indecent liberties with a child under the age of sixteen years, mayhem, kidnapping, robbery, burglary, voluntary manslaughter, extortion or blackmail accompanied by threats of violence, arson, assault with intent to commit any offenses, assault with a dangerous weapon, or an attempt or conspiracy to commit any of the foregoing offenses.

D.C. Code § 23-1331(4) (1981). See also Lucio-Lucio, 347 F.3d at 1205.

In accordance with this legislative history, the Supreme Court has ruled that Congress "provided in § 16 a general definition of the term 'crime of violence' to be used throughout the Act," including "for defining the elements of particular offenses [such as] 18 U.S.C. § 1959 (prohibiting threats to commit crimes of violence in aid of racketeering activity.")." Leocal v. Ashcroft, 543 U.S. 1, 6 (2004). Because Congress intended the definition of a "crime of violence" under Section 1959 to be governed by the definition of that term under 18 U.S.C. § 16, it is not necessary to determine the "generic" definition of a "crime of violence." Rather, any federal or state statutory offense that satisfies the definition of a "crime of violence" under 18 U.S.C. § 16 may constitute a predicate crime of violence under Section 1959.

In Leocal v. Ashcroft, 543 U.S. 1 (2004), the Supreme Court provided a framework for determining whether a violation satisfies the definition of a "crime of violence" under Section 16. There, the petitioner was convicted of driving under the influence of alcohol (DUI) and causing serious bodily injury, resulting from an accident, in violation of Florida Law. See Fla. Stat. § 316.193(3)(c)(2) (2003). Because this conviction was classified a "crime of violence" under 18 U.S.C. § 16, and therefore an "aggravated felony" under the Immigration and Nationality Act, petitioner was ordered to be deported.[85]

The Supreme Court examined the required elements of the Florida violation to determine whether it fell within the ambit of Section 16's definition of a "crime of violence." The Court began its analysis with the language of Section 16, stating that "[t]he plain text of § 16(a) states that an offense, to qualify as a crime of violence, must have 'as an element the use, attempted use, or threatened use of physical force against the person or property of another.'" 543 U.S. at 8. The Supreme Court found it significant that the Florida violation "does not require proof of any particular mental state." 543 U.S. at 7. The Court explained that "[t]he key phrase in § 16(a) - - the 'use . . . of physical force against the person or property of another - - most naturally suggests a higher degree of intent than negligent or merely accidental conduct." 543 U.S. at 9. The Court concluded that petitioner's DUI offense did not satisfy Section 16(a)'s definition because it did not require a higher degree of *mens rea* than mere negligence or accidental conduct. 543 U.S. at 9-10.[86]

The Court further noted that although "Section 16(b) sweeps more broadly than § 16(a), defining a crime of violence as including 'any other offense that is a felony and that, by its nature, involves a substantial risk that physical force against the person or property of another may be used in the course of committing the offense,'" petitioner's DUI offense did not fall within this definition. 543 U.S. at 10. In that regard, the Supreme Court explained:

> [Section] 16(b) does not thereby encompass all negligent misconduct, such as the negligent operation of a vehicle. It simply covers offenses that naturally involve a person acting in disregard of the risk that physical force might be used against another in committing an offense. The reckless disregard in § 16 relates *not* to the general

---

[85] Frequently, issues involving the construction of 18 U.S.C. § 16 arise in deportation cases.

[86] The Court added that "[t]his case does not present us with the question, whether a state or federal offense that requires proof of the *reckless* use of force against a person or property of another qualifies as a crime of violence under 18 U.S.C. § 16." 543 U.S. at 13.

conduct or to the possibility that harm will result from a person's conduct, but to the risk that the use of physical force against another might be required in committing a crime. The classic example is burglary. A burglary would be covered under § 16(b) *not* because the offense can be committed in a generally reckless way or because someone may be injured, but because burglary, by its nature, involves a substantial risk that the burglar will use force against a victim in completing the crime.

Thus, while § 16(b) is broader than § 16(a) in the sense that physical force need not actually be applied, it contains the same formulation we found to be determinative in § 16(a): the use of physical force against the person or property of another. Accordingly, we must give the language in § 16(b) an identical construction, requiring a higher *mens rea* than the merely accidental or negligent conduct involved in a DUI offense. This is particularly true in light of § 16(b)'s requirement that the "substantial risk" be a risk of using physical force against another person "in the course of committing the offense." In no "ordinary or natural" sense can it be said that a person risks having to "use" physical force against another person in the course of operating a vehicle while intoxicated and causing injury.

543 U.S. at 10-11 (footnotes omitted).

The Supreme Court concluded that:

Thus, § 16(b) plainly does not encompass all offenses which create a "substantial risk" that injury will result from a person's conduct. The "substantial risk" in § 16(b) relates to the use of force, not to the possible effect of a person's conduct. Compare § 16(b) (requiring a "substantial risk that physical force against the person or property of another may be used") with United States Sentencing Commission, Guidelines Manual § 4B1.2(a)(2) (Nov. 2003) (in the context of a career-offender sentencing enhancement, defining "crime of violence" as meaning, *inter alia*, "conduct that presents a serious potential risk of physical injury to another"). The risk that an accident may occur when an individual drives while intoxicated is simply not the same thing as the risk that the individual may "use" physical force against another in committing the DUI offense. See, e.g., United States v. Lucio-Lucio, 347 F.3d 1202, 1205-1207 (CA 10 2003); Bazan-Reyes v. INS, 256 F.3d 600, 609-610 (CA 7 2001).

543 U.S. at 10 fn. 7.

Leocal v. Ashcroft imposes several limitations upon the application of 18 U.S.C. § 16. First, to determine whether a statutory offense constitutes a "crime of violence" under § 16, the dispositive issue is whether the **elements** of the statutory offense at issue, and not the charged conduct or the particular factual circumstances of the case, satisfy Section 16's definition of a "crime of violence."[87] Second, Sections 16(a) and (b) both require a *mens rea* higher than that of mere negligence or accident. Third, Section 16(b) "does not encompass all offenses that create a 'substantial risk' that injury will result from a person's [charged] conduct." 543 U.S. at 10 fn. 7. Rather, Section 16(b) embraces only those offenses whereby their required elements there is "a substantial risk that physical force against the person or property may be used in the course of committing the offense." Id. With these principles in mind, OCRS will next discuss the scope of Sections 16(a) and (b).

   a. **Section 16(a) - - the Use, Attempted Use, or Threatened Use of Physical Force Against the Person or Property of Another.**

In accordance with Section 16(a)'s explicit legislative history (see supra p. 82), courts have held that Section 16(a), unlike Section 16(b), is not limited to felonies, but also includes

---

[87] In that regard, it is particularly significant that Section 16(a) explicitly provides that a "'crime of violence' means (a) an offense **that has as an element** the use, attempted use, or threatened use of physical force against the person or property of another" and Section 16(b) explicitly defines a "crime of violence" as "any other offense that is a felony **and that by its nature**, involves a substantial risk" of the use of physical force (emphasis added). Accordingly, courts have uniformly adopted a so-called "categorical approach" to determine whether a statutory offense falls within Section 16's definition of a crime of violence, which turns on the elements of the offense, or its "intrinsic nature", and not on the particular factual circumstances of the case. Therefore, courts have consistently held that Section 16(a) does not encompass an offense unless that offense includes an essential element of the use or attempted or threatened use of physical force, and that Section 16(b) does not include an offense unless its intrinsic nature, by examining its elements, involves a substantial risk of the use of physical force against the person or property of another, even though the particular factual circumstances of the case involved the use, attempted, or threatened use of physical force, or a substantial risk of the use of physical force. See, e.g., Szucz-Toldy v. Gonzales, 400 F.3d 978, 981-82 (7th Cir. 2005); Zaidi v. Ashcroft, 374 F.3d 357, 360-61 (5th Cir. 2004); Nguyen v. Ashcroft, 366 F.3d 386, 389 (5th Cir. 2004); United States v. Vargas-Duran, 356 F.3d 598, 605 (5th Cir. 2004) (en banc); Flores v. Ashcroft, 350 F.3d 666, 669-671 (7th Cir. 2003); Chery v. Ashcroft, 347 F.3d 404, 407 (2d Cir. 2003); Chrzanoski v. Ashcroft, 327 F.3d 18, 196 (2d Cir. 2003); Jobson v. Ashcroft, 326 F. 3d 367, 371-72 (2d Cir. 2003); United States v. Gracia-Cantu, 302 F.3d 308, 312 (5th Cir. 2002); United States v. Galvan-Rodriguez, 169 F.3d 217, 219 (5th Cir. 1999); United States v. Velazquez, 100 F.3d 418, 420 (5th Cir. 1996); United States v. Rodriguez-Guzman, 56 F.3d 18, 20 & n. 14 (5th Cir. 1995); United States v. Aragon, 983 F.2d 1306, 1312 (4th Cir. 1993); Santapaola v. Ashcroft, 249 F. Supp. 2d 181, 187-189 (D. Conn. 2003).

misdemeanors that satisfy 16(a)'s definition.[88] Courts also have held that a wide variety of offenses fall within the scope of Section 16(a)'s definition of a crime of violence. See, e.g., United States v. Morgan, 380 F.3d 698, 704 (2d Cir. 2004) (attempted murder under New York law); Reyes-Alcaraz v. Ashcroft, 363 F.3d 937, 941 (9th Cir. 2004) (California offense that "requires, as an element, that the defendant have drawn or exhibited a firearm or other deadly weapon and that the defendant have done so with an intent to resist, or prevent a peace officer from effecting, an arrest . . . necessarily involves a threatened use of physical force" within the ambit of § 16(a)); Dickson v. Ashcroft, 346 F.3d 44, 48-53 (2d Cir. 2003) (holding that a New York offense for the unlawful restraint or imprisonment of a competent adult falls with Section 16(a) and (b) because it must be accomplished by some degree of physical force, whereas the unlawful restraint of an incompetent person or child under 16 "is not a crime of violence under § 16, because it neither has as an element the use of force nor categorically involves a substantial risk that force may be used." Id. at 51); Bovkun v. Ashcroft, 283 F.3d 166, 169-171 (3d Cir. 2002) (Pennsylvania law proscribing terrorist threats "to commit any crime of violence with intent to terrorize another or to cause evacuation of a building, place of assembly, or facility of public transportation, or otherwise to cause serious public inconvenience, or in reckless disregard of the risk of causing such terror or inconvenience"); United States v. Maddalena, 893 F.2d 815, 819 (6th Cir. 1990) (robbery).

In several noteworthy cases, courts have held that offenses do **not** fall within the coverage of Section 16(a). See, e.g., Szucz-Toldy v. Gonzales, 400 F.3d 978, 981-82 (7th Cir. 2005) (Illinois offense for harassment by telephone not covered because its elements did not require proof of the use or threatened use of physical force); United States v. Vargas-Duran, 356 F.3d 598 (5th Cir. 2004) (en

---

[88] See, e.g., Flores, 350 F.3d at 669; Chrzanoski, 327 F.3d at 196; Bovkun v. Ashcroft, 283 F.3d 166, 169-171 (3d Cir. 2002).

banc) (holding that Section 16(a) requires the intentional use, attempted use or threatened use of physical force, and that even though the Texas offense of "intoxication assault" included an element of the use of force it did not fall within Section 16(a) because it did not include an element for **intentional** use of force); Flores v. Ashcroft, 350 F.3d 669, 670-72 (7th Cir. 2003) (holding that an Indiana battery offense which proscribes "any touching in a rude, insolent, or angry manner" was not covered by Section 16(a) because the Indiana offense did not include an element requiring the **use**, attempted **use** or threatened **use of physical force** even though the evidence indicated that the defendant had attacked and beaten his wife. The court also rejected the argument that any "touching" constituted "force" within the meaning of Section 16, lest every "battery" would fall within Section 16(a)); Chrzanoski v. Ashcroft, 327 F.3d 188, 191-97 (2d Cir. 2003) (Connecticut third degree assault offense for intentionally causing physical injury was not covered by § 16(a) because the Connecticut statute did not require an element of the use of force and one could intentionally cause physical injury in violation of the Connecticut statute without the use or threatened use of physical force); United States v. Gracia-Cantu, 302 F.3d 308, 311-312 (5th Cir. 2002) (Texas offense of causing bodily injury to a child, elderly individual or disabled individual not covered by § 16(a) "because the statutory definition of the offense does not explicitly require the application of force as an element"); United States v. Cruz, 805 F.2d 1464, 1469 n. 5 (11th Cir. 1996) ("Drug trafficking crimes are clearly not crimes of violence within the meaning of 18 U.S.C. § 16(a). The use of physical force is not an element of the crime. Only possession and distribution are required.").

  **b.**  **Section 16(b) --Felony Offenses Involving a Substantial Risk that Physical Force Against the Person or Property of Another May Be Used**

Although Section 16(b) is limited to felonies, its definition of a crime of violence sweeps more broadly than Section 16(a). Moreover, courts have ruled that it is not necessary that the risk of the use of force occur in every instance; rather, it is sufficient that the crime by its nature creates a strong probability that physical force will be used in the commission of the offense. See, e.g., Patel v. Ashcroft, 401 F.3d 400, 409-411 (Illinois offense for aggravated criminal sexual abuse, which required "the use of force or threat of force" covered by Section 16(b)); Zaidi v. Ashcroft, 374 F.3d 357, 360-61 (5th Cir. 2004) (Oklahoma offense "sexual battery" which has as a required element "the intentional touching, mauling or feeling of the body or private parts of any person sixteen (16) years of age or older, in a lewd and lascivious manner and without the consent of that other person"); Nguyen v. Ashcroft, 366 F.3d 386, 388-90 (5th Cir. 2004) (Oklahoma offense for using "any vehicle to facilitate the intentional discharge of any kind of firearms"); Chery v. Ashcroft, 347 F.3d 404, 407-09 (2d Cir. 2003) (Connecticut offense criminalizing sexual intercourse with an underage victim who is legally incapable of giving consent); United States v. Galvan-Rodriguez, 169 F.3d 217, 218-220 (5th Cir. 1999) (unauthorized use of a motor vehicle qualifies as a crime of violence under § 16(b) because there is "a strong probability that the event, in this case the application of physical force during the commission of the crime, will occur"); United States v. Velazquez-Overa, 100 F.3d 418, 420-23 (5th Cir. 1996) (Texas law proscribing sexual contact with a child involves "a significant likelihood that physical force may be used to perpetrate the crime," id. at 422) (citing similar rulings); United States v. Rodriguez-Guzman, 56 F.3d 18, 20-21 (5th Cir. 1995) (burglary of a nonresidential building or a vehicle, by its nature, creates a substantial risk of the use of force against the property of another); United States v. Guadaro, 40 F.3d 102, 104-05 (5th Cir. 1994) (Texas offense for burglary of a habitation) (citing similar rulings); United States v. Reyes-Castro, 13 F.3d 377, 379 (10th Cir. 1993) (attempted sexual abuse of a child); United States v. Aragon, 983 F.3d 1306, 1311-15 (4th Cir. 1993) (assisting a prisoner to escape); Maddalena, 893 F.2d at 819-20 (robbery); United States v. Flores, 875 F.2d 1110, 1113 (5th Cir. 1989) (burglary of a residence); Ramirez v. Ashcroft, 361 F. Supp. 2d

650, 653-657 (S.D. Texas 2005) ("unauthorized use of a motor vehicle carries a substantial risk of damage or destruction to the vehicle in the commission of the offense, by breaking into the vehicle, or vandalizing the vehicle in order to use it without the owner's consent"); United States v. Lepore, 304 F. Supp. 2d 183, 186-189 (D. Mass 2004) (indecent assault and battery on a person fourteen or older in violation of Mass. Gen. Laws Ch. 265 § 13H); Hongsathirath v. Ashcroft, 322 F. Supp. 2d 203 (D. Conn. 2004) (injury to a child and sexual assault in the fourth degree in violation of Conn. Gen. Stat. § 53a-73a); Santapola v. Ashcroft, 249 F. Supp. 2d 181, 194-203 (D. Conn. 2003) (same).

For cases holding that particular offenses were **not** covered by Section 16(b), see, e.g., Tran v. Gonzales, 414 F.3d 464, 465, 469-70 (3d Cir. 2005) (Pennsylvania crime of "reckless burning or exploding" is not covered by Section 16(b) because "pure" recklessness is not sufficient mens rea; rather specific intent is required); Jobson v. Ashcroft, 326 F.3d 367, 371-76 (2d Cir. 2003) (manslaughter in the second degree for recklessly causing the death of another person under New York Penal Law § 125.15(1) not covered by Section 16(b) because the New York "offense encompasses many situations in which the defendant applies no physical force to the victim, and more importantly, situations that do not involve any risk that the defendant will apply force to the victim" and "an unintentional accident caused by recklessness cannot properly be said to involve a substantial risk that a defendant will use physical force . . . [A] predicate offense cannot satisfy the above requirements of Section 16(b) without requiring some intentional conduct." Id. at 373-74); Gracia-Cantu, 302 F.3d at 312-13 (Texas offense of causing bodily injury to a child, elderly individual or disabled individual not covered by § 16(b) "[b]ecause the offense of injury . . . is results-oriented, many convictions involve an omission rather than . . . the substantial likelihood of an intentional use of force"); United States v. Lucio-Lucio, 347 F.3d 1202, 1204-05 (10th Cir. 2003) (driving while intoxicated not covered by

§ 16(b)) (collecting cases); United States v. Cervantez-Nava, 281 F.3d 501, 506 (5th Cir. 2002) (same); Cruz, 805 F.2d at 1468-1475 (conducting a continuing criminal enterprise involved in drug trafficking, conspiracy to possess cocaine with intent to distribute and possession with intent to distribute are not within the scope of Section 16(b)) (cites similar rulings); United States v. Diaz, 778 F.2d 86 (2d Cir. 1985) (drug trafficking offenses not within scope of Section 16(b)).

### 2. Section 1959 Cases Charging a Threat to Commit a Crime of Violence

The foregoing authority demonstrates that many types of offenses fall within the meaning of a "crime of violence" under 18 U.S.C. § 16. However, Section 1959 does not, per se, proscribe the commission of all such crimes of violence. Rather, Section 1959's reference to a crime of violence is limited to "threats" to commit a crime of violence. Therefore, establishing a crime of violence by itself is not sufficient under Section 1959; the United States must also establish a "threat" to commit a crime of violence that falls within the scope of 18 U.S.C. §§ 16 and 1959. Furthermore, the threat itself must violate state or federal law. For example, the state in which the threat occurred must have enacted a statute prohibiting such threats.

Only a few published decisions in Section 1959 prosecutions have involved predicate crimes alleging a threat to commit a crime of violence. For example, in United States v. Aragon, 983 F.2d 1306, 1311-1313 (4th Cir. 1993), the court joined the numerous courts (see supra n. 87) that have adopted a "categorical approach" to determine whether a particular statutory offense qualifies as a crime of violence, which focuses on the elements or instrinsic nature of the statutory offense, and not on the particular factual circumstances of the case. The court also held that whether an offense constitutes a crime of violence is an issue of law for the court, and not the jury, to decide. 983 F.2d at 1311.

The court further held that "the crime of rescue or attempting to rescue or assist in the escape of a federal prisoner, as defined in 18 U.S.C. § 752, is categorically a 'crime of violence' under 18 U.S.C. § 16(b)." 983 F.2d at 1313. The Court explained:

> Initially, it derives from common sense that events structured for the rescue or escape of a prisoner are supercharged with the potential that, in being played out, physical force will be exerted against some person or some property... Even in those situations where rescue is attempted or effectuated by stealth, there still exists a *substantial risk* that physical force will be used against people or property due to the custodial setting.

Id. at 1313.

Similarly, in United States v. Innie, 7 F.3d 840, 849 (9th Cir. 1993), the court applied the so-called "categorical approach" to determine whether the defendant's conviction for accessory after the fact to murder for hire (under 18 U.S.C. §§ 1959 and 3) was a crime of violence.[89] The court concluded that accessory after the fact to murder is not a crime of violence under 18 U.S.C. § 16(a) because:

> 18 U.S.C. § 3 does not require, as an element, the use, attempted use, or threatened use of physical force against the person or property of another. Nor must the use or threat of force be proven in every case to sustain a conviction as an accessory after the fact.

Innie, 7 F.3d at 850. The court further held, 7 F.3d at 850-53, that accessory after the fact to murder did not fall within the ambit of Section 16(b), stating:

> We simply cannot say that, by its nature, receiving, comforting or assisting someone who has committed an offense against the United States in order to hinder or prevent his apprehension, trial or punishment, involves a substantial risk in every case that physical force may be used.

Id. at 850.[90]

---

[89] The Court stated: "In doing so, we 'do not look to the specific conduct which occasioned [the defendant's] conviction, but only to the statutory definition of the crime.'" Innie, 7 F.3d at 849.

[90] See also, United States v. Dhinsa, 243 F.3d 635, 673-77 (2d Cir. 2001) (reversing defendant's conviction for threatening to commit murder in violation of 18 U.S.C. § 1959(a)(4), because the evidence was insufficient to establish the Section 1959 predicate crime of violence,
(continued...)

L.  **Attempts and Conspiracies**

1. As discussed in Section II (E) above, Congress intended to incorporate into Section 1959 **substantive** state statutory offenses for murder, kidnapping, maiming, assault with a dangerous weapon, and assault resulting in serious bodily injury that substantially conform to generic definitions of those crimes, and that state law governs any such substantive state statutory offense. However, Section 1959 explicitly includes predicate offenses for attempts and conspiracies to commit an underlying crime of violence,[91] and it is not settled whether state or federal law applies to such attempts and conspiracies. In United States v. Khalil, 279 F.3d 358 (6th Cir. 2002), the Sixth Circuit

---

[90](...continued)
coercion in the first degree, in violation of N.Y. Penal Law § 135.65); United States v. Wilson, 116 F.3d 1066, 1078-79 (5th Cir. 1997) (affirming the defendant's Section 1959 conviction for threatening to kill a police officer).

[91] See, e.g., United States v. Spinelli, 352 F.3d 48, 50 (2d Cir. 2003) (affirming conviction for conspiracy to murder under Section 1959); Pimentel, 346 F.3d at 297-99 (finding evidence of attempted murder under New York law insufficient as to one defendant, but sufficient as to another defendant); United States v. Desena, 287 F.3d 170; 177-79 (2d Cir. 2002) (affirming defendant's conviction for attempted murder under New York law); Khalil, 279 F.3d at 368-370 (affirming defendant's conviction for aiding and abetting an attempted assault with a dangerous weapon and to cause serious bodily injury under Ohio law); United States v. Vasquez, 267 F.3d 79 (2d Cir. 2001) (affirming defendant's conviction for conspiracy to murder under New York law); Desena, 260 F.3d at 154-156 (reversing conviction for conspiracy to assault with a dangerous weapon; see infra); United States v. James, 239 F.3d 120 (2d Cir. 2000) (affirming defendant's conviction for conspiracy to murder under New York law); Carrillo, 229 F.3d at 182-86 (affirming defendant's conviction for conspiracy to murder under New York law); United States v. Reyes, 157 F.3d 949, 954-55 (2d Cir. 1998) (affirming defendant's conviction for conspiracy to murder under New York law); Rolett,
151 F.3d at 792 (rejecting defendant's argument that his acquittal on the murder-in-aid of racketeering charge was inconsistent with, and vitiated, his conviction for conspiracy to murder in aid of racketeering); United States v. Wilson, 116 F.3d 1066, 1079-1080 (5th Cir. 1997) (affirming defendant's convictions for conspiracy to assault with a dangerous weapon); Orena, 32 F.3d at 713-14 (affirming defendant's conviction for conspiring to murder under New York law); United States v. Rosa, 11 F. 3d 315, 340-41 (2d Cir. 1993) (affirming defendant's conviction for conspiracy to murder); Cuong Gia Le, 310 F. Supp. 2d at 782-84 (holding that an indictment charging conspiracies to commit various crimes of violence under state law need not charge an overt act).

applied federal law of "attempt" to determine the sufficiency of the evidence of an attempted assault with a dangerous weapon, in violation of Ohio law, stating:

> To establish liability for an attempt, the government must prove both specific intent to engage in the criminal activity and the commission of an overt act that **constitutes a substantial step towards the commission of the crime.**

Khalil, 279 F.3d at 369 (emphasis added).[92]

Whereas in Cuong Gia Le, 310 F. Supp. 2d at 783, the district court stated that it appeared that "§ 1959 incorporates state law with respect to attempts and conspiracies." However, the court added that it was not necessary to decide the issue because neither the charged conspiracy offenses under Virginia and Maryland law, nor Section 1959, required proof of an overt act.[93] Therefore, the district court found that there was no material difference between state or federal law regarding attempts in that case. Id. at 782-84.

The Second Circuit has held that state law of attempts applies to attempts to commit state crimes of violence charged under Section 1959 and has strongly suggested that state law of conspiracy

---

[92] Applying this standard, the Sixth Circuit upheld the defendant's conviction for aiding and abetting an attempted assault with a dangerous weapon. The defendant, National President of the Avengers Motorcycle Club, directed club members to seek and assault members of a rival motorcycle club, the Iron Coffins. The evidence also showed that "on at least two occasions, members of the Avengers assembled into groups and traveled to local bars with the intention of engaging the Iron Coffins in a violent confrontation. On at least one of these occasions, the [Avengers'] club members were armed [with clubs]." Khalil, 279 F.3d at 368.

[93] The Supreme Court has held repeatedly that, "where Congress had omitted from the relevant conspiracy provision any language expressly requiring an overt act, the Court would not read such a requirement into the statute." Rather, the Court has held that, "absent contrary indications, Congress intends to adopt the common law definition of statutory terms," and that the common law understanding of conspiracy does not require proof of an overt act. Whitfield v. United States, 543 U.S. 209, 213-14 (2005) (citations omitted). Accord United States v. Shabani, 513 U.S. 10, 13-14 (1994); Singer v. United States, 323 U.S. 338, 340 (1945); Nash v. United States, 229 U.S. 373, 378 (1913). Therefore, because Section 1959 does not expressly require proof of an overt act to establish a conspiracy charge, such proof is not required.

also applies to conspiracies to commit state offenses charged under Section 1959. For example, in Pimentel, 346 F.3d at 297-299, the Second Circuit held that under New York law there was insufficient evidence to establish that co-conspirator Garcia attempted to murder one Santiago. The court explained that to establish an "attempt," New York courts require the government to "prove the defendant engaged in conduct that came *dangerously near* commission of the completed crime." Pimentel, 346 F.3d at 298, quoting United States v. Desena, 287 F.3d 170, 178 (2d Cir. 2002).[94] The Second Circuit added "to satisfy the 'dangerously near' standard, the defendant must have carried the project forward to within 'dangerous proximity of the intended crime, though he need not take the final step to effectuate that crime.'" Pimentel, 346 F.3d at 298 (citations omitted).[95]

In Pimentel, 346 F.3d at 298, the evidence "established only that (1) Garcia was armed when he spent an evening in the vicinity of a park, which Santiago was known to frequent, looking for him so he could shoot and kill him; and (2) Garcia abandoned his attempt to kill Santiago after he failed to locate him." The Second Circuit concluded that this evidence was not sufficient to satisfy New York's "dangerously near/dangerous proximity" test for attempts. Id. at 299. The Court reasoned

---

[94] In Desena, 287 F.3d at 177 n. 1, the Second Circuit stated that it did not decide whether "§ 1959 imports state law of *attempt and conspiracy* or whether federal law governs . . . because the defendant [did] not raise it as an issue and both parties have assumed that New York law of attempt governs." The court went on to hold that the evidence was sufficient to establish an attempted assault with a dangerous weapon under New York law. See supra pp. 73-74.

[95] New York's standard to prove an attempt is stricter than the federal law of attempt, which requires the commission of a "substantial step towards the commission of the crime." See, e.g., United States v. Crowley, 318 F.3d 401, 407-08 (2d Cir. 2003). (A "substantial step must be something more than mere preparation, yet may be less than the last act necessary before the actual commission of the substantive crime"), quoting United States v. Manely, 632 F.2d 978, 987 (2d Cir. 1980). Accord Khalil, 279 F.3d at 369; United States v. Doyon, 194 F.3d 207, 210-12 (1st Cir. 1999); United States v. Nelson, 66 F.3d 1036, 1042-44 (9th Cir. 1995); United States v. Cruz-Jiminez, 977 F.2d 95, 101-04 (3d Cir. 1992); United States v. Forbrich, 758 F.2d 555, 557 (11th Cir. 1985); United States v. Mandujano, 499 F.2d 370, 376-78 (5th Cir. 1974).

that:

> In the context of attempted murder prosecutions factually analogous to the case at bar, New York courts have consistently held that, to survive a-sufficiency-of-the-evidence challenge, the Government must establish that the defendant pointed a weapon at a victim and was about to kill him with it.

Id. at 298.

In Carrillo, 229 F.3d at 182-186, the Second Circuit indicated that it believed that the district court erred when it failed to instruct the jury that it must find an overt act in furtherance of the charged murder conspiracy, as required under New York law. (See supra pp. 25-26). However, the Second Circuit ruled that it was not necessary to decide that issue, because any error was harmless inasmuch as the defendant had conceded that for each conspiracy to murder or attempted murder charge, the jury found that the defendant committed the murder or attempted murder that was the object of the particular conspiracy. "Thus, the jury necessarily found that [the defendant] had committed an 'overt act' of murder or attempted murder in furtherance of each conspiracy to murder." Carrillo, 229 F.3d at 186.

OCRS believes that the Second Circuit's view that Section 1959 incorporates state law of attempt and conspiracy, when the underlying substantive crime of violence is a violation of state law, is wrong. Section 1959 provides, in relevant part, that it is a crime for anyone who "murders, kidnaps, maims, assaults with a dangerous weapon, commits assault resulting in serious bodily injury upon . . . any individual in violation of the laws of any state or the United States, or attempts or conspires so to do." It is particularly significant that this provision explicitly requires the list of generic crimes[96] to be in violation "**of the laws of any state or the United States**," but the phrase "or attempts or conspires so to do" comes **after**, not **before**, the requirement that the list of generic crimes be "in

---

[96] See supra Sections II (E)-(J).

violation of the laws of any state." Had Congress intended Section 1959 to incorporate state law of attempts and conspiracies, it could have provided in straightforward language that it was a crime for anyone who "murders, kidnaps, maims, assaults with a dangerous weapon, commits assault resulting in serious bodily injury upon . . . any individual, **or attempts or conspires so to do**, in violation of the laws of any state or the United States . . . . " Thus, Congress' placement of the phrase "or attempts or conspires so to do" **after** the phrase "in violation of the laws of any state" indicates that Congress intended that only the substantive generic crimes listed in Section 1959 be "in violation of the laws of any state," and that Congress created uniform offenses under federal law for attempts and conspiracies to commit those generic offenses.

The legislative history regarding Section 1959 confirms that Congress intended to apply federal law of attempts and conspiracies under Section 1959. In describing the generic offenses incorporated into Section 1959, the Committee responsible for Section 1959 stated that:

> While Section [1959] proscribes murder, kidnapping, maiming, assault with a dangerous weapon, and assault resulting in serious bodily injury in violation of federal or State law, it is intended to apply to these crimes in a generic sense, whether or not a particular State has chosen those precise terms for such crimes.

129 Cong. Rec. 22, 906 (98th Cong. 1st Sess. Aug. 4, 1983).

It is especially significant that the above-quoted list of "generic offenses" in violation of state law that are incorporated under Section 1959 does not include attempts and conspiracies, which indicates that Congress intended to incorporate only the generic offenses for substantive violations involving "murder, kidnapping, maiming, assault with a dangerous weapon, and assault resulting in serious bodily injury." Moreover, the Senate Report regarding Section 1959 states that:

> Racketeering activity is defined to incorporate the definition set forth in present Section 1961. **Attempted murder, kidnaping, maiming and assault are also covered**.

S. Rep. 98-225 at 307. This passage indicates that attempts to commit the listed generic offenses are included under Section 1959 regardless of whether state law proscribes attempts to commit the listed generic offenses. If Congress had wanted to limit Section 1959's coverage to attempts to commit the generic offenses under state law, it could have manifested that intent by either providing that "attempts in violation of state laws are also covered" or "attempts within the generic definition of attempts under state law are covered." However, Congress did not so provide; rather, Congress provided that "attempts or conspiracies" to commit the listed generic offenses are also included under Section 1959. See, 18 U.S.C. § 1959(a). This language does not impose any limitation that attempts and conspiracies to commit the generic list of crimes are proscribed **only** when the attempt or conspiracy violates state law.

Furthermore, OCRS' interpretation of the scope of Section 1959 promotes uniformity of the application of federal law: all attempts and conspiracies to commit the generic crimes of violence listed under Section 1959 are proscribed, regardless of the vagaries of state law.

For the foregoing reasons, OCRS believes that the Second Circuit's decisions that Section 1959 incorporates state law of attempts and conspiracies are wrong. Of course, however, prosecutors in the Second Circuit must follow these decisions. OCRS recommends that prosecutors in other circuits argue that federal law of attempts and conspiracies applies to Section 1959. However, OCRS also recommends that, if the only material difference between federal and state law of conspiracy is that state law requires proof of an overt act in furtherance of the conspiracy, the prudent course, absent clear circuit court precedent that federal law applies, is to allege and prove an overt act, and instruct the jury that the government must prove an overt act in furtherance of the conspiracy. Such a requirement is not an onerous burden; indeed, it would be a rare case, if ever, where OCRS would approve a conspiracy charge under Section 1959 when the government could not prove an overt act in furtherance of the conspiracy.

On the other hand, the differences between federal law of attempt, which requires a "substantial step" toward completion of the substantive offense, and state laws on attempt, like New York, that require acts coming "dangerously close" to completion of the substantive offense, are more problematic because the differences between state and federal law regarding attempts are more significant than is the case regarding conspiracies. OCRS recommends that prosecutors outside the Second Circuit argue that federal law of attempt applies. However, prosecutors should consider an alternative fallback position in appropriate cases. That is, when satisfaction of stricter requirements of attempt under state law would necessarily also satisfy the lesser requirements of attempt under federal law, it may be prudent to instruct the jury under the state law of attempt. In such cases, if the court rules that State law of attempt governs, the conviction may be affirmed. However, if the court rules that federal law of attempt governs, we may argue that the jury's conviction of the defendant under the state law of attempt necessarily means that the jury found all the elements of attempt under federal law as well.

2. Several Section 1959 prosecutions involve noteworthy issues. In <u>Wilson</u>, 116 F.3d at 1080, the Fifth Circuit held that "'conspiracy to commit attempted murder' is not a cognizable offense under 18 U.S.C. § 1959, both as a matter of statutory construction and common sense," explaining that "it would be the height of absurdity to conspire to commit an attempt, an inchoate offense, and simultaneously conspire to fail at the effort" (citation omitted). However, the court held that the defective allegation in the indictment was harmless error because the court found that, since the government did not introduce any evidence of "a conspiracy to attempt," the jury necessarily must have convicted the defendant on two other valid grounds alleged in the defective count and supported by the evidence: conspiracy to commit murder and assault with a deadly weapon. <u>Id.</u> at 1080.

In Dhinsa, 243 F.3d at 672-676, the defendant's 1959 charge was based upon a threat to commit a crime of violence; that is, Coercion in the First Degree, in violation of New York PENAL LAW § 135.65, which makes it a crime for one who "compels or induces a person to engage in conduct which [he] has a legal right to abstain from engaging in" "by instilling in the victim a fear that [the defendant] will cause physical injury to a person." The theory of the government's case was that the defendant threatened to kill Balwant Singh unless Singh arranged a meeting between the defendant and another person, Surander Parmar, and therefore violated § 135.65 because the defendant, by instilling in Singh a fear of physical injury, compelled or induced Singh to "engage in the conduct" from which he was entitled to refrain, that is arranging the meeting. The Second Circuit held that the evidence was insufficient to establish a completed violation of Section 135.65 because the victim, Singh, did not yield to the defendant's demand that he arrange the meeting, and hence the victim did not "engage in the conduct" from which he was entitled to refrain.

The Second Circuit also rejected the government's argument that the defendant's conviction, nonetheless, could be sustained on the ground that he committed the lesser included offense of attempted coercion in the first degree because "the district court failed to instruct the jury that it could find [the defendant] guilty of the lesser offense of attempted coercion in the first degree." Id. at 676. The Second Circuit's decision in this regard conflicts with the decisions of at least the Fifth, Sixth, Eight, Tenth and District of Columbia Circuits, which have held that the courts of appeals may enter a judgment of conviction on a lesser included offense which is supported by sufficient evidence where the defendant would not suffer undue prejudice, even if the jury was not specifically instructed on that lesser included offense.[97]

---

[97] See, e.g., United States v. Hunt, 129 F.3d 739, 745-46 (5th Cir. 1997) (collecting cases);
(continued...)

In Desena, 260 F.3d at 154-56, the Second Circuit held that there was insufficient evidence to support the defendant's conviction for conspiracy to assault with a dangerous weapon under Section 1959. The defendant, a member of the Pagans Outlaw Motorcycle Club (the "Pagans"), was charged under Section 1959 with conspiring to assault members of the Hell's Angels Motorcycle Club ("the Hell's Angels") with dangerous weapons (firearms, axe handles and motor vehicles), and to cause serious bodily injury, in violation of N.Y. Penal Law §§ 105.10 and 120.10. Id. at 154. The government relied primarily on evidence that Pagan recruits were told about an ongoing war with the Hell's Angels at weekly meetings of the chapter to which the defendant belonged, and there were statements that if Pagan members "ever saw someone wearing a Hell's Angels shirt he should 'take the shirt or get the Hell's Angel. Any way [he] could." Id. at 155[sic].

The Second Circuit found such evidence insufficient, stating that:

> None of this amounts to anything. In the context of rival motorcycle gangs, the talk of "war" and grabbing shirts would not remotely convey an ongoing campaign of assault with dangerous weapons and murder. But even assuming that [Pagan witnesses'] indoctrination amount to induction into a criminal conspiracy, nothing links [the defendant] to it. [The defendant] did not participate in the indoctrination. He had already been a member for some unspecified period, so no inference is available that the state of war and shirt-grabbing existed whenever [the defendant] was inducted.

---

[97](...continued)
United States v. Hunt, 1998 WL 432475, at *6 (6th Cir. July 15, 1998) (unpublished); United States v. Lamartina, 584 F.2d 764, 766-67 (6th Cir. 1978); United States v. Cobb, 558 F.2d 486, 489 and n. 5 (8th Cir. 1977); United States v. Duran, 1998 WL 115865 at *3 (10th Cir. March 16, 1998) (unpublished); United States v. Smith, 13 F.3d 380, 383 (10th Cir. 1993); United States v. Seegers, 445 F.2d 232, 233-34 (D.C. Cir. 1971). The rationale of these decisions is that, when the jury convicts a defendant on the greater offense, it necessarily must have found all the elements of any lesser included offense. See also Rutledge v. United States, 517 U.S. 292, 306 (1996) ("federal appellate courts appear to have uniformly concluded that they may direct the entry of judgment for a lesser included offense when a conviction for a greater offense is reversed on grounds that affect only the greater offense"); Rule 31(c), Fed. R. Crim. P. ("A defendant may be found guilty of any of the following: (1) an offense necessarily included in the offense charged; (2) an attempt to commit the offense charged; or (3) an attempt to commit an offense necessarily included in the offense charged, if the attempt is an offense in its own right.").

> And even assuming that the Pagans constitution was part of [the defendant's] induction, there is no evidence that its provisions reflect an agreement to assault members of the Hell's Angels.

Id. at 155.

### M. The Underlying Crimes of Violence Must Be Committed For One of Two Purposes

Section 1959 provides that the underlying crimes of violence must be committed for either one of two purposes: (1) the receipt of, or as consideration for a promise or agreement to pay, anything of pecuniary value from an enterprise, **or** (2) gaining entrance to or maintaining or increasing position in an enterprise. See United States v. Fernandez, 388 F.3d 1199, 1232-33 (9th Cir. 2004). As long as the evidence establishes one of these two alternative purposes, such purpose need not be the defendant's only or primary purpose, and therefore it is immaterial whether the defendant committed the crime of violence for personal reasons.[98] Moreover, a Section 1959 conviction may not rest on a particular purpose unless the indictment alleges that particular purpose and that theory is presented to the jury. See, e.g., Polanco, 145 F.3d at 540 n.2; Thai, 29 F.3d at 818; Concepcion, 983 F.2d at 385.

#### 1. Receipt of, or as Consideration for A Promise or Agreement to Pay, Anything of Pecuniary Value From An Enterprise

Section 1959(a) provides, in relevant part: "Whoever, as consideration for the receipt of, or as consideration for a promise or agreement to pay, anything of pecuniary value from an enterprise engaged in racketeering activity" commits any one of the listed crimes of violence shall be punished. This provision, in essence, proscribes "contract murders" and other crimes of violence in exchange

---

[98] See, e.g., United States v. Smith, 413 F.3d 1253, 1277 (10th Cir. 2005); United States v. Bruno, 383 F.3d 65, 83 (2d Cir. 2004); Pimentel, 346 F.3d at 295-96; Ferguson, 246 F.3d at 134; United States v. James, 239 F.3d 120, 124 n. 5 (2d Cir. 2000); United States v. Johnson, 219 F.3d 349; 355 (4th Cir. 2000); United States v. Rahman, 189 F.3d 88, 127 (2d Cir. 1999); Diaz, 176 F.3d at 94-95; Tse, 135 F.3d at 206; Wilson, 116 F.3d at 1078; Tipton, 90 F.3d at 891; Thai, 29 F.3d at 817; Concepcion, 983 F.2d at 381.

for, or a promise to pay, anything of pecuniary value. S. Rep. No. 98-225 at 306. See also cases cited infra p. 103 and n. 100. Although Section 1959 does not define "anything of pecuniary value," the Senate Report regarding Section 1959 states that the "Committee intends that 'anything of pecuniary value' have the same meaning as in section [1958]." S. Rep. No. 98-225 at 306 n. 6. 18 U.S.C. § 1958(b)(1) provides:

> (1) "anything of pecuniary value" means anything of value in the form of money, a negotiable instrument, a commercial interest, or anything else the primary significance of which is economic advantage.

Although it is "not necessary to prove that the [defendant] was himself a part of the enterprise engaged in racketeering activity,"[99] the government must prove that the enterprise paid, agreed or promised to pay, something of pecuniary value to the defendant as consideration for the commission of an underlying crime of violence.[100] Evidence that the defendant received payment, or was promised payment, from a person "acting as an agent of the enterprise, not in his personal capacity," is sufficient to establish the requisite payment from an enterprise. Andino, 101 F. Supp. 2d at 175.

For example, in Johnson, 219 F.3d at 355, the court held that the requisite evidence of payment from an enterprise was established by evidence that the Johnson brothers, who operated a drug trafficking enterprise, agreed to pay a member of their drug enterprise to murder several "'weak links' in the organization." See also Rolett, 151 F.3d at 791-92 (Davidson, the leader of a criminal enterprise involving auto theft, arson, insurance fraud and drug distribution, promised to give the defendant, who stole materials to assist the enterprise, a truck for killing Marlene Holt, who had become "a problem"

---

[99] Rolett, 151 F.3d at 790; see also Concepcion, 983 F.2d at 384.

[100] See, e.g., Johnson, 219 F.3d 355; Gray 137 F.3d at 772; United States v. Andino, 101 F. Supp. 2d 171, 175 (S.D.N.Y. 2000); United States v. Ferguson, 49 F. Supp. 2d 321, 324 (S.D.N.Y. 1999), aff'd, 246 F.3d 129 (2d Cir. 2001).

"because Holt was strung out on drugs, was acting erratic and Davidson was concerned that Holt might tell about his involvement in a murder-for-hire"); Muyet, 994 F.Supp. at 519 ("Corona testified that he overheard John Muyet discuss hiring the freelancers to 'take care' of the Salcedos. Following the shootings, Corona overheard John Muyet discuss the payment to Feliciano and Camacho . . . [This evidence] was sufficient to allow a reasonable jury to determine that Feliciano was promised or received payment for his role in the Salcedo shootings").[101]

## 2. Gaining Entrance to or Maintaining or Increasing Position in an Enterprise

a. Section 1959(a) also covers underlying crimes of violence committed "for the purpose of gaining entrance to or maintaining or increasing position in an enterprise." The defendant need not be a member of the enterprise, nor is the government required to prove that the defendant committed the crime of violence to gain entrance himself or to increase or advance his own position in an enterprise. Rather, it is sufficient that the defendant committed the requisite crime of violence to assist another person to gain entrance or to maintain or increase such person's position in an enterprise.[102]

United States v. Concepcion, 983 F.2d 369 (2d Cir. 1992), is the seminal case that sets forth the criteria to determine whether an underlying crime of violence was committed for the purpose of

---

[101] Several courts have found the evidence of payment from an enterprise for a crime of violence insufficient. See, e.g., Ferguson, 246 F.3d at 136-37 (holding that evidence that the enterprise's leader gave the defendant "a wad of bills one to two weeks after the Mercado shooting in front of [Enterprise] members and evidence that the enterprise leader paid other shooters was insufficient to prove "that the payment to [the defendant] was for a shooting . . . [because] the circumstances of the payment to [the defendant] are equally consistent with an innocent purpose or even a criminal purpose unrelated to [the shooting]"); Andino, 101 F. Supp. 2d at 175-177 (holding that there was insufficient evidence "that Castro acted on behalf of [the enterprise] when he gave Andino money for his participation in Castro's attempt to murder Totito" (id. at 177), when Castro merely associated with, but was not a member of, the enterprise and Castro had a personal motive of revenge to murder Tito that was not related to the enterprise's activities).

[102] See, e.g., United States v. Frampton, 382 F.3d 213, 222-23 (2d Cir. 2004); cf., Fernandez, 388 F.3d at 1232-33; see also infra Section III (A).

gaining entrance to or maintaining or increasing someone's position in an enterprise. Concepcion ruled that such purpose need not be "the defendant's sole or principal motive." Id. at 381. Rather, it is sufficient that the crime of violence was committed "'as an integral aspect of membership' in such enterprise." Id.[103] The Concepcion court went on to hold that the requisite purpose to maintain and improve the defendant's leadership position in a drug trafficking enterprise was established by evidence that the leader of the enterprise and several members shot or killed several competitor drug dealers to eliminate competition at a particular locations. Id. at 382-85.[104]

Numerous decisions, adopting the principles set forth in Concepcion, have upheld the sufficiency of the evidence that a crime of violence was committed for the purpose of gaining entrance to or maintaining or increasing a position in an enterprise. For example, in United States v. Smith, 413 F.3d 1253, 1277-78 (10th Cir. 2005), the enterprise was a violent street gang known as the King Mafia Disciples ("KMD"), and the evidence established that "acts of violence were a common part of KMD's culture and that members were expected to retaliate against acts of violence committed on fellow members." Id. at 1278. The court held that the murder of a person believed to be a rival gang member fell within Section 1959 "when the underlying crime was sanctioned by a high ranking leader of the RICO enterprise, if the high-ranking leader was expected to act and any failure to do so would have undermined his position in the enterprise." Id.[105]

---

[103] See S. Rep. No. 98-225 at 304 (Section 1959 "proscribes murder and other violent crimes committed . . . as an integral aspect of membership in an enterprise engaged in racketeering activity.").

[104] Other courts have likewise held that acts of violence to eliminate competition in drug trafficking were undertaken to enhance or maintain a position in a drug trafficking enterprise. See, e.g., James, 239 F.3d at 124 n.5; Reyes, 157 F.3d at 955; Wilson, 116 F.3d at 1078.

[105] In other Section 1959 cases involving enterprises consisting of violent street gangs or
(continued...)

Furthermore, in Dhinsa, 243 F.3d at 670-72, the court rejected the defendant's argument that his crimes involving fraud, murder, kidnapping and other offenses could not have been committed to maintain or enhance his position in the enterprise because he was the leader of the enterprise. The court explained that the evidence established that he committed these crimes to protect his criminal enterprise by murdering and threatening to murder persons he suspected were cooperating with the authorities, and that the defendant's failure to retaliate against those persons would have undermined his position in the enterprise.[106]

In United States v. Rahman, 189 F.3d 188, 125-27 (2d Cir. 1999), the court affirmed the Section 1959 convictions of various defendants who were members of a radical "Jihad Organization" (the enterprise), including defendant Nosair for murdering Rabbi Meir Kahane. Nosair argued, among other matters, that the murder of a private Israeli citizen (Kahane) "could not further the goals of an organization whose primary purpose was to levy war on the United States," and therefore could not have furthered the defendant's position in the enterprise. Id. at 126.

The court rejected Nosair's claims, noting that the indictment alleged that the Jihad Organization, was "opposed to nations, governments, institutions and individuals that did not share

---

[105](...continued)
motorcycle clubs, courts have likewise found, under the principles announced in Concepcion, that violent crimes committed to retaliate against rival gang members, eliminate competition, or because the perpetrator knew it was expected of him by reason of his membership in the enterprise were committed for the purpose of maintaining or enhancing a position in the enterprise within the ambit of Section 1959. See, e.g., Fernandez, 388 F.3d at 1232-33; Crenshaw, 359 F.3d at 992-93; Philips, 239 F.3d at 845; Diaz, 176 F.3d at 93-96; Mapp, 170 F.3d at 336; Wilson, 116 F.3d at 1078; Tipton, 90 F.3d at 89; Fiel, 35 F.3d at 1004-05.

[106] Other courts have likewise held that evidence of such retaliation against persons who pose a threat to an enterprise by a leader or member of a criminal enterprise is sufficient to establish that such crimes were committed to maintain or enhance one's position in the enterprise. See, e.g., Tse, 135 F.3d at 206; Tipton, 90 F.3d at 891; Thai, 29 F.3d at 817; Vasquez-Velasco, 15 F.3d at 842-43; Concepcion, 983 F.2d at 282-83.

the group's particular radical interpretation of Islamic law," and that objectives of this group included "to carry out, and conspire to carry out, acts of terrorism--including bombings, murders, and the taking of hostages--against various governments and government officials, including the United States government and its officials." In light of these purposes of the enterprise, the court concluded that the murder of Kahane did not "stray" from the purposes of the Jihad Organization, and in fact was entirely consonant therewith. Id. at 126. The court also found that there was sufficient evidence to establish that the murder of Kahane, as well as related violent crimes, were committed "in furtherance of" Nosair's membership in the Jihad Organization because such crimes of retaliation against Jewish emigration to Israel related to the goals of the enterprise to allow "Muslims to repossess their sacred lands in the hands of the enemies of God." Id. at 127.[107]

Moreover, it is especially significant that several courts have held that as long as the requisite statutory purpose for the commission of the crime of violence is established, it is immaterial that the actual victim of the violence was not the intended victim. For example, in Concepcion, 983 F.2d at 374, the defendant went to a location to shoot rival drug dealers in order to control drug trafficking

---

[107] See also, Pimentel, 346 F.3d at 295-96 (evidence sufficient where an enterprise's leader ordered a murder "to preserve and cement both her authority as a leader of the [enterprise] and her control over the discipline of the [enterprise's] members"); Crenshaw, 359 F.3d at 996-97 (shooting of a rival gang member to "gain stripes" in order to become a member of the street-gang enterprise); Johnson, 219 F.3d at 355 (member of a drug trafficking enterprise murdered "weak links" in the enterprise); Bracy, 67 F.3d at 1430 (defendants beat and kidnapped victim to collect debts victim owed to a drug trafficking enterprise); United States v. Hoyte, 51 F.3d 1239, 1245 (4th Cir. 1995) (same); Brady, 26 F.3d at 289-290 (holding that a defendant need not be a "made" member of the enterprise, the Colombo LCN family, and that the evidence sufficiently established that the defendant participated in the murder conspiracy to move from an associate to a made member of the Colombo family enterprise); United States v. Locascio, 6 F.3d 924, 940-42 (2d Cir. 1993) (holding that jury was entitled to: (1) find that Sammy Gravano committed various crimes of violence to maintain discipline within the enterprise, the Gambino LCN family, and to maintain his position in the enterprise, and (2) reject John Gotti's defense that the crimes were committed to advance Gravano's personal interests).

at that location. During the ensuing gun battle, the defendant and his cohorts shot three innocent bystanders, who were not members of the rival drug gang, killing one of them. The court rejected the defendant's claim "that the government must prove that the victim of the violence was the defendant's intended target" because "[t]he concept of transferred intent is well established in the criminal law." Id. at 381. Accord Smith, 413 F.3d at 1271; Rahman, 189 F.3d at 140-42; Mapp, 170 F.3d at 335-36; Malpeso, 115 F.3d at 163-64.

b.  In several prosecutions under Section 1959, courts have found the evidence insufficient to establish that the crimes of violence were committed to gain entrance to or maintain or increase a position in an enterprise. Perhaps most troubling is the Second Circuit's decision in United States v. Bruno, 383 F.3d 65, 72-77, 81-86 (2d Cir. 2004). In Bruno, the defendant Carmine Polito was an associate of the Genovese LCN family in the crew of Joe Zito, and defendant Fortunato allegedly was also an associate of the Genovese LCN family. Defendants Polito and Fortunato were convicted under Section 1959 for killing Sabatino Lombardi and shooting Michael D'Urso, both associates of the Genovese LCN family also in the crew of Joe Zito.

Defendant Polito, a cousin of Lombardi, incurred large gambling debts and borrowed substantial amounts of money from Genovese Family loansharks, including Lombardi and D'Urso, which Polito was unable to repay. Id. at 72-74. In late 1993, defendants Polito and Fortunato participated in a scheme to rob a bank with members of a Genovese LCN family crew led by a capo "Alley Shades" Malangone. Following the bank robbery, defendant Polito began spending more time with members of Malangone's crew "so that he could participate in more significant crimes, repay his outstanding gambling debts, and eventually become a 'made' member of the Genovese Family." Id. at 13-74. However, "Joe Zito told Malangone that he didn't want Polito hanging out with

Malangone's crew," and Malangone agreed that he would stop it. Id. at 74. In 1994, defendant Polito recruited Fortunato and several others to kill Lombardi and D'Urso, including Anthony Bruno who agreed to participate in the murder scheme to enhance his standing with organized crime figures. Id. at 74.

The Second Circuit stated that the evidence showed that Polito had several motivations for wanting to kill Lombardi and D'Urso: "Polito owed them significant amounts of money from loansharking; he believed that D'Urso had previously 'set him up' for a robbery; and he wanted to switch from Zito's crew to Malangone's crew to increase his chances of securing ill-gotten gains." Id. at 84. The Second Circuit rejected the government's argument that this last motivation satisfied the "'position related' element of § 1959" for several reasons, stating:

> First, it cites no authority - and we have found none - for the proposition that an associate of an organized crime family switching from one crew to another is per se evidence of maintaining or increasing his position in a criminal enterprise. Absent any such authority, we think it simply too tenuous to conclude that switching from a temporarily less active crew to a more active crew within the same organized crime family was likely to result in Polito maintaining or advancing his position in that enterprise.
>
> Second, even when the evidence is construed in the light most favorable to the Government, no rational juror could conclude that killing Lombardi and/or D'Urso would have resulted in Polito's being able to switch crews. Polito was not a made member of the Genovese Family; nor was he acting on the orders of a made member (or anyone else) in that organization. Polito was merely an associate of the Genovese Family whose principal ties to that organization were in his capacity as a gambling and loansharking customer. Lombardi and D'Urso also were associates and not made members of the Geonvese Family. Thus, the Government failed to establish through the conclusory, uncorroborated, biased, and illogical testimony of D'Urso how the killing of Lombardi and/or D'Urso would have resulted in Zito or Aparo "releasing" Polito so that he could switch crews. Nor was there any evidence that Malangone, to whose crew Polito desired to switch, had authorized the Shootings, nor that Polito would have been accepted by Malangone into his crew after the Shootings. Thus, even crediting D'Urso's testimony that Polito wanted to switch to Malangone's temporarily "more active crew," there is no evidence from which a rational juror could conclude that Polito participated in the murder of Lombardi and the attempted murder of D'Urso to enable him to switch crews.

> Third, there was significant evidence that Polito's shooting of Lombardi and D'Urso was done in contravention of Genovese Family protocols and that Polito's role in the Shootings actually *decreased* his standing in the Genovese Family.

Id. at 84-85. OCRS believes that this decision is wrong. If a defendant believes that committing a crime will maintain or increase his position in an enterprise, and commits the crime with that subjective intent, then the requisite purpose is established even if his subjective assessment turns out to be wrong. Nothing in the text of Section 1959 or its legislative history indicates that under Section 1959 Congress required the defendant's subjective intent to be objectively correct.[108]

## III. ALTERNATIVE THEORIES OF LIABILITY

### A. Aiding and Abetting

The Senate Report regarding Section 1959 states that any person who aids and abets a violation of the listed underlying crimes of violence is also liable for a Section 1959 violation "under 18 U.S.C. § 2" in addition to "the person who actually commits or attempts the offense." S. Rep. No. 98-225 at 307. Thus, Congress manifested its intent that federal law of aiding and abetting applies

---

[108] See also, Ferguson, 246 F.3d at 134-36 (affirming the district court's granting of a new trial, finding that the evidence was insufficient to establish that the defendant's participation in a conspiracy to murder a rival gang leader and drug dealer was undertaken to gain entrance to or to maintain or increase a position in the Power Rules Gang, a drug trafficking enterprise, where the evidence showed that the defendant "was an outside hit man who did not belong to or seek to join Power Rules"; id. at 135); Polanco, 145 F.3d at 539-40 (holding that the evidence was insufficient to establish that the defendant participated in a murder to gain entrance to or maintain or increase a position in a drug trafficking enterprise where the defendant, who was not a member of the enterprise, supplied the enterprise and its leader with guns, including a gun that the enterprise's leader used to kill an innocent motorist to test the gun, and noting the defendant's relationship with the enterprise "did not exceed a vendor-vendee relationship"); Thai, 29 F.3d at 817-18 (holding that evidence that a leader of an enterprise, a street gang known as Born to Kill ("BTK"), was paid $10,000 to bomb a restaurant was not sufficient to establish that the defendant committed the offense to maintain or increase his position in the BTK where there was no evidence "that the bombing was to be a response to any threat to the BTK organization or to [the defendant's] position as BTK's leader, nor any evidence that he thought that as a leader he would be expected to bomb the restaurant.").

to Section 1959. In accordance with this legislative history, all of the courts that have decided the issue have held that a person may be liable for a Section 1959 violation on the ground of aiding and abetting.[109]

Therefore, a defendant may be liable under Section 1959 for the commission of a crime of violence to aid and abet another person's efforts to gain entrance to, or maintain or increase that person's position in, an enterprise, even though the defendant does not seek to gain entrance to, or maintain or increase his own position in, an enterprise. See, e.g., Frampton, 382 F.3d at 222-23. This principle not only flows from the law on aiding and abetting, but also stems from the well settled principal that a defendant may be liable for a conspiracy to violate a law even if he may not be liable for a substantive violation of the law because he does not fall within the category of persons who could commit the substantive offense directly. See, e.g., Salinas v. United States, 522 U.S. 52, 64 (1977) ("[A] person . . . may be liable for conspiracy even though he was incapable of committing the substantive offense.") (citing United States v. Rabinovich, 238 U.S. 78, 86 (1915)).[110]

---

[109] See, e.g., Frampton, 382 F.3d at 222-23 (applying 18 U.S.C. § 2); Khalil, 279 F.3d at 367-370; (same); Diaz, 176 F.3d at 96-97; Houlihan, 92 F.3d at 1293; Matta-Ballesteros, 71 F.3d at 765 n. 8, 771; Hoyte, 51 F.3d at 1245; Locascio, 6 F.3d at 941; Concepcion, 983 F.2d at 383-84 (applying 18 U.S.C. § 2). Cf., Marino, 277 F.3d at 29-32 (suggesting, but not holding, that state law applies).

[110] For example, the Hobbs Act, 18 U.S.C. § 1951, makes it a crime for public officials to extort property under "color of official right." Nevertheless, private citizens have been convicted of Hobbs Act conspiracy, i.e., extortion under "color of official right," where they have conspired with public officials to violate the Hobbs Act even though they are not within the class of persons who may be liable for the substantive Hobbs Act violation. See, e.g., United States v. Collins, 78 F.3d 1021, 1031-32 (6th Cir. 1992); United States v. Torcasio, 959 F.2d 503, 505-06 (4th Cir. 1992); United States v. Marcy, 777 F. Supp. 1393, 1396-97 (N.D. Ill. 1991). See also United States v. Jones, 938 F.2d 737, 741-42 (7th Cir. 1991) (conspiracy charge legally sufficient against defendant who was not a financial institution, although underlying substantive statutes, 31 U.S.C. §§ 5313, 5322, proscribe the failure to file Currency Transaction Reports with the Internal Revenue Service only by financial institutions); United States v. Hayes, 827 F.2d 469, 472-73 (9th Cir. 1987) (same);
(continued...)

"To be found guilty of the crime of aiding and abetting a criminal venture, a defendant must associate himself with the venture in a manner whereby he participates in it as something that he wishes to bring about and seeks by his acts to make succeed." Khalil, 279 F.3d at 369, quoting United States v. Martin, 920 F.2d 345, 348 (6th Cir. 1990).[111] See also Concepcion, 983 F.2d at 383 ("To secure a conviction on a theory of aiding and abetting in violation of [18 U.S.C. § 2(a)], the government must prove that the underlying crime was committed by a person other than the defendant and that the defendant acted, or failed to act in a way that the law required the defendant to act, with the specific purpose of bringing about the underlying crime . . . . Under § 2(a), an aider and abettor must share in the principal's essential criminal intent, [and] the principal must be shown to have had the essential criminal intent.") (internal quotations and citations omitted).

This requirement that the defendant must share the same criminal intent as the principal is especially significant as it applies to aiding and abetting a Section 1959 violation because "[t]he intent necessary to support a conviction for aiding and abetting goes beyond the mere knowledge that the defendant's action would tend to advance some nefarious purpose of the principal. Rather, the

---

[110](...continued)
United States v. Sans, 731 F.2d 1521, 1531-32 (11th Cir. 1984) (defendant could be convicted of conspiracy to defraud United States, in violation of Currency and Foreign Transactions Reporting Act, 31 U.S.C. §§ 1058, 1081, although he was not a specified party required to file reports under the Act).

Similarly, a defendant may be liable for conspiring to violate RICO even if he is not among the class of persons who participates in the operation or management of the enterprise, provided that the defendant knowingly agrees to facilitate a scheme that would violate RICO involving at least one other conspirator who would participate in the operation or management of the enterprise. See, e.g., Smith v. Berg, 247 F.3d 532, 537-38 (3d Cir. 2001); United States v. Viola, 35 F.3d 34, 42-43 (2d Cir. 1994); United States v. Quintanilla, 2 F.3d 1469, 1484-85 (7th Cir. 1993).

[111] In Khalil, the court affirmed the defendant's Section 1959 conviction for aiding and abetting an assault with a dangerous weapons. See supra p. 74.

defendant must act with the specific intent of facilitating or advancing the principal's commission of the underlying crime." Frampton, 382 F.3d at 223. Accordingly, for example, the government must prove that at the time the defendant participated in the underlying crime of violence, the defendant knew that the principal he was aiding and abetting was seeking to gain entrance to, or maintain or increase his position in, the enterprise and "acted toward that end." Frampton, 382 F.3d at 223.[112] Therefore, OCRS will not approve a proposed Section 1959 charge based on an aiding and abetting theory of liability unless the admissible evidence conclusively demonstrates that, among other matters, the aider and abettor either knew that the principal was acting for pecuniary gain or knew that the principal was seeking to gain entrance to, or maintain or increase his position in, the charged enterprise.

### B. Pinkerton Liability

In Pinkerton v. United States, 328 U.S. 640 (1946), defendant Daniel Pinkerton and his brother were charged with conspiracy to violate the tax laws and with two substantive tax violations. Although no evidence was introduced showing that Daniel Pinkerton participated directly in the commission of the substantive offenses, the district court instructed the jury that each defendant could be found guilty of the other's substantive offenses if they were both part of the same criminal conspiracy and "the acts referred to in the substantive counts were acts in furtherance of the unlawful conspiracy or object of the unlawful conspiracy." Id. at 645 and n. 6. The Supreme Court upheld Daniel Pinkerton's conviction under a theory of co-conspirator liability, but cautioned that the case would be different "if the substantive offense committed by one of the conspirators was not in fact

---

[112] In Frampton, 382 F.3d at 222-23, the court held that the evidence was insufficient to establish that at the time the defendant attempted to murder a person at the behest of co-defendant Frampton, the defendant knew that Frampton was seeking to maintain or increase his position in the charged enterprise.

done in furtherance of the conspiracy, did not fall within the scope of the unlawful project, or was merely a part of the ramifications of the plan which could not be reasonably foreseen as a necessary or natural consequence of the unlawful agreement." Id. at 647-648.

The instruction upheld in Pinkerton did not explicitly state that a defendant is liable under the Pinkerton doctrine for the substantive acts of his co-conspirators only if those acts were "reasonably foreseeable." Some circuits, however, have indicated that a Pinkerton instruction must explicitly include "reasonable foreseeability" language even though that language did not, in fact, appear in the jury instruction in Pinkerton itself.[113] In any event, the common and better practice is to include such "reasonable foreseeability" language in a Pinkerton instruction. Moreover, the government may not rely on the Pinkerton doctrine unless the jury is "instructed in terms of that theory." Pereira v. United States, 347 U.S. 1, fn. at 10 (1954). Accord Nye & Nissen v. United States, 336 U.S. 613, 618 (1949). Applying these principles, courts have held in Section 1959 prosecutions that a defendant may be convicted of an underlying crime of violence in violation of state law under the federal Pinkerton doctrine. See, e.g., Diaz, 176 F.3d at 99-100; Tse, 135 F.3d at 206-07; United States v. Katona, 204 F. Supp. 2d 410, 412 (E.D.N.Y. 2002). Cf., United States v. Carrozza, 55 F.Supp. 2d 84, 87-89 (D. Mass. 1999).[114]

### C. Accessory After the Fact

---

[113] See, e.g., United States v. Turcks, 41 F.3d 893, 897 (3d Cir. 1994); United States v. Broadwell, 870 F.2d 594, 603 (11th Cir. 1989).

[114] It is noteworthy that unlike Section 1959, liability for the commission of predicate racketeering acts under RICO may not be based on the Pinkerton theory of vicarious liability because to establish a substantive RICO violation, the government must prove that each defendant **personally** committed at least two racketeering acts that constitute a pattern. This requirement under RICO is inconsistent with Pinkerton's rationale of **vicarious** liability. However, this RICO requirement is not a required element of a Section 1959 prosecution.

Section three of Title 18, United States Code, provides, in relevant part:

**Accessory after the fact**

Whoever, knowing that an offense against the United States has been committed, receives, relieves, comforts or assists the offender in order to hinder or prevent his apprehension, trial or punishment, is an accessory after the fact.

Courts have held that under this provision, a defendant may be convicted as an accessory after the fact to a violation of Section 1959, provided the government proves:

(1) the commission of an underlying offense against the United States [i.e., § 1959] by [another person],
(2) the defendant's knowledge of that offense, and
(3) assistance by the defendant, in order to prevent the apprehension, trial, or punishment of the offender.

Cuong Gia Le, 310 F. Supp. 2d at 779. Accord United States v. Malpeso, 115 F.3d 155, 163-64 (2d Cir, 1997).[115]

Moreover, because 18 U.S.C. § 3 relies on a completed federal crime, the government must ensure that all policy and legal requirements relating to the underlying completed offense have been met. Therefore, all proposed charges for accessory after the fact to a Section 1959 violation must go through the approval process described in Section I(B) above.

## IV. MISCELLANEOUS LEGAL ISSUES AND PROCEDURAL MATTERS

### A. Venue

---

[115] In Cuong Gia Le, 310 F. Supp. 2d at 779-781, the district court upheld the sufficiency of the indictment's allegations that "the charged defendants, 'knowing that offenses against the United States had been committed' by Le, 'did receive, relieve, comfort and assist the offender, Cuong Gia Le, in order to hinder or prevent the offender's apprehension trial, and punishment.'" Id. at 779. In Malpeso, 115 F.3d at 159-160, 163-64, the court held that the evidence was sufficient to support the defendant's conviction for accessory after the fact when the perpetrators of a murder told the defendant what had happened, and thereafter the defendant hid one of the perpetrators and the defendant wiped down the getaway car to obliterate any fingerprints and "pulled the ignition out to make it appear as though it had been stolen and abandoned." Id. at 160.

Article III of the Constitution requires that "[t]he Trial of all Crimes shall be held in the State where the said Crimes shall have been committed." Art. III, § 2, cl. 3. Furthermore, the Sixth Amendment requires, in relevant part, that "[i]n all criminal prosecutions, the accused shall enjoy the right to a speedy and public trial, by an impartial jury of the State and district wherein the crime shall have been committed." These constitutional principles are embodied in Rule 18, Fed. R. Crim. P., which provides that criminal "prosecution shall be had in a district in which the offense was committed."

The Supreme Court has explained that the place where a crime is deemed to have occurred, or the locus delicti, "must be determined from the nature of the crime alleged and the location of the act or acts constituting it." United States v. Cabrales, 524 U.S. 1, 6-7 (1998) (citation omitted). "In performing this inquiry, a court must initially identify the conduct constituting the offense (the nature of the crime) and then discern the location of the commission of the criminal acts." United States v. Rodriquez-Moreno, 526 U.S. 275, 279 (1999). Moreover, the principal venue statute, 18 U.S.C. § 3237(a), provides as follows:

> (a) Except as otherwise expressly provided by enactment of Congress, any offense against the United States begun in one district and completed in another, or committed in more than one district, may be inquired of and prosecuted in any district in which such offense was begun, continued, or completed.

Consistent with the above-referenced authority, courts have uniformly held that a Section 1959 violation constitutes a "continuing offense" that may be brought in any district where the enterprise conducted its affairs as well as the district where the underlying crime of violence occurred.[116] These

---

[116] See, e.g., United States v. Saavedra, 223 F.3d 85, 88-94 (2d Cir. 2000); United States v. Williams, 181 F. Supp. 2d 267, 290-92 (S.D.N.Y. 2001); United States v. Aiken, 76 F. Supp. 2d 1346, 1349-51 (S.D. Fla. 1999); United States v. DeJesus, 48 F. Supp. 2d 275, 278 (S.D.N.Y. 1998); United States v. Perez, 940 F. Supp. 540, 547-49 (S.D.N.Y. 1996).

courts explain that a section 1959 offense is not limited to the commission of the underlying crime of violence that may be a discrete act committed in one district, but rather also encompasses such crimes of violence committed to gain entrance to, or maintain or increase a position in, an **enterprise**. The existence of an enterprise is an essential element of a Section 1959 offense, and as noted above in Section II(B), an association-in-fact enterprise is proven "by evidence of an **ongoing organization**, formal or informal, and by evidence that the various associates function as a **continuing unit**." Turkette, 452 U.S. at 583 (emphasis added). Thus, the enterprise element of a Section 1959 offense necessarily requires some degree of **continuing** or **ongoing** activity, which triggers application of 18 U.S.C. § 3237(a).

For example, in Saavedra, 223 F. 3d at 86-88, 93, the charged enterprise was the Latin Kings, a violent street gang headquartered in Manhattan in the Southern District of New York where the enterprise held its regular meetings to plan its acts of violence and conduct its business and to collect dues for memberships in the enterprise. However, the charged predicate offense, conspiring to assault a person with a dangerous weapon and attempt to assault him, took place entirely in Brooklyn in the Eastern District of New York. The Second Circuit rejected the defendants' argument that venue did not properly lie in the Southern District of New York, and that venue was limited to the Eastern District of New York, where the predicate offense was entirely committed. The court explained that the charged offense was not a "simple attempted assault," but rather was an underlying crime of violence committed **in furtherance** or **in aid** of a racketeering enterprise" Id. at 91-92. "As a consequence, defendants' trial was properly venued in the Southern District of New York because the racketeering element of their § 1959 violations serves as a continuing thread between Manhattan, the epicenter of the Latin Kings' racketeering operations, and Brooklyn, the site where the conspiracy in this case was formed and the assault against Sierra was planned to take place." Id. at 92.

Moreover, the Second Circuit did not end its inquiry with finding that Section 1959 was a "continuing offense;" it also applied the "Substantial Contacts Test," which considers "four main factors: (1) the site of the crime, (2) its elements and nature, (3) the place where the effect of the criminal conduct occurs, and (4) suitability of the venue chosen for accurate fact finding." Id. at 93. Applying this test, the court concluded that venue was proper in the Southern District of New York because the charged racketeering enterprise was primarily located in the Southern District of New York where it held its regular meetings to conduct the affairs of the enterprise. Id. at 93.

**B. Extraterritorial Application of Section 1959**

1. The principal of "extraterritoriality" permits a sovereign nation to criminalize conduct that occurs outside the nation's territorial limits. Significantly, "[t]here is no constitutional bar to the extraterritorial application of penal laws." Chua Han Mow v. United States, 730 F.2d 1308, 1311 (9th Cir. 1984). Accord Vasquez-Velasco, 15 F.3d at 839; United States v. Felix-Gutierrez, 940 F.2d 1200, 1204 (9th Cir. 1991). See also EEOC v. Arabian American Oil Co., 499 U.S. 244, 248 (1991) ("Congress has the authority to enforce its laws beyond the territorial boundaries of the United States").

The Supreme Court has explained that whether Congress has exercised its authority to apply a statute beyond its territorial boundaries "is a matter of statutory construction." EEOC v. Arabian American Oil Co., 499 U.S. at 248. Several principles of statutory construction govern that question. First, it is presumed "that legislation of Congress, unless a contrary intent appears, is meant to apply only within the territorial jurisdiction of the United States." Id. at 248, quoting Foley Bros., Inc. v. Filardo, 336 U.S. 281, 285 (1949). Express intent is not necessary to overcome this presumption. Rather, Congress' intent to apply a law extraterritorially may be gleaned from the law's legislative history, the purposes to be achieved, the interests of the United States, or by considering the nature of the proscribed conduct. See, e.g., United States v. Bowman, 260 U.S. 94, 97-98 (1922) ("The necessary *locus*, when not specially defined, depends upon the purpose of Congress as evinced by the description and nature of the crime and upon the territorial limitations upon the power and jurisdiction of a government to punish crime under the law of nations").[117]

For example, in Bowman, the Supreme Court explained that the presumption against extraterritorial application of law:

> should not be applied to criminal statutes which are, as a class, not logically dependent on their locality for the Government's jurisdiction, but are enacted because of the right of the Government to defend itself against obstruction, or fraud wherever perpetrated, especially if committed by its own citizens, officers or agents. Some such offenses can only be committed within the territorial jurisdiction of the Government because of the local acts required to constitute them. Others are such that to limit their *locus* to the strictly territorial jurisdiction would be greatly to curtail the scope and usefulness of the statute and leave open a large immunity for frauds as easily committed by citizens on the high seas and in foreign countries as at home. In such cases, Congress has not thought it necessary to make specific provision in the law that the *locus* shall include the high seas and foreign countries, but allows it to be inferred from the nature of the offense.

Bowman, 260 U.S. at 98.

If it is determined as a matter of statutory construction that Congress intended to apply a penal statute extraterritorially, then considerations of international law pertain. As a general rule, Congressional legislation should not "be construed to violate the law of nations if any other possible construction remains." McCulloch v. Sociedad Nacional de Marineros de Honduras, 372 U.S. 10, 21 (1963). "Nonetheless, in fashioning the reach of our criminal law, Congress is not bound by international law. If it chooses to do so, it may legislate with respect to conduct outside the United

---

[117] See also, United States v. Kim, 246 F.3d 186, 189 (2d Cir. 2001) (To determine Congressional intent, a court is allowed to "consider all available evidence about the meaning of the statute, including its text, structure, and legislative history") (quotations and citations omitted).

States, in excess of the limits posed by international law." United States v. Yousef, 327 F.3d 56, 86 (2d Cir. 2003) (internal quotations and citations omitted).

International law recognizes five principal bases on which a nation may exercise its criminal jurisdiction over citizens and non-citizens for conduct committed outside that nation's territorial limits:

> (1) the "objective territorial principle," which provides for jurisdiction over conduct committed outside a State's borders that has, or is intended to have, a substantial effect within its territory; (2) the "nationality principle," which provides for jurisdiction over extraterritorial acts committed by a State's own citizens; (3) the "protective principle," which provides for jurisdiction over acts committed outside the State that harm the State's interests; (4) the "passive personality principle," which provides for jurisdiction over acts that harm a State's citizens abroad; and (5) the "universality principle," which provides for jurisdiction over extraterritorial acts by a citizen or non-citizen that are so heinous as to be universally condemned by all civilized nations.

Yousef, 327 F.3d at 91 n. 24 (citations omitted). Accord Vazquez-Velasco, 15 F.3d at 840; Chua Han Mow, 730 F.2d at 1311 (collecting cases).[118]

---

[118] Pursuant to the foregoing authority, courts have applied penal laws extraterritorially in a variety of circumstances, including where sovereign interests of the United States or its citizens may be adversely affected. See, e.g., United States v. Cohen, 427 F.3d 164, 168 (2d Cir. 2005) (drug conspiracy laws); Yousef, 327 F.3d at 79-82, 86-98 (conspiracy to bomb United States - flag aircraft that served routes in southeast Asia, in violation of 18 U.S.C. § 32(a)); United States v. Plummer, 221 F.3d 1298, 1304-06 (11th Cir. 2000) (attempt under 18 U.S.C. § 545, which proscribes smuggling of goods into the United States); United States v. Chen, 2 F.3d 330, 332-34 (9th Cir. 1993), cert. denied, 511 U.S. 1039 (1994) (alien smuggling and other immigration laws apply extraterritorially); United States v. Layton, 855 F. 2d 1388, 1394 (9th Cir. 1988), cert. denied, 489 U.S. 1049 (1989) (applying 18 U.S.C. § 356, which proscribes killing of any member of Congress, extraterritorially to the murder of a Congressman in a foreign country); United States v. Wright-Barker, 784 F.2d 161, 166-68 (3rd Cir. 1986) (extraterritorial application of drug statutes warranted, as failure to apply statutes in such fashion would greatly diminish statutes' utility and effectiveness); Chua Han Mow, 730 F.2d at 1311-13 (applying drug conspiracy and distribution statutes (21 U.S.C. §§ 846 and 963) extraterritorially where foreign national engaged in conspiracy to smuggle drugs into U.S. although defendant's conduct occurred entirely outside U.S., "noting that drug smuggling compromises a sovereign's control of its own borders," quoting Untied States v.
(continued...)

2. Applying the foregoing principles, courts have held that Section 1959 applies extraterritorially in some circumstances. For example, the Ninth Circuit has applied Section 1959 to the murder and kindnapping of DEA Agent Enrique Camarena and a DEA informant, which offenses defendants committed in Mexico to protect their drug-trafficking enterprise, and to a defendant's conviction under 18 U.S.C. § 3 to accessory after the fact to those crimes. See United States v. Lopez-Alvarez, 970 F.2d 583, 596 (9th Cir. 1992); Felix-Gutierrez, 940 F.2d at 1203-06.[119] The Ninth Circuit explained that since drug smuggling by its very nature always requires some conduct in a foreign country:

> [i]t follows that United States agents involved in the investigations of international organizations seeking to smuggle drugs into the United States will, when foreign governments are willing to cooperate, conduct a portion of their activities outside the territorial bounds of the United States. We have no doubt that whether the kidnapping and murder of such federal agents constitutes an offense against the United States is **not** dependant upon the locus of the act. We think it clear that Congress intended to apply statutes proscribing the kidnapping and murder of DEA agents extraterritorially.

Felix-Gutierrez, 940 F.2d at 1204.

The Ninth Circuit also ruled that "the crime of 'accessory after the fact' gives rise to extraterritorial jurisdiction to the same extent as the underlying offense" (Section 1959) because "both

---

[118](...continued)
Schmucker-Bula, 609 F. 2d 399, 403 (7th Cir. 1980)); United States v. Noriega, 746 F. Supp. 1506, 1516-1517 (S.D. Florida 1990) (holding that the RICO statute applied extraterritorially to drug trafficking because based upon the Statement of Findings and Purpose, Pub. L. No. 91-452, 84 Stat. 992 (1970), Congress intended the RICO statute to be read expansively as a means of attacking organized crime at every level); United States v. Bin Laden, 92 F. Supp. 2d 189, 191-204 (S.D.N.Y. 2000) (holding that 18 U.S.C. §§ 844 (f)(1), (f)(3), (h) and (n), 942(c), 930(c), 1114 and 2155 apply extraterritorially to schemes to murder United States nationals, to destroy United States buildings and property and to destroy United States defense facilities).

[119] For other Section 1959 prosecutions arising from the conspiracy to murder and torture DEA Agent Camarena and an informant, see Matter of Ballesteros, 71 F.3d at 760-62, 71-73; Zund-Arce, 44 F.3d at 1423-26.

extraterritorial offenses injure the government," and "[l]imiting jurisdiction to the territorial bounds of the United States would greatly curtail the scope and usefulness of the accessory after the fact statute in cases in which extraterritorial crimes occur." Felix-Gutierrez, 940 F.2d at 1205. Moreover, the Ninth Circuit ruled that three principles of international law permitted extraterritorial application of Section 1959 and 18 U.S.C. § 3: (1) the "passive personality" principle because the victim DEA agent was a United States citizen, (2) the "territorial" principle because the defendant's unlawful conduct "created a significant detrimental effect in the United States and adversely affected the national interest," and (3) the "protective" principle because the defendant's unlawful conduct "directly hindered United States efforts to prosecute an alleged murder of a government agent." Felix-Gutierrez, 940 at 1205-06.

Under a similar rationale in Vasquez-Velasco, 15 F.3d at 839-41, the Ninth Circuit held that Section 1959 applied extraterritorially to the murder in Mexico of United States citizens mistakenly believed to be DEA agents who were investigating the defendant's drug-trafficking enterprise. The court stated that these murders, "like the murder of agent Camarena, were performed to further the [enterprise's] drug smuggling activities by intimidating the DEA from continuing its enforcement activities against the [enterprise's] drug trafficking," and hence "has an equally direct and adverse impact on our nation's security interests in combating the importation and trafficking of illegal narcotics. Id. at 841.[120]

### C. Drafting the Indictment and Related Issues

1. Consistent with the general rule on sufficiency of an indictment's allegations, courts

---

[120] Moreover, the United States has brought other Section 1959 charges predicated on crimes of violence committed in a foreign country, but the published opinions do not address extraterritorial application of Section 1959. See, e.g., Rahman, 189 F.3d at 126-30, 140-42 (murder of private citizens in Israel).

have held that a count alleging a Section 1959 violation is sufficient when it tracks Section 1959's statutory language as to all the required elements and includes some supporting factual allegations.[121] OCRS, however, disfavors "bare bones" allegations, and hence to ensure adequate notice to the defendant, OCRS requires more specificity in Section 1959 charges than minimally required by law. For example, OCRS requires that a Section 1959 charge explicitly allege that an association-in-fact enterprise "constituted an ongoing organization whose members functioned as a continuing unit for a common purpose of achieving the objectives of the enterprise." Furthermore, a Section 1959 charge must describe with specificity the nature of the enterprise, including its purposes and means and methods. Therefore, where an alleged enterprise had a particular structure or its members performed distinct roles in the enterprise, the indictment should describe the enterprise's structure and the various roles performed by the defendants.

A Section 1959 charge must also specify whether the defendant committed the underlying crime of violence for the purpose of either pecuniary gain, or to gain entrance to, or maintain or enhance a position in, an enterprise, or both. Failure to allege the particular purpose may preclude the government from relying on that purpose. See supra p. 102.

Moreover, although a Section 1959 count need not allege with specificity the racketeering acts engaged in by the enterprise,[122] the count at minimum must describe "generically" the types of racketeering activity in which the enterprise engaged, i.e., acts involving murder, extortion, robbery, etc., and identify the applicable statutory violations.

---

[121] See, e.g., Fernandez, 388 F.3d at 1219-20; United States v. Martinez, 136 F.3d 972, 978 (4th Cir. 1998); Orena, 32 F.3d at 714; Cuong Gia Le, 310 F. Supp. 2d at 777-780; United States v. Baez, 62 F. Supp. 2d 557, 559 (D. Conn. 1999). Cf., United States v. Cutolo, 861 F. Supp. 1142, 1147 (E.D.N.Y. 1994).

[122] See, e.g., Cuong Gia Le, 310 F. Supp. 2d at 778-780.

A Section 1959 charge must also allege with specificity the predicate crime of violence, including naming all the defendants charged with the offense, the approximate date of the offense, the location where the offense was committed, the elements of the Section 1959 violation and cite to the specific underlying state or federal statutory violation.[123]

Moreover, each underlying crime of violence constitutes a separate offense and may give rise to separate Section 1959 counts. Therefore, to avoid problems of duplicity,[124] as a general rule, the indictment should allege a separate count for each underlying crime of violence. For example, separate Section 1959 counts may be charged for (1) an assault resulting in serious bodily injury, and (2) assault with a dangerous weapon, arising from the same course of conduct. However, in some circumstances it may be permissible to combine two underlying crimes of violence in a single Section 1959 count, provided that the prosecutor obtains a special verdict requiring the jury to specify which underlying crimes of violence it found that the defendant committed.[125]

2. Several Section 1959 cases have addressed issues arising from amendments or

---

[123] Model Section 1959 charges are included in Appendix D.

[124] Duplicity is the joining of two or more distinct and separate offenses into a single count. The two principal problems posed by a duplicitous pleading are: (1) a general verdict of not guilty does not reveal whether the jury found the defendant not guilty of one crime or not guilty of both; (2) a general verdict of guilty does not disclose whether the jury found the defendant guilty of one crime or both. See United States v. Pungitore, 910 F.2d 1084, 1135 (3d Cir. 1990).

[125] See e.g., Pungitore, 910 F. 2d at 1135-36 (holding that even if charging alternative theories of murder, attempt, and conspiracy to murder under one predicate act of RICO racketeering constituted duplicitous pleading, no prejudicial error occurred where special verdicts were used and the jury decided on sub-predicates unanimously); United States v. Biaggi, 675 F. Supp. 790, 799 (S.D.N.Y. 1987) (court refused to dismiss a RICO sub-predicated racketeering act charging extortion, bribery, mail fraud and receipt of a gratuity arising from the same conduct where any duplicity problem could be solved by use of a special verdict form and adequate jury instructions).

constructive amendments to the indictment. In Owens, 236 F. Supp. 2d at 137-140, the district court rejected the defendant's argument that the district court constructively amended the Section 1959 Count, which alleged that the defendant had committed first degree "premeditated" murder, by permitting the jury to convict the defendant for second degree murder, which did not require premeditation. See supra, pp. 43-44.

In United States v. Wilson, 116 F.3d 1066, 1079-80 (5th Cir. 1997), the court ruled that although the indictment improperly charged a "conspiracy to commit attempted murder," which is not a cognizable offense, it was not reversible error to allow the jury to convict the defendant of attempted murder. The court reasoned that the evidence supported the attempted murder charge, and since "no evidence was ever presented to support the legally flawed charge, there is little danger that the jury convicted on that impermissible ground." Id. at 1080.

However, in Dhinsa, 243 F.3d at 664-670, the Second Ciruit held that it was reversible error to allow the government to obtain an amended indictment from the grand jury near the end of the defendant's trial to substitute federal kidnapping charges under 18 U.S.C. § 1201(a)(1), in place of the kidnapping charges originally brought under Section 1959 based on a violation of New York Penal Law § 135.20 (kidnapping in the Second Degree). Near the end of the government's case-in-chief, the district court questioned the sufficiency of the government's proof as to two elements of a Section 1959 violation: the interstate commerce nexus and that the kidnapping was undertaken to maintain the defendant's position in the charged enterprise. After the government rested its case-in-chief and shortly before the end of the trial, the government obtained an amended indictment, alleging a violation of the federal kidnapping statute, which unlike the Section 1959 charge, does not require proof that a kidnapping was committed to maintain a position in the enterprise. The court reasoned that the defendant was prejudiced by the late amendment of the indictment because the defendant was deprived of an opportunity to cross-examine the government's witness as regarding the new kidnapping charge.

### D. Double Jeopardy and Collateral Estoppel

### 1. Double Jeopardy

It is well established that the test for determining whether two offenses are the "same offense" for Double Jeopardy purposes is the "same-elements" or "Blockburger" test.[126] Thus, the Supreme Court stated:

> [W]here the two offenses for which the defendant is punished or tried cannot survive the "same-elements" test, the Double Jeopardy bar applies... The same-elements test, sometimes referred to as the "Blockburger" test, inquires whether each offense contains an element not contained in the other; if not, they are the "same offence" and Double Jeopardy bars additional punishment and successive prosecution.

United States v. Dixon, 509 U.S. 688, 696 (1993) (internal citations omitted). Under the Blockburger test, RICO and Section 1959 violations arising from the same course of conduct are not the same offense, and hence may be the basis for successive prosecutions and multiple punishment.[127]

Moreover, in United States v. Williams, 155 F. 3d 418, 419-22 (4th Cir. 1998), the court held that the defendant's Section 1959 prosecution for conspiring to murder John Jones in aid of racketeering, in violation of 18 U.S.C. § 1959(a)(5) and murdering Jones in aid of racketeering, in violation of 18 U.S.C. § 1959(a)(1), was not barred by the defendant's prior conviction for conspiring to retaliate against witnesses, in violation of 18 U.S.C. § 1513(a), which alleged the murder of John

---

[126] See Blockburger v. United States, 284 U.S. 299 (1932).

[127] See, e.g., Marino, 277 F.3d at 39; Polanco, 145 F.3d at 542. See also United States v. Johnson, 219 F. 3d 349, 358-59 (4th Cir. 2000) (holding that under the Blockburger test, a defendant was properly sentenced consecutively under both Section 1959(a)(1) and 18 U.S.C. § 924(j) for the murder of four persons because each offense requires proof of an element that the other does not.

Jones as an overt act in furtherance of that conspiracy. The court rejected the defendant's argument that Double Jeopardy principles barred his second prosecution because it relied on evidence of the same murder and enterprise that were proven in his first prosecution. The court concluded that since the Blockburger test was satisfied, such overlap in evidence was immaterial.

Under the dual sovereignty doctrine, courts have held that neither principles of Double Jeopardy nor alleged violations of the Department of Justice's *Petite* policy barred Section 1959 prosecutions because the defendants previously had been acquitted of the charged underlying state crimes of violence in state courts even though the federal and state authorities cooperated in those prosecutions. See, e.g., United States v. Williams, 181 F. Supp. 2d 267, 292-93 (S.D.N.Y. 2001); United States v. Claiborne, 92 F. Supp. 2d 503, 506-510 (E.D. Va. 2000).[128]

### 2. Collateral Estoppel

Collateral Estoppel is a component of Double Jeopardy protections. Collateral Estoppel "means simply that when an issue of ultimate fact has once been determined by a valid and final judgment, that issue cannot again be litigated between the same parties in any future lawsuit." Ashe v. Swenson, 397 U.S. 436, 443 (1970). Accord United States v. Console, 13 F.3d 641, 664 (3d Cir.

---

[128] Under the dual sovereignty doctrine, the Supreme Court has consistently held that the Double Jeopardy Clause does not bar successive federal and state prosecutions for offenses arising from the same acts, even where there was substantial cooperation between state and federal authorities. The Supreme Court has reasoned that the same act is an offense against both the federal and state sovereignty, and hence may be prosecuted by both. See United States v. Wheeler, 435 U.S. 1313 (1978); Abbate v. United States, 359 U.S. 187 (1959); Bartkus v. Illinois, 359 U.S. 121 (1959); United States v. Lanza, 260 U.S. 377 (1922). Cf., Heath v. Alabama, 474 U.S. 82 (1985).

The *Petite* policy "establishes guidelines for the exercise of discretion by appropriate officers of the Department of Justice in determining whether to bring a federal prosecution based on substantially the same acts or transactions involved in a prior state or federal proceeding." United States Attorneys' Manual § 9-2.03 (A). See also Petite v. United States, 361 U.S. 529 (1960).

1993) ("The double jeopardy clause protects against relitigation of an issue necessarily determined in the defendant's favor by a valid and final judgment").

Moreover, a defendant bears the burden of demonstrating that the issue of fact whose litigation he seeks to foreclose was actually decided in his favor by a valid and final judgment in an earlier proceeding. See Dowling v. United States, 493 U.S. 342, 350-51 (1990); Console, 13 F.3d at 665, n. 28. A defendant's burden in that regard is onerous. "A criminal defendant seeking to benefit from collateral estoppel has the burden of proving 'by clear and convincing evidence that the fact sought to be foreclosed was necessarily determined by the jury against the government in the prior trial.'" United States v. Uselton, 927 F.2d 905, 907 (6th Cir. 1991), quoting United States v. Benton, 852 F.2d 1456, 1466 (6th Cir. 1988). Accord United States v. Boldin, 818 F.2d 771, 775 (11th Cir. 1987). Thus, "it is not enough that the fact **may** have been determined in the former trial." United States v. Irwin, 787 F.2d 1506, 1515 (11th Cir. 1986). Accord Marino, 200 F.3d at 10-11 (holding that collateral estoppel must be denied where the government and the defendant offer "plausible competing" theories regarding the jury's factual findings at issue); United States v. Lanoue, 137 F.3d 656, 662 (1st Cir. 1998) ("Where it is impossible to determine whether the particular issue was previously resolved in a defendant's favor, preclusive effect must be denied."), (quoting United States v. Aguilar-Aranceta, 957 F.2d 18, 23 (1st Cir. 1992)).

To determine whether the defendant has carried his burden of establishing that a jury in a prior prosecution necessarily resolved a particular fact in his favor, "requires a court to 'examine the record of a prior proceeding, taking into account the pleadings, evidence, charge, and other relevant matter, and conclude whether a rational jury could have grounded its verdict upon an issue other than that which the defendant seeks to foreclose from consideration.'" Ashe, 397 U.S. at 44 (citation deleted). Accord Dowling, 493 U.S. at 350; Console, 13 F.3d at 665, n. 28. Thus, "[i]f the court concludes that a rational jury could have grounded its verdict upon an issue other than that which the defendant seeks to foreclose, then collateral estoppel does not apply." Boldin, 818 F.2d at 775.

Several significant Collateral Estoppel issues have arisen in Section 1959 prosecutions. For example, in United States v. Merlino, 310 F. 3d 137 (3rd Cir. 2002), the Third Circuit rejected the defendant's argument that Collateral Estoppel precluded his Section 1959 prosecution for conspiring to murder, and aiding and abetting the murder of, Joseph Sodano to maintain and increase the defendant's position in the charged enterprise, the Philadelphia LCN family, on the ground that a jury allegedly had found that the defendant did not participate in Sodano's murder in a previous RICO prosecution which charged the defendant with a RICO predicate act for conspiring to murder, and murdering, Joseph Sodano, in furtherance of the affairs of the same enterprise alleged in the Section 1959 prosecution. 310 F. 3d at 139-140.

In the earlier RICO prosecution, the jury returned a special verdict indicating on the verdict sheet "Not Proven" for defendant Merlino's participation in the Sodano murder predicate act. Therefore, defendant Merlino argued that the jury had acquitted him on that predicate act and Collateral Estoppel precluded the government from relitigating the issue of his participation in the Sodano murder and murder conspiracy in the subsequent Section 1959 prosecution. During the jury's deliberations, the jury submitted the following question to the district court:

> Racketeering Acts. Once we determine that the defendant has committed one unlawful collection of debt or two or more racketeering acts, do we need to decide proven or not proven on all the racketeering acts?

The judge responded, "Yes."

Two days later, the jury requested additional clarification on this issue. It sent a note asking:

> If, on a given racketeering act that has no bearing on the count decision we cannot come to a unanimous decision, is it within the law to unanimously decide that the act is "not proven"?

Over the objections of the government, the judge again told them, "Yes."

Id. at 140.

The Third Circuit held that the defendant did not carry his burden of establishing that the jury in the earlier RICO trial had acquitted him on the Sodano murder related racketeering act because the jury's verdict was ambiguous in light of the trial court's instructions. The Third Circuit explained:

> [The trial court's second] instruction makes the jury's vote ambiguous because we cannot tell from the face of the verdict sheet whether the vote was unanimously "Not Proven" or whether the jury unanimously decided that they were unable to reach a unanimous decision as to "Proven" or "Not Proven," *i.e.*, whether they were "hung" on that issue.
>
> Only the first of these interpretations of the jury note would bar the current case against Merlino because only the first is a unanimous acquittal and only the first resolves the issue Merlino wants to preclude from consideration in the New Jersey prosecution. The second interpretation of the note is not a unanimous acquittal and therefore is not a final judgment in favor of the defendant. Because Merlino cannot prove which is the actual jury vote, he cannot preclude the issue of his participation in the Sodano murder.

Id. at 143.[129]

---

[129] The district court in Merlino erroneously instructed the jury that it could return a verdict of "Not Proven" if it could not reach a unanimous decision. Rather, the correct instruction would have been to inform the jury that it could not return a verdict of "Not Proven" unless it unanimously agreed that the government did not prove beyond a reasonable doubt the racketeering act at issue. If the jury were unable to reach a unanimous decision of either "Proven" or "Not Proven" on a particular racketeering act, then they were "hung" on the act, and a retrial is permissible. See, e.g., Johnson v. Louisiana, 406 U.S. 356, 363 (1972) ("[W]hen a jury in a federal court... cannot agree unanimously upon a verdict, the defendant is not acquitted, but is merely given a new trial."). Accord United States v. Yeaman, 194 F.3d 442, 453 (3d Cir. 1999); United States v. Scalzitti, 578 F.2d 507, 512 (3d Cir. 1978). When a jury cannot unanimously decide that the defendant is either guilty or not guilty, then the jury is deemed "hung" and a retrial is permissible. See
(continued...)

Similarly, in Marino, 200 F.3d at 8-10, appellants argued that Collateral Estoppel barred their retrial on count three, which charged them with conspiring to murder fourteen individuals in aid of racketeering activity, because the jury acquitted them on count four, which charged them with using or carrying a firearm in furtherance of the murder conspiracy charged in count three. The district court in Marino, 200 F.3d at 10, instructed the jury not to reach a verdict on count four until it had reached a verdict on count three and that it could find the defendant guilty on count four only if it found that the defendant was a member of the conspiracy charged in count three. However, the jury did not reach a verdict on count three, but rather was deadlocked. Nevertheless, the jury acquitted the defendants on count four. The First Circuit stated that since the jury did not find the defendant guilty on count three, "but deadlocked instead, we are left to divine an interpretation of the charge which might explain its rationale." 200 F.3d at 10. The appellants contended that the jury must have acquitted them on count four because it found either that the count three conspiracy did not exist or that appellants were not members of that conspiracy. The First Circuit noted that the government had offered a plausible alternative interpretation, stating:

> Since the instruction - that the jury not consider count 4 prior to count 3 - was given immediately after the *Pinkerton* instruction, the jury may have understood (mistakenly) that the prohibition (against considering count 4 before count 3) applied only to its consideration of the *Pinkerton* criminal liability theory, not its consideration of the earlier "direct" liability or "aiding and abetting" theories. After deadlocking on count 3, however, the jury may have proceeded to count 4 - presuming that it need not consider whether the government had proven *Pinkerton* coconspirator liability - and then determined that the government had not proven either direct liability or aiding and

---

[129](...continued)
Richardson v. United States, 468 U.S. 317, 324 (1984) ("[W]e have constantly adhered to the rule that a retrial following a 'hung jury' does not violate the Double Jeopardy Clause."); Console, 13 F.3d at 664-65 ("[A] response to a special interrogatory regarding an element of a 'hung' count is neither a 'final' judgment nor a determination 'necessary' to a final judgment, such a response would not preclude the government from relitigating an issue.") (footnote deleted).

abetting beyond a reasonable doubt. In other words, the jury may have acquitted simply because it found that a codefendant (*i.e.*, not the defendant under consideration) had used or carried the firearm, or because the defendant under consideration had not known to a "practical certainty" that a codefendant was using a gun.

200 F.3d at 11.

The First Circuit stated that because of ambiguous jury instructions, "the more difficult it may be for defendants to demonstrate unequivocally on appeal that the jury necessarily predicated its verdict on a particular finding." Id. at 10. The court rejected appellants' Collateral Estoppel claims, stating that it could not "determine with any reasonable degree of reliability that the jury interpreted the pertinent aspects of its charge in the manner asserted by appellants." Id. The court concluded that since the government and appellants offered "plausible" competing theories, appellants did not carry "their burden to prove 'unequivocally'" that the jury necessarily acquitted him on count three. Id.[130]

### E. Joinder and Severance

Rule 8(b), Fed. R. Crim. P., permits joinder of defendants in a single indictment where the defendants participated in the same act or transaction or in the same series of acts or transactions constituting an offense. As is the case under RICO[131], the requirements of Rule 8(b) may be satisfied by establishing the existence of an enterprise and that the defendants' charged crimes related to the affairs of the same enterprise, and in such cases defendants not charged with a Section 1959 offense

---

[130] See also United States v. Fiel, 35 F.3d 997, 1006 (4th Cir. 1994) (refusing to exclude evidence that the defendant participated in surveillance of a rival motorcycle gang's members because the defendant was acquitted of aiding and abetting the murders of those gang members, explaining that the jury could have found that the defendant "was involved in the surveillance, but that his involvement did not rise to the level of aiding and abetting or attempting to murder" those gang members).

[131] See RICO Manual at 233-34.

may be joined in the same indictment.[132]

Also, as is the case under RICO, courts have repeatedly rejected defendants' claims that their charges should be severed from defendants charged with crimes of violence under Section 1959 to avoid prejudicial spillover from disparity of the evidence, evidence of the predicate violent crimes and the existence of an ongoing criminal enterprise, especially where limiting instructions to consider the evidence separately against each defendant may minimize the risk of undue prejudice.[133]

### F. Statute of Limitations

"A five year statute of limitations applies to federal non-capital crimes, unless specifically provided otherwise. See 18 U.S.C. § 3282." United States v. Gigante, 982 F. Supp. 140, 154 (E.D.N.Y. 1997). Accordingly, a five year statute of limitations applies to all Section 1959 prosecutions for non-capital crimes of violence, and the statute of limitations period begins to run for a substantive offense when the underlying crime of violence has been completed, and for a conspiracy offense when all the objectives of the conspiracy have been achieved or abandoned. See, e.g., United States v. Owens, 965 F. Supp. 158, 164-65 (D. Mass. 1997); Gigante, 982 F. Supp. at 154-159, 168-73. Cf. Desena, 287 F. 3d at 179-180.

---

[132] See, e.g., Matta-Ballesteros, 71 F.3d at 770-71; United States v. Darden, 70 F.3d 1507, 1526-27 (8th Cir. 1995); Vasquez-Velasco, 15 F.3d at 843-44; Felix-Gutierrez, 940 F.2d at 1208-09.

[133] See, e.g., Fernandez, 388 F.3d at 1241-44; United States v. Spinelli, 352 F.3d 48, 54-55 (2d Cir. 2003); Phillips, 239 F.3d at 837-840; Diaz, 176 F.3d at 102-103; Houlihan, 92 F.3d at 1295-96; Matta-Ballesteros, 71 F.3d at 771; Bracy, 67 F.3d at 1433-34; Vasquez-Velasco, 15 F.3d at 845-46; United States v. Rosa, 11 F.3d 315, 341-42 (2d Cir. 1993); Cuong Gia Le, 316 F. Supp. 2d at 339-341; United States v. Aiken, 76 F. Supp. 2d 1346, 1356-58 (S.D. Fla. 1999); United States v. Muyet, 943 F. Supp. 586, 595-98 (S.D.N.Y. 1996); Perez, 940 F. Supp. at 546-47. But see United States v. Williams, 181 F. Supp. 2d 267, 301-03 (S.D.N.Y. 2001) (severing defendant who was charged only in a narcotics conspiracy count from other defendants charged with RICO, Section 1959 violations and death-penalty eligible counts.)

On September 13, 1994, Section 1959 was amended to render any murder in violation of Section 1959 subject to a maximum penalty of death. See Violent Crime Control and Law Enforcement Act of 1994, Pub. L. No. 103-322, § 60003(a)(12), 108 Stat. 1796, 1969-70. Because 18 U.S.C. § 3281 provides that "[a]n indictment for any offense **punishable by death** may be found at any time without limitations" (emphasis added), any murder committed on or after September 13, 1994 that was chargeable under Section 1959 when committed is subject to the maximum penalty of death, and therefore is not subject to any limitations period regardless of whether the death penalty is actually sought. See, e.g., Owens, 965 F. Supp. at 164-65.

### G. Sentencing and Punishment in Non-Capital Cases

As set forth below, Section 1959(a) imposes different sentences depending upon the underlying crime of violence that is the basis for the defendant's conviction. Moreover, U.S.S.G. § 2E1.3 provides that the base offense level for a Section 1959 violation is the greater of 12 or "the offense level applicable to the underlying crime or racketeering activity."

#### 1. Murder and Kidnapping

Section 1959(a)(1) provides the following punishment:

(1) for murder, by death or life imprisonment, or a fine under this title, or both; and for kidnapping, by imprisonment for any term of years or for life, or a fine under this title, or both.

Under this provision, a defendant convicted of a predicate crime of murder may not be sentenced to a term of years. Rather, the permissible sentence is either death or a mandatory minimum of life imprisonment.[134] Moreover, a defendant is "subject to the same sentence under Section 1959,

---

[134] See, e.g., United States v. James, 239 F. 3d 120, 126-27 & n.7 (2d Cir. 2000) (the court also rejected the defendant's argument that Section 1959(a)(1) permits a fine in lieu of imprisonment); Feliciano, 223 F.3d at 124-25 (same); Rahman, 189 F.3d at 148-49; Vasquez-
(continued...)

either as a primary participant, aider and abettor, or conspirator" under the Pinkerton theory of liability. See, e.g., Matta-Ballesteros, 71 F.3d at 772. Furthermore, for sentencing purposes it is immaterial what degree of murder is the basis for the defendant's conviction under Section 1959 provided that the elements of the murder offense charged fall within the generic definition of murder.[135]

### 2. Maiming

Section 1959(a)(2) provides that the sentence for maiming is "imprisonment for not more than thirty years or a fine under this title, or both." As of this writing, there are no reported decisions addressing sentencing for maiming under Section 1959.

### 3. Assault Offenses

Section 1959 (a)(3) provides the following punishment:

> (3) for assault with a dangerous weapon or assault resulting in serious bodily injury, by imprisonment for not more than twenty years or a fine under this title, or both.

---

[134](...continued) Velasco, 15 F.3d at 847; Duarte v. United States, 289 F. Supp. 2d 487, 491 (S.D.N.Y. 2003) (the court also held that "Apprendi" principles (Apprendi v. New Jersey, 530 U.S. 466 (2000)) were not implicated because no additional fact finding was necessary to impose life imprisonment beyond the jury's guilty verdict for a Section 1959 murder); Marino, 277 F.3d at 38 (same).

[135] See, e.g., Tolliver, 61 F. 3d at 1220-21 (affirming the defendant's sentence for life imprisonment for Section 1959 murder and rejecting defendant's claim that the trial court should have used the federal sentencing guideline for second degree murder because the underlying state crimes were murder in the second degree under Louisiana law, and finding that the federal sentencing guideline for first degree murder under 18 U.S.C. § 1111 was the federal crime most analogous to the Louisiana second degree murder statute.); Guzman v. United States, 277 F. Supp. 2d 255, 260 (S.D.N.Y. 2003) (holding that for sentencing guidelines purposes, first degree murder under 18 U.S.C. § 1111 was the most analogous federal offense to second-degree murder under New York Law).

In <u>Phillips</u>, 239 F.3d at 835, 847-48, the defendant was convicted under Section 1959 of assaulting Charlotte Flemming, age 4, in a drive by shooting. Ms. Flemming was injured by metal fragments from an aluminum storm door striking her face when shots penetrated into her house. The court ruled that under U.S.S.G. § 2A2.2 for aggravated assault, the base level offense was 15. The court also upheld a six level enhancement for "permanent or life-threatening bodily injury" pursuant to U.S.S.G. § 2A2.2 (b)(3) because Ms. Flemming "suffered permanent and disfiguring scars on her face." 239 F.3d at 848. Accord <u>United States v. Agostini</u>, 365 F. Supp. 530, 537 (S.D.N.Y. 2005). <u>See</u> also <u>United States v. McCall</u>, 915 F.2d 811, 814-816 (2d Cir. 1990) (holding that the trial court must apply the offense level (U.S.S.G. § 2A2.2, aggravated assault) applicable to the crime for which the defendant was convicted (here assault with a dangerous weapon), and not for his "real conduct" - determined by the court to be assault with intent to commit murder.).

### 4. Threats to Commit A Crime of Violence

Section 1959(a)(4) provides that the punishment "for threatening to commit a crime of violence, [is] imprisonment for not more than five years or a fine under this title, or both." As of this writing, there are no reported decisions addressing sentencing for threatening to commit a crime of violence under Section 1959.

### 5. Attempts or Conspiracies to Commit Murder or Kidnapping

Section 1959(a)(5) provides the following punishment:

> (5) for attempting or conspiring to commit murder or kidnapping, by imprisonment for not more than ten years or a fine under this title, or both;

<u>See</u>, <u>e.g.</u>, <u>United States v. Felipe</u>, 148 F.3d 101, 112 (2d Cir. 1998). Under U.S.S.G. 2A1.5, the predicate offense of conspiracy to murder has a base offense level of 28, or a base offense level of 43 if death resulted. <u>See</u>, <u>e.g.</u>, <u>Marino</u>, 277 F.3d at 36. Pursuant to U.S.S.G. §§ 2A1.5(c) and 2A2.1, the

predicate crime of attempted murder has a base offense level of 28 if the object of the offense would have constituted first degree murder, or 22 otherwise.

Moreover, pursuant to the interplay among U.S.S.G. §§ 2E1.3, 2A4.1 and 2X1.1, the predicate crimes of conspiring and attempting to commit kidnapping have a base level offense of 29, subject to modifications. See generally United States v. DiGiorgio, 193 F.3d 1175, 1176-77 (11th Cir. 1999).

### 6. Attempts or Conspiracies to Commit Maiming or Assault Offenses

Section 1959(a)(6) provides the following punishment:

(6) for attempting or conspiring to commit a crime involving maiming, assault with a dangerous weapon, or assault resulting in serious bodily injury, by imprisonment for not more than three years or a fine of under this title, or both.

Pursuant to the interplay among U.S.S.G. §§ 2E1.3, 2A2.2(a) and 2X1.1, the predicate offenses of conspiracy or attempt to assault with a dangerous weapon and conspiracy or attempt to commit maiming or an assault resulting in serious bodily injury have a base offense level of 14, subject to modifications. See, e.g., United States v. DeJesus, 75 F. Supp. 2d 141, 142 (S.D.N.Y. 1999).

### H. Jury Instructions

Cases involving various jury instructions have been discussed in the preceding sections. In that respect, courts have upheld instructions setting forth the elements of a Section 1959 violation[136], as well as Pinkerton instructions imposing vicarious liability[137], and instructions regarding the requisite

---

[136] See cases cited supra, n. 9 and Locascio, 6 F.3d at 940-41.

[137] See, e.g., Diaz, 176 F.3d at 99-100; Tse, 135 F.3d at 206-07; Katona, 204 F. Supp. 2d at 412; see also supra, Section III(B).

nexus to interstate or foreign commerce.[138] Moreover, it bears repeating that the trial court must instruct the jury on the state substantive law applicable to the charged predicate offense[139], and the government may not rely on a purpose for which the predicate crime was committed unless the jury is instructed on that purpose.[140] See also Frampton, 382 F.3d at 222 n. 8 (upholding instructions that track the applicable statutory language on "enterprise" and "racketeering activity"); Phillips, 239 F.3d at 843-44 (upholding instructions on "enterprise" and "racketeering activity"); Tipton, 90 F.3d at 887-88 (same).

## I. Admission of Uncharged Crimes

It is well established that to prove RICO substantive and conspiracy charges, uncharged unlawful conduct or racketeering acts may be proven to establish the requisite continuity and pattern of racketeering activity,[141] and the existence of the charged RICO enterprise or conspiracy, and the defendant's participation in either or both.[142] Similarly, courts have held that to prove Section 1959

---

[138] See, e.g., Fernandez, 388 F.3d at 1249-50l; Marino, 277 F.3d at 34-35; Vasquez, 267 F.3d at 86-90; Feliciano, 223 F.3d at 117-19; see also supra, Section II (C).

[139] See supra Section II(E)(2).

[140] See supra Section II(M), p. 102.

[141] See, e.g., United States v. Richardson, 167 F.3d 621, 625-26 (D.C. Cir. 1999); Tabas v. Tabas, 47 F.3d 1280, 1294-95 (3d Cir. 1995) (en banc); United States v. Alkins, 925 F.2d 552, 551-53 (2d. Cir. 1991); United States v. Coiro, 922 F.2d 1008, 1017 (2d Cir. 1991); United States v. Gonzalez, 921 F.2d 1530, 1544-45 & n.23 (11th Cir. 1991); United States v. Link, 921 F.2d 1523, 1527 (11th Cir. 1991); United States v. Kaplan, 866 F.2d 536, 543 (2d Cir. 1989).

[142] See, e.g., United States v. Keltner, 147 F.3d 662, 667-68 (8th Cir. 1998); United States v. Salerno, 108 F.3d 730, 738-39 (7th Cir. 1997); United States v. Miller, 116 F.3d 641, 682 (2d. Cir. 1997); United States v. Krout, 66 F.3d 1420, 1425 (5th Cir. 1995); United States v. DiSalvo, 34 F.3d 1204, 1221 (3d Cir. 1994); United States v. Clemente, 22 F.3d 477, 483 (2d Cir. 1994); United States v. Coonan, 938 F.2d 1553, 1561 (2d Cir. 1991); United States v. Eufrasio, 935 F.2d 553, 572-73 (3d. Cir. 1991); United States v. Ellison, 793 F.2d 942, 949 (8th Cir. 1986); United States v.
(continued...)

charges, uncharged crimes are admissible to prove the enterprise or conspiracy and a defendant's membership in either or both.[143]

### J. Constitutional Challenges

### 1. Vagueness Challenges

Several courts have rejected vagueness challenges to Section 1959. For example, in Feliciano, 223 F.3d at 125, the defendant argued that Section 1959 "is unconstitutional on its face because: it fails to provide constitutionally sufficient notice as to what conduct is prohibited; it impermissibly imputes the conduct of third parties (the other members of the enterprise) to the defendant; it fails to assure that organized crime will be the subject of prosecution; and it impermissibly predicates a defendant's criminal liability on the basis of his status." The defendant also argued that Section 1959 "was unconstitutionally applied in this case because the district court failed to require proof of temporal, relational, and/or quantitative relationships that [the defendant] asserts were required by various elements of [Section 1959], and because the district court failed . . . to require that the enterprise be engaged in interstate commerce at the time the underlying violent crime was committed." Id. at 125.

The Second Circuit held that the defendant waived these claims because he did not raise them in the district court, and that in any event there was no plain error. In that regard, the Second Circuit stated:

---

[142](...continued)
Murphy, 768 F.2d 1518, 1534-35 (7th Cir. 1985); United States v. Gonzalez, 921 F.2d 1530, 1545-47 (11th Cir. 1991).

[143] See, e.g., Fernandez, 388 F.3d at 1245-46; United States v. Baez, 349 F.3d 90, 93-94 (2d Cir. 2003); United States v. Delatorre, 157 F.3d 1205, 1209-10 (10th Cir. 1998); Tse, 135 F.3d at 207-08; United States v. Nosov, 153 F. Supp. 2d 477, 481 (S.D.N.Y. 2001).

> None of the various notice problems raised by [the defendant] are problems alleged to infect the charges of murder and conspiracy, based on Connecticut law, of which he was convicted. None of [the defendant's] arguments raise the possibility that he could not have known that he was committing a very serious felony when he participated in the murder of Edwin Ramos. All of the challenges go to the issue of federal jurisdiction. The only issue hinging on the success of [the defendant's] challenges, therefore, is whether he should have been tried in federal or state court. We do not find that this issue implicates the fairness, integrity or public reputation of judicial proceedings in the circumstances of this case.

223 F.3d at 125 (footnote omitted).

In Cutolo, 861 F. Supp. at 1145-46, the district court rejected a claim that Section 1959's element of "an enterprise engaged in racketeering activity" was vague as applied where the indictment alleged that the enterprise was the Colombo Family of the LCN that engaged in various criminal activities "including the operation of illegal gambling businesses, the extortionate extensions and collections of credit, and the generation of income from various businesses through illegal means, including the exploitation of the Colombo Family's corrupt control of union officials." Id. at 1146.

Similarly, in United States v. Wei, 862 F. Supp. 1129, 1138-39 (S.D.N.Y. 1994), the district court rejected the defendants' claims that Section 1959 was vague as applied "because an enterprise cannot engage in racketeering activity" and it fails to provide adequate notice "when an enterprise has, in fact, 'engaged in racketeering activity.'" 862 F. Supp. at 1138. The district court explained that the defendants had adequate notice of the charged unlawful conduct because the indictment alleged that all the defendants "were members of the White Tigers, whose purposes were unlawful conduct like the acts of murder, arson, robbery, and narcotics trafficking charged against defendants." Id. at 1139.

### 2. Ex Post Facto Challenges

In Guzman v. United States, 277 F. Supp. 2d 255, 260-262 (S.D.N.Y. 2003), the district court rejected the defendant's argument that his rights under the *Ex Post Facto* Clause were violated because the district court sentenced him to a mandatory life sentence on the Section 1959 count pursuant to a version of Section 1959 that became effective after the date of the charged murder. The district court reasoned that under the version of Section 1959 and the Sentencing Guidelines in effect when the charged murder was committed, life imprisonment was mandatory, and therefore the defendant did not receive greater punishment than applicable at the time the murder was committed. Id. at 61-62. See also Garfinkle, 842 F. Supp. at 1293-95 (holding that a retroactive application of the law defining racketeering activity under RICO (18 U.S.C. § 1961(1)) was irrelevant to the defendant's Section 1959 conviction because Section 1959 does not require proof of a second racketeering act).

### 3. Tenth Amendment Challenges

In Kehoe, 310 F.3d at 588, the Eighth Circuit rejected the defendant's claim that because his Section 1959 "conviction for the [predicate] murders rest solely on Arkansas substantive law [his prosecution] for state law offenses in federal court. . . improperly encroached upon state sovereignty." The court reasoned that federal prosecution of the defendant did not encroach upon state sovereignty because it does not bar the state from prosecuting the defendant for the state law crimes.[144]

---

[144] Moreover, courts have rejected claims that Section 1959 exceeds Congress' authority under the Commerce Clause. See cases cited supra, p. 13, n. 18.

# APPENDIX A

# Excerpts of Senate Report No. 98-225, 98th Cong. 1st Sess. pp. 1-2, 304-314, 322-323

| 98TH CONGRESS | SENATE | REPORT |
| 1st Session | | No. 98-225 |

# COMPREHENSIVE CRIME CONTROL ACT OF 1983

# REPORT

OF THE

## COMMITTEE ON THE JUDICIARY
## UNITED STATES SENATE

ON

## S. 1762

together with

ADDITIONAL AND MINORITY VIEWS

SEPTEMBER 14 (legislative day, SEPTEMBER 12), 1983.—Ordered to be printed

U.S. GOVERNMENT PRINTING OFFICE
WASHINGTON : 1983

## COMMITTEE ON THE JUDICIARY

STROM THURMOND, South Carolina, *Chairman*

CHARLES McC. MATHIAS, Jr., Maryland
PAUL LAXALT, Nevada
ORRIN G. HATCH, Utah
ROBERT DOLE, Kansas
ALAN K. SIMPSON, Wyoming
JOHN P. EAST, North Carolina
CHARLES E. GRASSLEY, Iowa
JEREMIAH DENTON, Alabama
ARLEN SPECTER, Pennsylvania

JOSEPH R. BIDEN, Jr., Delaware
EDWARD M. KENNEDY, Massachusetts
ROBERT C. BYRD, West Virginia
HOWARD M. METZENBAUM, Ohio
DENNIS DeCONCINI, Arizona
PATRICK J. LEAHY, Vermont
MAX BAUCUS, Montana
HOWELL HEFLIN, Alabama

VINTON DeVANE LIDE, *Chief Counsel and Staff Director*
DEBORAH K. OWEN, *General Counsel*
PAUL C. SUMMITT, *Special Counsel*
MARK H. GITENSTEIN, *Minority Chief Counsel*

---

### SUBCOMMITTEE ON CRIMINAL LAW

PAUL LAXALT, Nevada, *Chairman*

STROM THURMOND, South Carolina
ARLEN SPECTER, Pennsylvania
ROBERT DOLE, Kansas

JOSEPH R. BIDEN, Jr., Delaware
MAX BAUCUS, Montana

JOHN F. NASH, Jr., *Chief Counsel and Staff Director*
WILLIAM MILLER, *General Counsel*
KATHY J. ZEBROWSKI, *Minority Counsel*

# CONTENTS

| | Page |
|---|---|
| General statement | 1 |
| Title I—Bail reform | 3 |
| Title II—Sentencing reform | 37 |
| Title III—Forfeiture | 191 |
| Title IV—Offenders with mental disease or defect | 222 |
| Title V—Drug enforcement amendments | 255 |
| Title VI—Justice assistance | 274 |
| Title VII—Surplus Federal property amendments | 292 |
| Title VIII—Labor racketeering amendments | 297 |
| Title IX—Currency and foreign transactions reporting amendments | 300 |
| Title X—Miscellaneous violent crime amendments | 304 |
|     Part A—Murder-for-hire and violent crime in aid of racketeering activity | 304 |
|     Part B—Solicitation to commit a crime of violence | 308 |
|     Part C—Felony-murder rule | 311 |
|     Part D—Mandatory penalty for the use of a firearm in a Federal crime of violence | 312 |
|     Part E—Armor piercing bullets | 315 |
|     Part F—Kidnaping of Federal officials | 318 |
|     Part G—Crimes against the family members of Federal officials | 320 |
|     Part H—Addition of maiming and involuntary sodomy to the major crimes act | 322 |
|     Part I—Destruction of motor vehicles | 324 |
|     Part J—Destruction of energy facilities | 325 |
|     Part K—Assault upon Federal officials | 327 |
|     Part L—Escape from custody resulting from civil commitment | 330 |
|     Part M—Extradition reform | 332 |
|     Part N—Arson amendments | 358 |
|     Part O—Pharmacy robbery and burglary | 360 |
| Title XI—Serious nonviolent offenses | 363 |
|     Part A—Child pornography | 363 |
|     Part B—Warning the subject of a search | 368 |
|     Part C—Program fraud and bribery | 369 |
|     Part D—Counterfeiting of State and corporate securities and forging of endorsements or signatures on United States securities | 371 |
|     Part E—Receipt of stolen bank property | 373 |
|     Part F—Bank bribery | 374 |
|     Part G—Bank fraud | 377 |
|     Part H—Possession of contraband in prison | 380 |
|     Part I—Livestock fraud | 383 |
| Title XII—Procedural amendments | 386 |
|     Part A—Prosecution of certain juveniles as adults | 386 |
|     Part B—Wiretap amendments | 394 |
|     Part C—Venue for threat offenses | 400 |
|     Part D—Injunctions against fraud | 401 |
|     Part E—Government appeal of post-conviction new trial orders | 403 |
|     Part F—Witness security program improvements | 407 |
|     Part G—Clarification of change of venue for certain tax offenses | 413 |
|     Part H—18 U.S.C. 951 amendments | 415 |
| Cost estimate | 415 |
| Committee proceedings | 422 |
| Regulatory impact evaluation | 422 |
| Changes in existing law | 426 |
|     Minority views of Senator Charles McC. Mathias, Jr | 792 |
|     Additional views of Senator John P. East | 794 |

| 98TH CONGRESS | SENATE | REPORT |
|---|---|---|
| 1st Session | | No. 98-225 |

# COMPREHENSIVE CRIME CONTROL ACT OF 1983

SEPTEMBER 14 (legislative day, SEPTEMBER 12), 1983.—Ordered to be printed

Mr. THURMOND, from the Committee on the Judiciary, submitted the following

# REPORT

together with

## ADDITIONAL AND MINORITY VIEWS

[To accompany S. 1762]

The Committee on the Judiciary, to which was referred the bill (S. 1762) to make comprehensive reforms and improvements in the Federal criminal laws and procedures, and for other purposes, having considered the same, reports favorably thereon and recommends that the bill do pass.

## GENERAL STATEMENT

The Comprehensive Crime Control Act of 1983 as reported by the Committee is the product of a decade long bipartisan effort of the Senate Committee on the Judiciary, with the cooperation and support of successive administrations, to make major comprehensive improvements to the Federal criminal laws. Significant parts of the measure, such as sentencing reform, bail reform, insanity defense amendments, drug penalty amendments, criminal forfeiture improvements, and numerous relatively minor amendments, have evolved over the almost two-decade consideration of proposals to enact a modern Federal criminal code.[1] In addition, specialized

---

[1] See, e.g., S. 1630, 97th Cong., 2d Sess. (S. Rept. No. 97 307); *Reform of the Federal Criminal Laws*, Hearings before the Committee on the Judiciary, United States Senate, 96th 97th Cong., Parts XIV XVI (1979 81) (hereinafter cited as Criminal Code Hearings); *Reform of the Federal Criminal Laws*, Hearings before the Subcommittee on Criminal Laws and Procedures of the Committee on the Judiciary, United States Senate, 92d-95th Cong., Parts I XIII (1971 77) (hereinafter cited as Subcommittee Criminal Code Hearings); Final Report of the National Commission on Reform of Federal Criminal Laws (1971); Working Papers, National Commission on Reform of Federal Criminal Laws, Vols. I III (1970).

hearings have been held on numerous subjects covered by the bill, such as sentencing,[2] bail reform,[3] the insanity defense,[4] forfeiture,[5] extradition,[6] child pornography,[7] and pharmacy robbery.[8] Moreover, this bill contains, with little significant change, most of the provisions of the Violent Crime and Drug Enforcement Improvements Act of 1982 (S. 2572) that passed the Senate on September 30, 1982, by a vote of 95 to 1, as well as a number of relatively minor noncontroversial matters designed to make current Federal criminal laws more effective.

The Committee also noted the major contribution to this bill by the Administration. On March 16, 1983, the President sent to the Congress a 42-point proposal with sixteen major titles entitled, as is this bill, the "Comprehensive Crime Control Act of 1983" (S. 829). In transmitting the proposal to the Congress, the Administration noted that it was "intended to serve as a reference document to set out, in a comprehensive fashion, all of the various criminal justice legislative reforms needed to restore a proper balance between the forces of law and the forces of lawlessness." Six days of hearings on S. 829 and other related bills were held—4 days by the Subcommittee on Criminal Law, 1 day jointly by the Subcommittees on Criminal Law and Juvenile Justice, and 1 day on the Tort Claims Act amendments by the Subcommittee on Administrative Practice and Procedure.[9]

On July 21, 1983, the Committee ordered reported a bill consisting of twelve titles dealing with bail (title I), sentencing (title II), forfeiture (title III), the insanity defense and related procedures (title IV), drug penalties (title V), justice assistance (title VI), surplus Federal property for corrections purposes (title VII), labor racketeering (title VIII), foreign currency transactions (title IX), miscellaneous violent crime amendments (title X), miscellaneous nonviolent offenses (title XI), and procedure amendments (title XII).[10] Each of these titles is discussed in order in detail below.

---

[2] Subcommittee Criminal Code Hearings, Part XIII.

[3] *Bail Reform*, Hearings before the Subcommittee on the Constitution of the Committee on the Judiciary, United States Senate, 97th Cong., 1st Sess. (1981).

[4] *The Insanity Defense*, Hearings before the Committee on the Judiciary, United States Senate, 97th Cong., 2d Sess. (1982); *Limiting the Insanity Defense*, Hearings before the Subcommittee on Criminal Law of the Committee on the Judiciary, United States Senate, 97th Cong., 2d Sess. (1982).

[5] *Forfeiture of Narcotics Proceeds*, Hearings before the Subcommittee on Criminal Justice of the Committee on the Judiciary, United States Senate, 96th Cong., 2d Sess. (1980).

[6] *Extradition Act of 1981*, Hearings before the Committee on the Judiciary, United States Senate, 97th Cong., 1st Sess. (1981).

[7] *Child Pornography*, Hearing before the Subcommittee on Juvenile Justice of the Committee on the Judiciary, United States Senate, 97th Cong., 2d Sess. (1982).

[8] *Pharmacy Robbery Legislation*, Hearings before the Subcommittee on Criminal Law of the Committee on the Judiciary, United States Senate, 97th Cong., 2d Sess. (1982).

[9] *The Comprehensive Crime Control Act of 1983*, Hearings before the Subcommittee on Criminal Law of the Committee on the Judiciary, United States Senate, 98th Cong., 1st Sess. (1983) (hereinafter cited as Crime Control Act Hearings); *Title XIII of S. 829 To Amend the Federal Tort Claims Act*, Hearing before the Subcommittee on Administrative Practice and Procedure of the Committee on the Judiciary, United States Senate, 98th Cong., 1st Sess. (1983).

[10] To enhance the potential for ultimate enactment of a comprehensive crime bill, the Committee decided to deal with a number of the more controversial pending issues in separate legislation. Accordingly, bills on habeas corpus (S. 1763), exclusionary rule (S. 1764), capital punishment (S. 1765), and to establish an Office for the Director of National and International Drug Operations and Policy (S. 1787) were introduced and reported to the Senate on August 4, 1983 (see, 129 Cong. Rec. pp. S11679 S11713 (daily ed.)).

# TITLE X—MISCELLANEOUS VIOLENT CRIME AMENDMENT

Title X consists of a group of miscellaneous violent crime amendments divided into sixteen parts. In summary, they relate to murder for hire and violent crimes in aid of racketeering (Part A); Solicitation to commit a Federal crime of violence (Part B); the felony-murder rule (Part C); mandatory penalties for use of a firearm during a Federal crime of violence (Part D); use of armor-piercing bullets to commit a crime of violence (Part E); kidnapping Federal officials (Part F); crimes against family members of Federal officials (Part G); additions to the Major Crimes Act applicable in Indian country (Part H); destruction of motor vehicles (Part I); destruction of energy facilities (Part J); assaults upon Federal officials (Part K); escape from custody resulting from civil commitment (Part L); international extradition (Part M); Federal explosives offenses (Part N); and robbery of a pharmacy or other registered possessor of controlled substances (Part O).

## PART A—MURDER-FOR-HIRE AND VIOLENT CRIME IN AID OF RACKETEERING ACTIVITY

### 1. In general

This Part of title X proscribes murder and other violent crimes committed for money or other valuable consideration or as an integral aspect of membership in an enterprise engaged in racketeering. It is similar to a provision contained in S. 2572 as passed by the Senate in the 97th Congress. Part A consists of two sections· the first defines the term "crime of violence", used here and elf where in the bill, while the second creates new offenses and ac tional definitions.

The offenses set forth in this Part are related but distinct. T. first is limited to murder and punishes the travel in interstate o. foreign commerce or the use of the facilities of interstate or foreign commerce or of the mails, as consideration for the receipt of anything of pecuniary value, with the intent that a murder be committed. The second extends to murder, kidnapping, or serious assault committed for anything of pecuniary value or for the purpose of gaining entrance into or maintaining or increasing one's position in an organized crime group.

With respect to the first offense, the Committee is aware of the concerns of local prosecutors with respect to the creation of concurrent Federal jurisdiction in an area, namely murder cases, which has heretofore been the almost exclusive responsibility of State and local authorities.[1] However, the Committee believes that the option

---

[1] See Crime Control Act Hearings (statement of the National District Attorney's Association, p. 27).

of Federal investigation and prosecution should be available when a murder is committed or planned as consideration for something of pecuniary value and the proper Federal nexus, such as interstate travel, use of the facilities of interstate commerce, or use of the mails, is present. This does not mean, nor does the Committee intend, that all or even most such offenses should become matters of Federal responsibility. Rather, Federal jurisdiction should be asserted selectively based on such factors as the type of defendants reasonably believed to be involved and the relative ability of the Federal and State authorities to investigate and prosecute. For example, the apparent involvement of organized crime figures or the lack of effective local investigation because of the interstate features of the crime could indicate that Federal action was appropriate. On the other hand, the Committee fully appreciates that many State and local police forces and prosecutors offices are quite capable of handling a murder for hire case notwithstanding the presence of some interstate aspects and regardless of the criminal backgrounds of the defendants. Cooperation and coordination between Federal and State officials should be utilized to ensure that the new murder-for-hire statute is used in appropriate cases to assist the States rather than to allow the usurpation of significant cases by Federal authorities that could be handled as well or better at the local level.

With respect to the second offense set out in Part A, the Committee concluded that the need for Federal jurisdiction is clear, in view of the Federal Government's strong interest, as recognized in existing statutes, in suppressing the activities of organized criminal enterprises, and the fact that the FBI's experience and network of informants and intelligence with respect to such enterprises will often facilitate a successful Federal investigation where local authorities might be stymied. Here again, however, the Committee does not intend that all such offenses should be prosecuted federally. Murder, kidnaping, and assault also violate State law and the States will still have an important role to play in many such cases that are committed as an integral part of an organized crime operation.

## 2. *Present Federal law*

Under current Federal law, the Interstate Travel in Aid of Racketeering (ITAR) statute, 18 U.S.C. 1952, covers murder and certain other crimes of violence if the perpetrator traveled in interstate or foreign commerce or used a facility of interstate or foreign commerce to commit it, and the crime was in furtherance of an unlawful activity involving offenses related to gambling, untaxed liquor, narcotics, prostitution, extortion, bribery, or arson. There is no general Federal proscription against murder even if interstate travel or the use of interstate facilities is involved in its commission. The general Federal murder statute, 18 U.S.C. 1111, applies mainly territorially, in the special maritime and territorial jurisdiction of the United States [2] and in the Indian Country [3] or if the victim is a

---

[2] 18 U.S.C. 7.
[3] 18 U.S.C. 1151.

person as to whom there is a particular Federal interest in vindicating the offense.[4]

### 3. Provisions of the bill, as reported

Part A adds two new sections, 1952A and 1952B, to title 18, United States Code. Section 1952A follows the format of present section 1952. Section 1952A reaches travel in interstate or foreign commerce or the use of the mails or of a facility in interstate or foreign commerce with the intent that a murder be committed in violation of State or Federal law. The murder must be carried out or planned as consideration for the receipt of "anything of pecuniary value." This term is defined to mean money, a negotiable instrument, a commercial interest, or anything else the primary significance of which is economic advantage. Thus, an option to purchase would clearly qualify as would a promise of future payment even if the contract were unenforceable as contrary to public policy. The term "facility of interstate commerce" is also defined to include means of transportation and communication. Thus, an interstate telephone call is sufficient to trigger Federal jurisdiction, as it is under the ITAR statute.[5] Both the person who ordered the murder and the "hit man" would be covered by the new section provided the interstate commerce or mail nexus is present. For example, if A pays money to B to go from State X to State Y to murder C, both A and B have violated the statute. In this situation, B's travel was caused by A.

The gist of the offense is the travel in interstate commerce or the use of the facilities of interstate commerce or of the mails with the requisite intent and the offense is complete whether or not the murder is carried out or even attempted. In such a case, the punishment extends to five years of imprisonment and a $5,000 fine. If, however, personal injury results, the punishment is up to twenty years of imprisonment and a $20,000 fine; and if death results, t¹ punishment can extend to life imprisonment and a $50,000 fine.

Section 1952B proscribes contract murders and other viol crimes by organized crime figures. Such crimes frequently do . involve interstate travel or the use of interstate facilities and a. sometimes not performed for money or other direct pecuniary benefit, but rather as an aspect of membership in a criminal organization. Therefore, the new section proscribes not only murder, kidnapping, maiming, serious assaults, and the other enumerated offenses when done as consideration for the receipt of or a promise or agreement to pay "anything of pecuniary value"[6] from an enterprise engaged in racketeering activity, but also such crimes when done for the purpose of gaining entrance to or maintaining or increasing position in such an enterprise. The term "enterprise" is defined as "any partnership, corporation, association, or other

---

[4] 18 U.S.C. 1116 (internationally protected persons). See also 18 U.S.C. 351 (members of Congress and of the Cabinet); 18 U.S.C. 1751 (the President and Vice President).

[5] See *United States* v. *Villano*, 529 F.2d 1046 (10th Cir.), cert. denied, 426 U.S. 953 (1976). The Committee intends that the full breadth of the phrase "any facility in interstate or foreign commerce" as used in the ITAR statute also be applicable here. See *Erlenbaugh* v. *United States*, 409 U.S. 239 (1972) (interstate newspaper).

[6] The Committee intends that "anything of pecuniary value" have the same meaning as in section 1952A.

legal entity, and any union or group of individuals associated in fact although not a legal entity, which is engaged in, or the activities of which affect, interstate or foreign commerce." The definition is very similar to that in 18 U.S.C. 1961, the Racketeer Influenced and Corrupt Organizations (RICO) statute, which has been held to include illegal organizations such as organized crime "families" as well as legitimate business organizations.[7] The Committee intends that the term enterprise here have the same scope. Racketeering activity is defined to incorporate the definition set forth in present section 1961. Attempted murder, kidnaping, maiming and assault are also covered. While section 1952B only covers the person who actually commits or attempts the offense as opposed to the person who requested or ordered it, the latter person would be punishable as an aider and abettor under 18 U.S.C. 2.

Section 1952B also covers threats to commit a "crime of violence." The term "crime of violence" is defined, for purposes of all of title 18, United States Code, in section 1001 of the bill (the first section of Part A of title X). Although the term is occasionally used in present law,[8] it is not defined, and no body of case law has arisen with respect to it. However, the phrase is commonly used throughout the bill,[9] and accordingly the Committee has chosen to define it for general application in title 18.

The definition is taken from S. 1630 as reported in the 97th Congress.[10] The term means an offense—either a felony or a misdemeanor—that has as an element the use, attempted use, or threatened use of physical force against the person or property of another, or any felony that, by its nature, involves the substantial risk that physical force against another person or property may be used in the course of its commission. The former category would include a threatened or attempted simple assault[11] or battery[12] on another person; offenses such as burglary in violation of a State law and the Assimilative Crimes Act[13] would be included in the latter category inasmuch as such an offense would involve the substantial risk of physical force against another person or against the property.

---

[7] *United States* v. *Turkette,* 452 U.S. 576 (1981).
[8] It is used in the ITAR statute, but no reported prosecutions appear to have been brought under this branch of 18 U.S.C. 1952.
[9] For example, "crime of violence" is used in title I (bail), in several other parts of title X, and in title XII, Part A (prosecution of certain juveniles as adults).
[10] See S. 1630, as reported, section 111; S. Rept. No. 97 307.
[11] 18 U.S.C. 113(e).
[12] 18 U.S.C. 113(d).
[13] 18 U.S.C. 13.

PART B—SOLICITATION TO COMMIT A CRIME OF VIOLENCE

*1. In general and present Federal law*

Part B of title X is designed to proscribe the offense of solicitation to commit a Federal crime of violence. It is derived from a provision in S. 2572 as passed by the Senate in the 97th Congress. The Committee believes that a person who makes a serious effort to induce another person to commit a crime of violence is a clearly dangerous person and that his act deserves criminal sanctions whether or not the crime of violence is actually committed. The principal purpose of the new section is to allow law enforcement officials to intervene at an early stage where there has been a clear demonstration of an individual's criminal intent and danger to society. Of course, if the person solicited actually carries out the crime, the solicitor is punishable as an aider and abettor.[1]

At the present time there is no Federal law that prohibits solicitation generally, although there are a few statutes defining specific offenses which contain language prohibiting solicitation. For example, the current bribery statute[2] prohibits soliciting the payment of a bribe. Moreover S. 1630, as approved by the Committee in the 97th Congress, included a solicitation offense that would have applied to a wide panoply of offenses,[3] not just to solicitations to commit a crime of violence covered by Part B.

*2. Provisions of the bill, as reported*

Part B of title X adds a new section 373 to title 18 to proscribe the soliciting, commanding, inducing, or otherwise endeavoring to persuade another person to engage in conduct constituting a crime of violence, with the intent that the crime actually be committed. The solicitation, command, or inducement must be under circumstances that strongly corroborate the person's intent that the other person actually engage in conduct constituting the crime of violence. The penalty is up to one-half the maximum prison term and fine that could be imposed for the crime solicited, and up to twenty years if that crime carries the sentence of death.

A lengthy discussion of the elements of the offense, which the Committee intends to apply to Part B, is contained in the Report on S. 1630 in the 97th Congress.[4] In general the solicitation or command must be made under circumstances showing that the actor is serious that the "crime of violence"[5] be carried out. Thus, a person

---

[1] 18 U.S.C. 2.
[2] 18 U.S.C. 201.
[3] See section 1003 of S. 1630 and the discussion at pages 179–186 of S. Rept. No. 97–307 (97th Cong., 1st Sess.).
[4] See, *id* at 182–184.
[5] The term "crime of violence" is defined in Part A of this title and the discussion in this Report thereon should be consulted.

at a baseball game who shouts "kill the umpire" would not be guilty of the offense since the circumstances would not bear out the conclusion that he genuinely wanted the result. On the other hand, a person who shouted encouragement to a mob surrounding a jail to lynch a prisoner might well be found to have intended that other persons engage in violent criminal conduct. Additionally, the defendant must engage in conduct characterizable as commanding, entreating, inducing, or endeavoring to persuade another person to act. For example, an order to commit an offense made by a person to another with whom he stands in a relationship of influence or authority would constitute a command. Threatening another person if he will not commit a offense would constitute a form of inducement or endeavoring to persuade as would offering to pay him to commit an offense.

While the section rests primarily on words of instigation to crime, the Committee wishes to make it clear that what is involved is legitimately proscribable criminal activity, not advocacy of ideas that is protected by the First Amendment right of free speech.[6] The Committee agrees with the following summary by a respected First Amendment scholar of the relationship between the First Amendment and criminal solicitation:[7]

> The problem is, indeed, no different from that involving the use of speech generally in the commission of crimes of action. Most crimes—certainly those in which more than one person participates—involve the use of speech or other communication. Where the communication is an integral part of a course of criminal action, it is treated as action and receives no protection under the First Amendment. Solicitation to crime is similar conduct, but in a situation where for some reason the contemplated crime does not take place. Solicitation involves a hiring or partnership arrangement, designed to accomplish a specific action in violation of law, where the communication is an essential link in a direct chain leading to criminal action, though the action may have been interrupted. In short, the person charged with solicitation must, in a direct sense, have been a participant in an abortive crime of action. Thus the crime of criminal solicitation may be seen as a particular instance of the more general category of criminal attempts. Here, also, the applicable legal doctrine undertakes to draw the line between "expression" and "action." The fact that issues of this nature rarely arise indicates that establishing the division between free expression and solicitation to crime has not created a serious problem.

Subsection (b) provides an affirmative defense of renunciation under the section. For the defense to apply, the defendant must have voluntarily and completely abandoned his criminal intent and actually prevented the commission of the crime (not merely made efforts to prevent it). The subsection specifically provides that a re-

---

[6] The Committee adopts the discussion of the tangential relationship of the First Amendment to the solicitation offense in S. Rept. No. 97 307, 97th Cong., 1st Sess., pp. 180 182.
[7] Emerson, *"Toward a General Theory of the First Amendment,"* p. 83 (1966).

nunciation is not complete and voluntary if it is motivated in whole or in part by a decision to postpone the commission of the crime to another time or to substitute another victim. If the defendant raises the defense of renunciation, he has the burden of proving it by a preponderance of the evidence.

Subsection (c) provides that the solicitor cannot successfully assert a defense that the solicitee could not be convicted of the crime of violence because he lacked the state of mind required or was incompetent or irresponsible, or is immune from or otherwise not subject to prosecution. The prohibition of this defense is based on the universally acknowledged principle that one is no less guilty of the commission of a crime because he uses the overt behavior of an innocent or irresponsible agent.[8] On the other hand, this provision does not mean that the irresponsibility or incompetence of the solicitee is never relevant. The lack of responsibility or competence of the person solicited may be highly relevant in determining the solicitor's intent. For example, an entreaty to a young child or to an imbecile may indicate the solicitor's lack of serious purpose.

---

[8] See e.g., *Nigro* v. *United States*, 117 F.2d 624 (8th Cir. 1941); *United States* v. *Brandenburg*, 155 F.2d 110 (8th Cir. 1946) (physician circulating illegal narcotics prescriptions guilty of sale by innocent druggist).

## Part C—Felony-Murder Rule

### 1. In general and present Federal law

Part C of title X expands the definition of felony murder. It is identical to a provision in S. 2572 as passed by the Senate in the 97th Congress. Under the common law, a murder committed during any felony was held to be committed with a sufficient degree of malice to warrant punishment as first degree murder. However, under present Federal law, 18 U.S.C. 1111, the felony murder doctrine only applies to killings committed during an actual or attempted arson, rape, burglary, or robbery. The Committee has concluded that limiting the felony-murder rule to these four offenses is too restrictive. For example, the current statute does not cover a killing committed during the crimes of treason, espionage, or sabotage, or during a kidnaping or prison escape, crimes which pose as great if not a greater threat to human life than the four already listed.

### 2. Provisions of the bill, as reported

Part C of title X amends 18 U.S.C. 1111(a), which presently provides that every willful, deliberate, malicious, and premeditated killing, or every killing "committed in the perpetration of, or attempt to perpetrate, any arson, rape, burglary, or robbery" is murder in the first degree. The amendment adds the offenses of escape, murder, kidnaping, treason, espionage, and sabotage to the four listed offenses. Thus the felony murder rule would apply to a killing occurring during one of these offenses and would constitute first degree murder. Murder is included in the list to cover a situation in which the defendant acts in the heat of passion in an attempt to kill A, but instead kills B. The Committee believes that the danger to innocent persons presented in this type of situation is so severe that the defendant should be charged with first degree murder even though if he had killed A he could only be charged with second degree murder.

PART D—MANDATORY PENALTY FOR THE USE OF A FIREARM IN A
FEDERAL CRIME OF VIOLENCE

## 1. *In general and present Federal law*

Part D of title X is designed to impose a mandatory penalty without the possibility of probation or parole, for any person who uses or carries a firearm during and in relation to a Federal crime of violence. Although present Federal law, section 924(c) of title 18, appears to set out a mandatory minimum sentencing scheme for the use or unlawful carrying of a firearm during any Federal felony, drafting problems and interpretations of the section in recent Supreme Court decisions have greatly reduced its effectiveness as a deterrent to violent crime.

Section 924(c) sets out an offense distinct from the underlying felony and is not simply a penalty provision.[1] Hence, the sentence provided in section 924(c) is in addition to that for the underlying felony and is from one to ten years for a first conviction and from two to twenty-five years for a subsequent conviction. However, section 924(c) is drafted in such a way that a person may still be given a suspended sentence or be placed on probation for his first violation of the section, and it is ambiguous as to whether the sentence for a first violation may be made to run concurrently with that for the underlying offense. Some courts have held that a concurrent sentence may be given.[2] Moreover, even if a person is sentenced to imprisonment under section 924(c), the normal parole eligibility rules apply.

In addition to these problems with present section 924(c), the Supreme Court's decisions in *Simpson* v. *United States*,[3] and *Busic* v. *United States*,[4] have negated the section's use in cases involving statutes, such as the bank robbery statute[5] and assault on Federal officer statute[6] which have their own enhanced, but not mandatory, punishment provisions in situations where the offense is committed with a dangerous weapon. These are precisely the type of extremely dangerous offenses for which a mandatory punishment for the use of a firearm is the most appropriate.

In *Simpson*, the defendants had been convicted of armed bank robbery involving the use of a dangerous weapon or device in violation of 18 U.S.C. 2113 (a) and (d), and of using firearms to commit the robbery in violation of 18 U.S.C. 924(c). They were sentenced to maximum terms of 25 years in prison on the aggravated robbery count and to 10-year consecutive prison terms on the firearms

---

[1] *Simpson* v. *United States*, 435 U.S. 6, 10 (1978).
[2] *United States* v. *Sudduth*, 457 F.2d 1198 (9th Cir. 1972); *United States* v. *Gaines*, 594 F.2d 541 (7th Cir. 1979).
[3] *Supra*, note 1.
[4] 446 U.S. 398 (1980).
[5] 18 U.S.C. 2113.
[6] 18 U.S.C. 111.

count. The Supreme Court held that the statutory construction and legislative history of section 924(c) rendered it inapplicable in cases where the predicate felony statute contains its own enhancement provision for the use of a dangerous weapon.

In *Busic*, the two defendants had been convicted, among other things, of narcotics offenses, and of armed assault on Federal officers resulting from a shoot-out with agents of the Drug Enforcement Administration, in violation of 18 U.S.C. 111. In addition, one defendant had been convicted of using a firearm in the commission of a felony, in violation of 18 U.S.C. 924(c)(1) and the other of carrying a firearm in the commission of a felony, under section 924(c)(1). Each was sentenced to a total of 30 years of imprisonment, of which five years resulted from concurrent sentences on the narcotics charges, five were the result of the assault charges, and 20 were imposed for the section 924(c) violations. Relying on *Simpson*, the Supreme Court held that where the predicate felony statute contains its own enhancement provision, section 924(c) "may not be applied at all * * *"[7] Thus, the twenty-year sentence was nullified.

The Committee has concluded that subsection 924(c) should be completely revised to ensure that all persons who commit Federal crimes of violence, including those crimes set forth in statutes which already provide for enhanced sentences for their commission with a dangerous weapon,[8] receive a mandatory sentence, without the possibility of the sentence being made to run concurrently with that for the underlying offense or for any other crime and without the possibility of a probationary sentence or parole.

## 2. Provisions of the bill, as reported

Part D of title X represents a complete revision of subsection 924(c) of title 18 to overcome the problems with the present subsection discussed above. As amended by Part D, section 924(c) provides for a mandatory, determinate sentence for a person who uses or carries a firearm during and in relation to any Federal "crime of violence," including offenses such as bank robbery or assault on a Federal officer which provide for their own enhanced punishment if committed by means of a dangerous weapon.[9] In the case of a first conviction under the subsection, the defendant would be sentenced to imprisonment for five years. For a second or subsequent conviction he would receive a sentence of imprisonment for ten years. In either case, the defendant could not be given a suspended or probationary sentence, nor could any sentence under the revised subsection be made to run concurrently with that for the predicate crime or with that for any other offense. In addition, the Committee intends that the mandatory sentence under the revised subsection 924(c) be served prior to the start of the sentence for the underlying or any other offense. For example, a person convicted of

---

[7] *Supra*, note 4 at 407.
[8] These statutes include 18 U.S.C. 111, 112, 113, 2113, 2114 and 2231. Enhancement tences varies widely among these sections and the terms called for are generally less than the penalty under section 924(c).
[9] The term "crime of violence" is defined in Part A of this title and the discussion in the Report thereon should be consulted here. In essence the term includes any offenses in which the use of physical force is an element and any felony which carries a substantial risk of such force. Thus, the section expands the scope of predicate offenses, as compared with current law, by including some violent misdemeanors, but restricts it by excluding non-violent felonies.

armed bank robbery in violation of section 2113 (a) and (d) and of using a gun in its commission (for example by pointing it at a teller or otherwise displaying it whether or not it is fired) [10] would have to serve five years (assuming it was his first conviction under the subsection) less only good time credit for proper behavior in prison, before his sentence for the conviction under section 2113 (a) and (d) could start to run. Finally, a person sentenced under the new subsection 924(c) would not be eligible for parole.

---

[10] Evidence that the defendant had a gun in his pocket but did not display it, or refer to it, could nevertheless support a conviction for "carrying" a firearm in relation to the crime if from the circumstances or otherwise it could be found that the defendant intended to use the gun if a contingency arose or to make his escape. The requirement in present section 924(c) that the gun be carried unlawfully, a fact usually proven by showing that the defendant was in violation of a State or local law, has been eliminated as unnecessary. The "unlawfully" provision was added originally to section 924(c) because of Congressional concern that without it policemen and persons licensed to carry firearms who committed Federal felonies would be subjected to additional penalties, even where the weapon played no part in the crime, whereas the section was directed at persons who chose to carry a firearm as an offensive weapon for a specific criminal act. See *United States* v. *Howard*, 504 F.2d 1281, 1285-1286 (8th Cir. 1974). The Committee has concluded that persons who are licensed to carry firearms and abuse that privilege by committing a crime with the weapon, as in the extremely rare case of the armed police officer who commits a crime, are as deserving of punishment as a person whose possession of the gun violates a State or local ordinance. Moreover, the requirement that the firearm's use or possession be "in relation to" the crime would preclude its application in a situation where its presence played no part in the crime, such as a gun carried in a pocket and never displayed or referred to in the course of a pugilistic barroom fight.

## Part H—Addition of Maiming and Involutary Sodomy to the Major Crimes Act

### 1. In general and present Federal law

Part H of title X adds two new offenses to those presently included in 18 U.S.C. 1153, the Major Crimes Act, which applies to offenses committed by Indians in the Indian Country.[1] The significance of section 1153 can best be understood by reference to section 1152. Under section 1152, the "general laws of the United States," i.e., those applicable in the special maritime and territorial jurisdiction of the United States, are made applicable to the Indian Country. However, the second paragraph of sectin 1152 provides an exception for offenses committed by one Indian against the person or property of another Indian. These offenses can generally only be prosecuted in tribal court where the maximum punishment is currently six months of imprisonment and a $500 fine.[2] Since tribal court punishment has long been felt to be inadequate for the most serious offenses committed by one Indian against another, the Major Crimes Act was enacted as an exception to the second paragraph of 18 U.S.C. 1152.[3] Section 1153 has been amended from time to time and now includes fourteen serious offenses. Not included, however, are maiming and involutary sodomy. An Indian who commits one of these offenses against another Indian is only subject to prosecution in tribal court.[4]

The Committee believes that both maiming and involuntary sodomy should be included in the Major Crimes Act. Maiming is one of the oldest of Federal crimes, having been first proscribed in 1790.[5] Although seldom prosecuted, the offense as currently defined is among the most heinous of crimes against the person. 18 U.S.C. 114 provides for seven years of imprisonment and a $1,000 fine for whoever in the special maritime and territorial jurisdiction "with intent to maim or disfigure, cuts, bites or slits the nose, ear, or lip, or cuts out or disables the tongue, or puts out or destroys an eye, or cuts off or disables a limb or any member of another person", or "throws or pours upon another person, any scalding water, corrosive acid, or caustic substance."

There seems no reason why this offense, presently applicable within the special maritime and territorial jurisdiction of the United States, is not included within the Major Crimes Act, the

---

[1] The term "Indian Country" is defined in 18 U.S.C. 1151 to include, inter alia, Indian reservations.
[2] 25 U.S.C. 1302(7).
[3] See Act of March 3, 1885, § 9, 23 Stat 385.
[4] Unfortunately this discriminates against Indian victims. This is so because if an Indian committed one of these crimes against a non-Indian he would be subject to prosecution under 18 U. 1152 and 114 in the case of maiming or under 1152 and 13 (the Assimilative Crimes Act), and State law in the case of sodomy. Only when the victim is another Indian is there an inability to bring the perpetrator to justice.
[5] 1 Stat 115.

purpose of which is to extend Federal jurisdiction over all serious offenses "against the person or property of another" that are committed by an Indian in Indian country. While an offense constituting maiming could usually be prosecuted under the Major Crimes Act as an "assault resulting in serious bodily injury" under 18 U.S.C. 113(f), the Committee believes it is appropriate to amend the Major Crimes Act to permit a prosecution for the more specific and serious offense of maiming, if such an opportunity arises, rather than using the general assault provisions in 18 U.S.C. 113.

The crime of forcible or involuntary sodomy, although one of the most serious sexual offenses known to our law, is not now within the Major Crimes Act.[6] Its absence represents a serious gap in felony coverage making it impossible to prosecute and punish (except by a tribal court at a petty offense level) this offense when committed against an Indian victim by an Indian in Indian country. In at least one case of which the Committee is aware, prosecution of an Indian for forcibly sodomizing his three-year old grandson had to be declined for failure of the Major Crimes Act to proscribe sodomy. Clearly, in a case where the victim and the offender are of the same family, such a result may have continuing tragic consequences since there may be no other practicable way to remove the offender from the situation and to protect the victim from his unwanted sexual attention.

*2. Provisions of the bill, as reported*

Part H of title X amends 18 U.S.C. 1153 by inserting the words "maiming" and "involuntary sodomy" into the list of offenses there set out for the reasons explained above.[7] In addition, the Committee struck out the word "larceny" that appears in present section 1153 and replaced it with the term "a felony under section 661 of this title." 18 U.S.C. 661 has been held to define "larceny" for purposes of section 1153.[8] Section 661 makes larcenies of $100 or less a misdemeanor punishable by a fine of up to $1,000 and up to a year in prison and makes all other larcenies felonies punishable by up to five years of imprisonment and a $5,000 fine. Federal jurisdiction over an Indian for committing petty larceny [9] is anomalous in light of the fact that the purpose of the Major Crimes Act is to cover only certain enumerated major offenses and that all of the other offenses in section 1153 are serious felonies such as murder, rape, and arson. Moreover, jurisdiction over petty larceny is unnecessary and virtually never asserted in light of tribal court jurisdiction over this offense. The Committee therefore believes it is appropriate to limit Major Crimes Act jurisdiction over larcenies to those larcenies that are felonies.

---

[6] Sodomy is not embraced within the concept of which embodies only the common law crime of forcible intercourse by a male with a female. *United States* v. *Smith*, 574 F.2d 988, 990 (9th Cir.), cert. denied, 439 U.S. 852 (1978). Likewise, although "incest," as defined by State law, is included withi the Major Crimes Act, sodomy is a distinct offense that is not typically covered by State incest laws.

[7] It is also provided that involuntary sodomy, like the present major crimes of burglary and incest, shall be defined and punished in accordance with the laws of the State in which the offense was committed. There is no Federal law defining these offenses but title 18 provides defini tions (at least by reference to common law) and punishments for all the others.

[8] See, e.g., *United States* v. *Gristeau*, 611 F.2d 181 (7th Cir. 1979), cert. denied 447 U.S. 907 (1980).

[9] See *United States* v. *Gilbert*, 378 F. Supp. 82, 89-93 (D. S. Dak. 1974).

# APPENDIX C
# State Assault Statutes

# APPENDIX C

# STATE ASSAULT STATUTES

1. **Alabama** - In 1984, ALA. CRIMINAL CODE §13A-6-20 (1977) provided as follows:

"Assault in the first degree.

> (a) A person commits the crime of assault in the first degree if:
> (1) With intent to cause serious physical injury to another person, he causes serious physical injury to any person by means of a deadly weapon or a dangerous instrument; or
> (2) With intent to disfigure another person seriously and permanently, or to destroy, amputate or disable permanently a member or organ of his body, he causes such an injury to any person; or
> (3) Under circumstances manifesting extreme indifference to the value of human life, he recklessly engages in conduct which creates a grave risk of death to another person, and thereby causes serious physical injury to any person; or
> (4) In the course of and in furtherance of the commission or attempted commission of arson in the first degree, burglary in the first or second degree, escape in the first degree, kidnapping in the first degree, rape in the first degree, robbery in any degree, sodomy in the first degree or any other felony clearly dangerous to human life, or of immediate flight therefrom, he causes a serious physical injury to another person."

ALA. CODE § 13A-1-2 (1977) contained the following definitions:

> "(9) Serious Physical Injury. Physical injury which creates a substantial risk of death, or which causes serious and protracted disfigurement, protracted impairment of health or impairment of the function of any bodily organ.
> (10) Deadly Physical Force. Physical force which, under the circumstances in which it is used, is readily capable of causing death or serious physical injury.
> (11) Deadly Weapon. A firearm or anything manifestly designed, made or adapted for the purposes of inflicting death or serious physical injury, and such term includes, but is not limited to, a pistol, rifle or shotgun; or a switch-blade knife, gravity knife, stiletto, sword or dagger; or any billy, black-jack, bludgeon or metal knuckles.
> (12) Dangerous Instrument. Any instrument, article or substance which, under the circumstances in which it is used, attempted to be used or threatened to be used, is highly capable of causing death or serious physical injury, and such term includes a "vehicle," as that term is defined in subdivision (13) of this section."

2. **Alaska** - ALASKA STAT. § 11.41.200 (1984) provided in relevant part:

"Assault in the first degree.

>(a) A person commits the crime of assault in the first degree if
>(1) that person recklessly causes serious physical injury to another by means of a dangerous instrument;
>(2) with intent to cause serious physical injury to another, the person causes serious physical injury to any person; or
>(3) the person intentionally performs an act that results in serious physical injury to another under circumstances manifesting extreme indifference to the value of human life.
>(b) Assault in the first degree is a class A felony."

As of 1978, section 11.81.900(b)(50) defined "serious physical injury" to mean "(A) physical injury caused by an act performed under circumstances that create a substantial risk of death; or (B) physical injury that causes serious and protracted disfigurement, protracted impairment of health, protracted loss or impairment of the function of a body member or organ, or that unlawfully terminates a pregnancy". ALASKA STAT. § 11.81900 (11) provided that "'dangerous instrument' means any deadly weapon or anything which, under the circumstances in which it is used, attempted to be used, or threatened to be used, is capable of causing death or serious physical injury."

3. **Arizona:** ARIZ. REV. STAT. § 13-1204 (1984) provided as follows:

"Aggravated Assault; classification

>A. A person commits aggravated assault if such person commits assault as defined in § 13-1203 under any of the following circumstances:
>1. If such person causes serious physical injury to another.
>2. If such person uses a deadly weapon or dangerous instrument.
>3. If such person commits the assault after entering the private home of another with the intent to commit the assault.
>4. If such person is eighteen years of age or more and commits the assault upon a child the age of fifteen years or under.

> 5. If such person commits the assault knowing or having reason to know that the victim is a peace officer, or a person summoned and directed by such officer while engaged in the execution of any official duties.
> 6. If such person commits the assault knowing or having reason to know the victim is a teacher or other person employed by any school and such teacher or other employee is upon the grounds of a school or grounds adjacent to such school or is in any part of a building or vehicle used for school purposes, or any teacher or school nurse visiting a private home in the course of his professional duties, or any teacher engaged in any authorized and organized classroom activity held on other than school grounds.
> 7. If such person is imprisoned in the custody of the department of corrections, a law enforcement agency, county or city jail, or adult or juvenile detention facility of a city or county or subject to the custody of personnel from such department, agency, jail or detention facility and commits the assault knowing or having reason to know the victim is an employee of such department, agency, jail or detention facility acting in an official capacity.
> 8. If such person commits the assault while the victim is bound or otherwise physically restrained or while the victim's capacity to resist is substantially impaired.
>
> B. Aggravated assault pursuant to subsection A, paragraph 1 or 2 of this section is a class 3 felony except if the victim is under fifteen years of age in which case it is a class 2 felony punishable pursuant to § 13-604.01. Aggravated assault pursuant to subsection A, paragraph 7 of this section is a class 5 felony. Aggravated assault pursuant to subsection A, paragraph 3, 4, 5, 6 or 8 of this section is a class 6 felony."

"'Serious physical injury' includes physical injury which creates a reasonable risk of death, or which causes serious and permanent disfigurement, serious impairment of health or loss or protracted impairment of the function of any bodily organ or limb." ARIZ. REV. STAT. § 13-105(31) (1984). "Dangerous instrument" means "anything that under the circumstances in which it is used, attempted to be used or threatened to be used is readily capable of causing death or serious physical injury." ARIZ. REV. STAT. § 13-105(7)(1982). *See, e.g., State v. Venegas*, 137 Ariz. 171, 175, 669 P. 2d 604, 608 (Ariz. Ct. App. 1983).

4.  **Arkansas** - In 1984, ARK. CODE ANN. § 41-1604 (1) provided: "Aggravated Assault" - "A person commits aggravated assault if, under circumstances manifesting extreme indifference to the value of human life, he purposely engages in conduct that creates a substantial danger of death or serious physical injury to another person." The Arkansas Code defined "serious physical injury" as "physical injury that creates a substantial risk of death or that causes protracted disfigurement, protracted impairment of health, or loss or protracted impairment of the function of any bodily member or organ." ARK. CODE. ANN.. § 5-1-102(19)(1984).

ARK. CODE ANN. § 16-90-121 (1984) provided that "Any person who is found guilty of or pleads guilty to a felony involving the use of a deadly weapon, whether or not an element of the crime, shall be sentenced to serve a minimum of ten (10) years in state prison . . . ." ARK. CODE ANN. § 5-1-102 (4) (1984) provided that "Deadly weapon" includes "Anything that in the manner of its use or intended use is capable of causing death or serious physical injury."

5.  **California** - In 1984, the California Penal Code included the following provision:

"Assault with deadly weapon or force likely to produce great bodily injury; punishment.

(a)(1) Every person who commits an assault upon the person of another with a deadly weapon or instrument other than a firearm or by any means of force likely to produce great bodily injury is punishable by imprisonment in the state prison for two, three or four years, or in a county jail not exceeding one year, or by fine not exceeding ten thousand dollars ($10,000), or by both such fine and imprisonment.

(2) Every person who commits an assault upon the person of another with a firearm is punishable by imprisonment in the state prison for two, three or four years, or in a county jail for a term of not less than six months and not exceeding one year, or by both a fine not exceeding ten thousand dollars ($10,000) and imprisonment.

(b) Every person who commits an assault with a deadly weapon or instrument, other than a firearm, or by any means likely to produce great bodily injury upon the person of a peace officer or fireman, and who knows or reasonably should know that the victim is a peace officer or fireman engaged in the performance of his or her duties, when the peace officer or fireman is engaged in the performance his or her duties shall be punished by imprisonment in the state prison for two, three, four, or five years.

(c) Every person who commits an assault with a firearm upon the person of a peace officer or fireman, and who knows or reasonably should know that the victim is a peace officer or fireman engaged in the performance of his or her duties, when the peace officer or fireman is engaged in the performance his or her duties shall be punished by imprisonment in the state prison for four, six, or eight years.

(d) When a person is convicted of a violation of this section, in a case involving use of a deadly weapon or instrument or firearm, and the weapon or instrument or firearm is owned by that person, the court shall order that the weapon or instrument or firearm be deemed a nuisance and it shall be confiscated and disposed of in the manner provided by Section 12028.

(e) As used in this section, "peace officer" refers to any person designated as a peace officer in Chapter 4.5 (commencing with Section 830) of Title 3 of Part 2."

CAL. PENAL CODE § 245 (West 1984).

The California Penal Code did not define "deadly weapon." Under California case law, a deadly weapon is one likely to produce death or great bodily injury. *See, e.g., People v. Lopez*, 135 Cal. 23, 66 P. 965 (Ca. Sup. Ct. 1901).

"Serious bodily injury" was added to § 243 in 1981 and is defined as "a serious impairment of physical condition, including, but not limited to, the following: loss of consciousness; concussion; bone fracture; protracted loss or impairment of function of any bodily member or organ; a wound requiring extensive suturing; and serious disfigurement." CAL. PENAL CODE § 243 (e)(5).

**6.     Colorado** - COLO. REV. STAT. ANN. § 18-3-202 (West 1984) provided in relevant part as follows:

"Assault in the first degree

(1) A person commits the crime of assault in the first degree if:
(a) With intent to cause serious bodily injury to another person, he causes serious bodily injury to any person by means of a deadly weapon; or
(b) With intent to disfigure another person seriously and permanently, or to destroy, amputate, or disable permanently a member or organ of his body, he causes such an injury to any person; or
(c) Under circumstances manifesting extreme indifference to the value of human life, he knowingly engages in conduct which creates a grave risk of death to another person, and thereby causes serious bodily injury to any person."

At the time §18-2-202 was enacted, the Colorado code also included the following definitions:

"(e) 'Deadly weapon' means any of the following which in the manner it is used or intended to be used is capable of producing death or serious bodily injury:
(I) A firearm, whether loaded or unloaded;
(II) A knife;
(III) A bludgeon; or
(IV) Any other weapon, device, instrument, material, or substance, whether animate or inanimate.

. . . .

(p) 'Serious bodily injury' means bodily injury which, either at the time of the actual injury or at a later time, involves a substantial risk of death, serious permanent disfigurement, protracted loss or impairment of the function of any part or organ of the body, or breaks, fractures, or burns of the second or third degree."

COLO. REV. STAT. ANN. §§ 18-1-901(3)(e) and (p) (West 1975).

**7.     Connecticut** - In 1984, CONN. GEN. STAT. ANN. § 53a-59 (West 1971) provided in relevant part as follows:

"Assault in the first degree: Class B felony.

(a) A person is guilty of assault in the first degree when:
(1) With intent to cause serious physical injury to another person,

he causes such injury to such person or to a third person by means of a deadly weapon or a dangerous instrument; or
(2) with intent to disfigure another person seriously and permanently, or to destroy, amputate or disable permanently a member or organ of his body, he causes such injury to such person or to a third person; or
(3) under circumstances evincing an extreme indifference to human life he recklessly engages in conduct which creates a risk of death to another person, and thereby causes serious physical injury to another person."

At the time § 53a-59 was enacted, the Connecticut code included the following definitions:

"(4) 'serious physical injury' means physical injury which creates a substantial risk of death, or which causes serious disfigurement, serious impairment of health or serious loss or impairment of the function of any bodily organ.

. . . .

(6) 'Deadly weapon' means any weapon, whether loaded or unloaded, from which a shot may be discharged, or a switchblade knife, gravity knife, billy, blackjack, bludgeon, or metal knuckles. The definition of "deadly weapon" in this subdivision shall be deemed not to apply to section 29-38 or 53-206;

(7) 'dangerous instrument' means any instrument, article or substance which, under the circumstances in which it is used or attempted or threatened to be used, is capable of causing death or serious physical injury, and includes a "vehicle" as that term is defined in this section."

CONN. GEN. STAT. ANN. §§ 53a-3(4), (6) and (7) (West 1971).

**8.** **Delaware** - In 1984, the Delaware code contained two felonious assault statutes that provided in relevant part as follows:

"Assault in the second degree; class C felony.

A person is guilty of assault in the second degree when:
(1) He intentionally causes serious physical injury to another person; or
(2) He intentionally causes physical injury to another person by means of a deadly weapon or a dangerous instrument; or
(3) He recklessly causes serious physical injury to another person by means of a deadly weapon or a dangerous instrument; or
(4) He intentionally causes physical injury to a law-enforcement officer or a

volunteer or full-time fireman who is acting in the lawful performance of his duty."

"Assault in the first degree; class B felony.

A person is guilty of assault in the first degree when:
(1) He intentionally causes serious physical injury to another person by means of a deadly weapon or a dangerous instrument; or
(2) He intentionally disfigures another person seriously and permanently, or intentionally destroys, amputates or disables permanently a member or organ of another person's body; or
(3) He recklessly engages in conduct which creates a substantial risk of death to another person, and thereby causes serious physical injury to another person; or
(4) In the course of or in furtherance of the commission or attempted commission of a felony or immediate flight therefrom, he intentionally or recklessly causes serious physical injury to another person; or
(5) He intentionally causes serious physical injury to a law-enforcement officer or a volunteer or full-time fireman who is acting in the lawful performance of his duty."

DEL. CODE ANN., tit. 11, §§ 612 and 613 (1974).

At the time these assault statutes were in force, the Deleware code included the following definitions:

(4) "'Dangerous instrument' means any instrument, article or substance which, under the circumstances in which it is used, attempted to be used or threatened to be used, is readily capable of causing death or serious physical injury.
(5) 'Deadly weapon' includes any weapon from which a shot may be discharged, a knife of any sort (other than an ordinary pocketknife carried in a closed position), switchblade knife, billy, blackjack, bludgeon, metal knuckles, slingshot, razor, bicycle chain or ice pick. For the purpose of this definition, an ordinary pocketknife shall be a folding knife having a blade not more than 3 inches in length.
. . . .
(21) 'Serious physical injury' means physical injury which creates a substantial risk of death, or which causes serious and prolonged disfigurement, prolonged impairment of health or prolonged loss or impairment of the function of any bodily organ."

DEL. CODE ANN., tit. 11, §§ 222(4), (5) and (21) (1974).

9. **Florida** - In 1984, the Florida code included two statutes prohibiting "aggravated assault" and "aggravated battery" as follows:

"Aggravated assault

(1) An 'aggravated assault' is an assault:
(a) With a deadly weapon without intent to kill; or
(b) With an intent to commit a felony.
(2) Whoever commits an aggravated assault shall be guilty of a felony of the third degree, punishable as provided in § 775.082, § 775.083, or § 775.084."

"Aggravated battery

(1) A person commits aggravated battery who, in committing battery:
(a) Intentionally or knowingly causes great bodily harm, permanent disability, or permanent disfigurement; or
(b) Uses a deadly weapon.
(2) Whoever commits aggravated battery shall be guilty of a felony of the second degree, punishable as provided in § 775.082, § 775.083, or § 775.084."

FLA. STAT. ANN., §§ 784.021 and 784.045 (West 1976).

At that time, the Florida code included the following definition:

"(13) 'Weapon' means any dirk, metallic knuckles, slungshot, billie, tear gas gun, chemical weapon or device, or any other deadly weapon except a firearm or a common pocketknife."

FLA. STAT. ANN., § 790.001 (West 1976).

The statute did not expressly define "great bodily harm" and the District Court of Appeals of Florida has held that "[w]hether the evidence . . . rises to the level of great bodily harm required by the statute is generally a question for the jury." *McKnight v. Florida*, 494 So.2d 450, 451 (Fl. 1986). The court continued, stating that "the term 'great bodily harm' does not lend itself to precise legal definition." *Id.*, see *Guthrie v. State*, 407 So.2d 357, 358 (Fla. Dist. Ct. App. 1981) ("Great bodily harm defines itself and means great as distinguished from slight, trivial, minor, or moderate harm, and as such does not include mere bruises as are likely to be inflicted in a simple assault and battery . . . . Whether the evidence describing such harm or injury is within the meaning of the Statute . . . is generally a question of fact for the jury.") (citing *Owens v. State*, 289 So.2d 472 (Fla. Dist. Ct. App. 1974)).

**10.   Georgia -**   In 1984, GA. CODE ANN., § 16-5-21, provided in relevant part: "Aggravated assault.

(a) A person commits the offense of aggravated assault when he assaults:
(1) With intent to murder, to rape, or to rob; or
(2) With a deadly weapon or with any object, device, or instrument which, when used offensively against a person, is likely to or actually does result in serious bodily injury.
(b) A person convicted of the offense of aggravated assault shall be punished by imprisonment for not less than one nor more than 20 years.
(c) A person who knowingly commits the offense of aggravated assault upon a peace officer while the peace officer is engaged in, or on account of the performance of, his official duties shall, upon conviction thereof, be punished by imprisonment for not less than five nor more than 20 years.
(d) Any person who commits the offense of aggravated assault against a person who is 65 years of age or older shall, upon conviction thereof, be punished by imprisonment for not less than three nor more than 20 years."

GA. CODE ANN., § 16-5-21 (Harrison 1983).

The statute did not define "serious bodily injury", but case law indicates that the term is broadly defined. *See Roberson v. State*, 349 S.E.2d 39, 40 (Ga. Ct. App. 1986) (finding "serious bodily injury" where "[t]he victim testified that she could hardly walk and had to crawl around the house after she was beaten by defendant . . . she was unable to work for 'quite a while' . . . [and] . . . she was so severely bruised that she could not endure chiropractic treatment (which she was undergoing for a previous injury)"); *Watkins v. State*, 328 S.E.2d 537, 539 (Ga. Ct. App. 1985) ("[T]here is no question that an injury which results in impairment of vision and hearing, removal of a portion of the frontal lobe of the brain, and a month-long hospital stay is a serious injury."). Furthermore, "[t]here is obviously no necessity for showing that the injuries inflicted were life-threatening or for a showing that the infliction of such injuries actually did result in serious bodily injury." *Gabler v. State*, 338 S.E.2d 469 (Ga. Ct. App. 1985).

**11.** **Hawaii** - In 1984, the Hawaii code prohibited two degrees of assault as follows:

"Assault in the first degree.

(1) A person commits the offense of assault in the first degree if he intentionally or knowingly causes serious bodily injury to another person.
(2) Assault in the first degree is a class B felony."

"Assault in the second degree.

(1) A person commits the offense of assault in the second degree if:
(a) He intentionally or knowingly causes bodily injury to another person with a dangerous instrument;
(b) He recklessly causes serious bodily injury to another person with a dangerous instrument; or
(c) He intentionally or knowingly causes bodily injury to a correctional worker, as defined in section 710-1031(2), who is engaged in the performance of duty or who is within a correctional facility."

HAW. REV. STAT. §§ 707-710 and 707-711 (1984).

HAW. REV. STAT. § 707-700(3) and (4) (1984) included the following definitions:

"(3) 'Serious bodily injury' means bodily injury which creates a substantial risk of death or which causes serious, permanent disfigurement, or protracted loss or impairment of the function of any bodily member or organ.

. . . .

(4) 'Dangerous instrument' means any firearm, or other weapon, device, instrument, material, or substance, whether animate or inanimate, which in the manner it is used or is intended to be used is known to be capable of

producing death or serious bodily injury."

**12.  Idaho** - IDAHO CODE § 18-905 (1979) provided as follows:

"Aggravated assault defined.

> An aggravated assault is an assault:
>
>> (a) With a deadly weapon or instrument without intent to kill; or
>>
>> (b) By any means or force likely to produce great bodily harm; or
>>
>> (c) With any vitriol, corrosive acid, or a caustic chemical of any kind.
>>
>> (d) 'Deadly weapon or instrument' as used in this chapter is defined to include any firearm, though unloaded or so defective that it can not be fired."

The Idaho statute did not further define "great bodily harm." Case law indicates that the term "great bodily harm" is broadly construed to include serious injuries, *see, e.g., State v. Crawford*, 110 Idaho 577, 716 P. 2d 1349 (Idaho Ct. App. 1986) and that a deadly weapon "is one likely to produce death or great bodily harm." *See, e.g., State v. Lenz*, 103 Idaho 632, 635, 651 P. 2d 566, 569 (Idaho Ct. App. 1982).

**13.  Illinois** - In 1984, ILL. COMP. STAT. Ch. 38 § 12-4 (West 1979) proscribed "aggravated battery" as follows:

"Aggravated Battery.

(a) A person who, in committing a battery, intentionally or knowingly causes great bodily harm, or permanent disability or disfigurement commits aggravated battery.
(b) A person who, in committing a battery, in committing a battery either:

(1) Uses a deadly weapon;
(2) Is hooded, robed or masked, in such manner as to conceal his identity;
(3) Knows the individual harmed to be a teacher or other person employed in any school and such teacher or other employee is upon the grounds of a school or

grounds adjacent thereto, or is in any part of a building used for school purposes;
(4) Knows the individual harmed to be a supervisor, director, instructor or other person employed in any park district and such supervisor, director, instructor or other employee is upon the grounds of the park or grounds adjacent thereto, or is in any part of a building used for park purposes;
(5) Knows the individual harmed to be a caseworker, investigator, or other person employed by the State Department of Public Aid or a County Department of Public Aid and such caseworker, investigator, or other person is upon the grounds of a Public Aid office or grounds adjacent thereto, or is in any part of a building used for Public Aid purposes, or upon the grounds of a home of a public aid applicant, recipient, or any other person being interviewed or investigated in the employee's discharge of his duties, or on grounds adjacent thereto, or is in any part of a building in which the applicant, recipient, or other such person resides or is located;
(6) Knows the individual harmed to be a peace officer, or a person summoned and directed by him, or a correctional institution employee, while such officer or employee is engaged in the execution of any of his official duties including arrest or attempted arrest;
(7) Knows the individual harmed to be a fireman engaged in the execution of any of his official duties;
(8) Is, or the person battered is, on or about a public way, public property or public place of accommodation or amusement;
(9) Knows the individual harmed to be the driver, operator, employee or passenger of any transportation facility or system engaged in the business of transportation of the public for hire and the individual assaulted is then performing in such capacity or then using such public transportation as a passenger or using any area of any description designated by the transportation facility or system as a vehicle boarding, departure, or transfer location;
(c) A person who administers to an individual or causes him to take, without his consent or by threat or deception, and for other than medical purposes, any intoxicating, poisonous, stupefying, narcotic or anesthetic substance commits aggravated battery.
(d) A person who knowingly gives to another person any food that contains any substance or object that is intended to cause physical injury if eaten, commits aggravated battery.
(e) Sentence.
Aggravated battery is a Class 3 felony."

The Penal Code did not define "bodily harm", and case law indicates that it is broadly defined. *See, e.g., People v. Costello*, 51 Ill. Dec. 178, 181 (1981) ("The term 'great bodily injury' referred to as an essential element of the offense of aggravated battery is not susceptible of a precise legal definition but it is an injury of a graver and more serious character than an ordinary battery."); *People v. Parks*, 8 Ill. Dec. 877, 880 (1977) (finding "bodily harm" where the victim testified that she was bleeding from a cut on her left hand after the attack and a police officer corroborated the testimony).

14. **Indiana** - In 1984, IND. CODE ANN. § 35-42-2-1 (Michie 1984) provided in relevant part as follows:

> "A person who knowingly or intentionally touches another person in a rude, insolent, or angry manner commits battery, a Class B misdemeanor. However, the offense is:
>
> . . . .
>
> (3) A Class C felony if it results in serious bodily injury to any other person or if it is committed by means of a deadly weapon."

The Indiana Code defined "serious bodily injury" as "bodily injury that creates a substantial risk of death or that causes serious permanent disfigurement, unconsciousness, extreme pain, or permanent or protracted loss or impairment of the function of a bodily member or organ. IND. CODE ANN. § 35-41-1-25 (Michie 1984). "Deadly weapon" was defined as

> "(1) A loaded or unloaded firearm; or
>
> (2) A weapon, device, equipment, chemical substance, or other material that in the manner it is used, or could ordinarily be used, or is intended to be used, is readily capable of causing serious bodily injury."

IND. CODE ANN. § 35-42-2-1 (Michie 1984).

**15.    Iowa** - In 1984, the Iowa Code contained an "assault provision," and an "assault while participating in a felony" provision. IOWA CODE ANN. § 708.1 (West 1988) provided that:

"A person commits an assault when, without justification, the person does any of the following:

1. Any act which is intended to cause pain or injury to, or which is intended to result in physical contact which will be insulting or offensive to another, coupled with the apparent ability to execute the act.

2. Any act which is intended to place another in fear of immediate physical contact which will be painful, injurious, insulting, or offensive, coupled with the apparent ability to execute the act.

3. Intentionally points any firearm toward another, or displays in a threatening manner any dangerous weapon toward another.

Provided, that where the person doing any of the above enumerated acts, and such other person, are voluntary participants in a sport, social or other activity, not in itself criminal, and such act is a reasonably foreseeable incident of such sport or activity, and does not create an unreasonable risk of serious injury or breach of the peace, the act shall not be an assault."

In 1984, IOWA CODE ANN. § 708.3 (West 1988) proscribed "assault while participating in a felony" as follows:

"Any person who commits an assault as defined in section 708.1 while participating in a felony is guilty of a class "C" felony if the person thereby causes serious injury to any person; if no serious injury results, the person is guilty of a class "D" felony.

Pursuant to IOWA CODE ANN. § 702.7 (West 1988):

"A 'dangerous weapon' is any instrument or device designed primarily for use in inflicting death or injury upon a human being or animal, and which is capable of inflicting death upon a human being when used in the manner for which it was designed. Additionally, any instrument or device of any sort whatsoever which is actually used in such a manner as to indicate that the defendant intends to inflict death or serious injury upon the other, and which, when so used, is capable of inflicting death upon a human being, is a dangerous weapon. Dangerous weapons include, but are not limited to, any offensive weapon, pistol, revolver, or other firearm, dagger, razor, stilletto, or knife having a blade of three inches or longer in length."

"Serious injury" was defined by IOWA CODE ANN. § 702.18 (West 1988) as follows:

"'Serious injury' means disabling mental illness, or bodily injury which creates a substantial risk of death or which causes serious permanent disfigurement, or protracted loss or impairment of the function of any bodily member or organ."

**16.     Kansas** - KAN. CRIM. CODE ANN. § 21-3414 (West 1984) provided:

> "Aggravated battery is the unlawful touching or application of force to the person of another with intent to injure that person or another and which either:
>
> (a) Inflicts great bodily harm upon him; or
>
> (b) Causes any disfigurement or dismemberment to or of his person; or
>
> (c) Is done with a deadly weapon, or in any manner whereby great bodily harm, disfigurement, dismemberment, or death can be inflicted.
>
> Aggravated battery is a class C felony."

The statute did not define "great bodily harm." The Kansas Supreme Court has noted that "[T]he language of the statute . . . is couched in language which is readily understandable, and there are no omissions of necessary language. Bodily harm or injury to the body is clear and unequivocal. Great distinguishes the bodily harm necessary in this offense from slight, trivial, minor or moderate harm, and as such it does not include mere bruises, which are likely to be sustained in simple battery. Whether the injury or harm is 'great' or not is generally a question of fact for the jury." *State v. Sanders*, 575 P.2d 533, 552 (Kan. 1978). In *State v. Hanks*, 236 Kan. 524, 537

(Sup. Ct. 1985), the court defined a "deadly weapon" as "an instrument which, from the manner in which it is used, is calculated or likely to produce death or serious injury."

17.   **Kentucky** - KY. REV. STAT. ANN. § 500.010 (Michie 1974) provided as follows:

"Assault in the first degree

> (1) A person is guilty of assault in the first degree when:
>> (a) He intentionally causes serious physical injury to another person by means of a deadly weapon or a dangerous instrument; or
>>
>> (b) Under circumstances manifesting extreme indifference to the value of human life he wantonly engages in conduct which creates a grave risk of death to another and thereby causes serious physical injury to another person."

"'Serious physical injury' means physical injury which creates a substantial risk of death, or which causes serious and prolonged disfigurement, prolonged impairment of health, or prolonged loss or impairment of the function of any bodily organ." KY. REV. STAT. ANN. § 500.080 (Michie 2001) (enacted 1974).

Kentucky law defined "deadly weapon" as:

(a) Any weapon from which a shot, readily capable of producing death or other serious physical injury, may be discharged; or

(b) Any knife other than an ordinary pocket knife or hunting knife; or

(c) Billy, nightstick, or club; or

(d) Blackjack or slapjack; or

(e) Nanchaku karate sticks; or

(f) Shuriken or death star; or

(g) Artificial knuckles made from metal, plastic or other similar hard material."

KY. REV. STAT. ANN. § 508.080(4) (Michie 1985). "'Dangerous instrument'" means any instrument, article, or substance which, under the circumstances in which it is used, attempted to be used, or threatened to be used, is readily capable of causing death or serious physical injury." KY. REV. STAT. ANN. § 508.080(3) (Michie 1985).

**18. Louisiana** - In 1984, LA. REV. STAT. ANN. § 37 (West 1987) provided as follows:

"Aggravated assault is an assault committed with a dangerous weapon.
Whoever commits an aggravated assault shall be fined not more than five hundred dollars or imprisoned for not more than six months, or both."

"Assault" and "dangerous weapon" were defined as follows: (1) An "[a]ssault is an attempt to commit a battery, or the intentional placing of another in reasonable apprehension of receiving a battery." LA. REV. STAT. ANN. § 36 (West 1987). "Battery is the intentional use of force or violence upon the person of another; or the intentional administration of a poison or other noxious liquid or substance to another." LA. REV. STAT. ANN. § 363 (West 1987).

(2) "'Dangerous weapon' includes any gas, liquid or other substance or instrumentality, which, in the manner used, is calculated or likely to produce death or great bodily harm." LA. REV. STAT. ANN. § 2 (3) (West 1987).

LA. REV. STAT. ANN. § 34.1 defined "serious bodily injury" as follows:

"For purposes of this article, serious bodily injury means bodily injury which involves unconsciousness, extreme physical pain or protracted and obvious disfigurement, or protracted loss or impairment of the function of a bodily member, organ, or mental faculty, or a substantial risk of death."

**19. Maine** -   In 1984, ME. REV. STAT. ANN. tit. 17-A, § 208 (West 1984) defined "aggravated assault" as follows:

"1. A person is guilty of aggravated assault if he intentionally, knowingly, or recklessly causes:

A. Serious bodily injury to another; or

B. Bodily injury to another with use of a dangerous weapon; or

C. Bodily injury to anther under circumstances manifesting extreme indifference to the value of human life. Such circumstances include, but are not limited to, the number, location or nature of the injuries, the manner or method inflicted, or the observable physical condition of the victim."

"Serious bodily injury" under Maine law "means a bodily injury which creates a substantial risk of death or which causes serious, permanent disfigurement or loss or substantial impairment of the function of any bodily member or organ, or extended convalescence necessary for recovery of physical health." ME. REV. STAT. ANN. tit. 17-A, § 2 (West 1984). "Bodily injury means physical pain, physical illness or any impairment of physical condition." ME. REV. STAT. ANN. tit. 17-A, § 2 (West 1984). "Use of a dangerous weapon" was defined as "the use of a firearm or other weapon, device, instrument, material or substance, whether animate or inanimate, which, in the manner it is used or threatened to be used is capable of producing death or serious bodily injury." ME. REV. STAT. ANN. tit. 17-A, § 2 (West 1984).

**20. Maryland** - In 1984, Maryland did not have statutory assault offenses comparable to either the Model Penal Code's offense for assault resulting in serious bodily injury or to the majority of states' definition of assault with a dangerous weapon. Rather, Maryland had assault offenses under the common law. Common law assault, under Maryland law, "encompasses two definitions: (1) an attempt to commit a battery or (2) an unlawful intentional act which places another in reasonable apprehension of receiving an immediate battery." *Harrod v. State*, 499 A.2d 959, 960 (1985) (citation omitted). "A battery is the unlawful application of force to the person of another." *Anderson v. State*, 487 A.2d 294, 295 (1985), *cert. denied*, 493 A.2d 349 (1985). However, the Maryland legislature "cut out of the herd for special treatment four assaults where the aggravating factor is a special *mens rea* or specific intent": assault with intent to rob, assault with intent to murder, assault with intent to commit either a rape or a sexual offense, and assault with intent to maim or disfigure. *Walker v. State*, 452 A.2d 1234, 1247-8 & n.11 (1982). *See also* MD. CODE ANN. Crimes and Punishments §§ 12 & 386 (1986).

In *Walker v. State*, 53 Md. 171, 197, 452 A.2d 1234, 1248 (Md. Ct. Spec. App. 1982), the court stated:

> "Many states have made assault with a deadly weapon a special crime. Maryland has not done so, but has trusted the wide discretion of the common law sentencing provisions to deal appropriately with such severely aggravated assaults. The aggravating factor might well be the harmful consequences of a particular assault ... a brutal beating that leaves its victim blinded, crippled, disfigured, in a wheelchair for life, in a psychiatric ward for life, is severely aggravated. Once again, Maryland has not dealt with this form of aggravation legislatively but has left it to the discretion of common law sentencing ... A common law assault is theoretically capable of being as aggravated as or more aggravated than any of our statutory assaults."

*See also Brooks v. State*, 314 Md. 585, 552 A.2d 872 (Md. Ct. App. 1989).

In 2002, Maryland overhauled its criminal code, by repealing the former code and re-designating all of the sections. Currently, Maryland punishes the offense of "assault in the first degree," which states that "(a)(1) A person may not intentionally cause or attempt to cause serious physical injury to another." MD. CODE. ANN., CRIM. § 3-202 (2002). "'Serious physical injury' means physical injury that: (1) creates a substantial risk of death; or (2) causes permanent or protracted serious: (I) disfigurement; (ii) loss of the function of any bodily member or organ; or (iii) impairment of the function of any bodily member or organ." MD. CODE. ANN., CRIM. § 3-201(d) (2002).

**21.** **Massachusetts** - Currently, Massachusetts' PENAL CODE punishes anyone who "commits an assault or an assault and battery . . . upon another and by such assault and battery causes serious bodily injury . . . ." MASS. GEN. LAWS ch. 265 § 13A (2002). The provision defines "serious bodily injury" as "bodily injury that results in a permanent disfigurement, loss or impairment of a bodily function, limb or organ, or a substantial risk of death." MASS. GEN. LAWS ch. 265, § 13A(c). Prior to 2002, the section did not include "serious bodily injury."

MASS. GEN. LAWS ch. 265, § 15A(b) (1984) provided: "Whoever commits assaults and battery upon another by means of a dangerous weapon shall be punished by imprisonment for not more than ten years. . . ." In *Commonwealth v. Appleby*, 380 Mass. 296, 303-08 (Supreme Judicial Ct. 1980), the court ruled that a "dangerous weapon" included weapons which under the circumstances in which they are used could cause serious bodily injury.

**22.** **Michigan** - In 1984, MICH. STAT. ANN. § 750.82 (1988) provided as follows:

"Any person who shall assault another with a gun, revolver, pistol, knife, iron bar, club, brass knuckles or other dangerous weapon, but without intending to commit the crime of murder, and without intending to inflict great bodily harm less than the crime of murder, shall be guilty of a felony."

"Dangerous weapon" included any instrument under the circumstances in which it is used is capable of causing death or serious bodily injury. S*ee, e.g, People v. Van Diver*, 80 Mich. App. 352, 263 N.W. 2d 370 (Mich. Ct. App. 1977).

MICH. STAT. ANN. § 750.84 - provided: "Assault with intent to do great bodily harm less than murder - - Any person who shall assault another with intent to do great bodily harm, less than the crime of murder, shall be guilty of a felony punishable by imprisonment in the state prison not more than 10 years, or by fine of not more than 5,000 dollars." *See People v. Van Diver*, *supra* (discussing § 750.84 and the distinction between simple assault and assault with intent to do great bodily harm). The Michigan Penal Code did not expressly define "great bodily harm."

**23.** **Minnesota** - In 1984, MINN. STAT. ANN. § 609.221 proscribed assault in the first degree for:

"Whoever assaults another and inflicts great bodily harm." Moreover, MINN. STAT. ANN. § 609.222 (West 1991) proscribed assault in the second degree as follows:

"Whoever assaults another with a dangerous weapon but without inflicting great bodily harm ..."

Under Minnesota law, "Assault" is:

"(1) An act done with intent to cause fear in another of immediate bodily harm or death; or
(2) The intentional infliction of or attempt to inflict bodily harm upon another."

MINN. STAT. ANN. § 609.022, subd. 10 (West 1991). "'Great bodily harm'" means bodily injury which creates a high probability of death, or which causes serious permanent disfigurement, or which causes a permanent or protracted loss or impairment of the function of any bodily member or organ or other serious bodily harm." MINN. STAT. ANN. § 609.022, subd. 8 (West 1991). *See also Peterson v. State*, 282 N.W.2d 878, 880 (Minn. 1979). "'Substantial bodily harm' means bodily injury which involves a temporary but substantial disfigurement, or which causes a temporary but substantial loss or impairment of the function of any bodily member or organ, or which causes a fracture of any bodily member." MINN. STAT. ANN. § 609.022, subd. 7a (West 1991). *See also State v. Stafford*, 340 N.W.2d 669, 670-71 (Minn. 1983). "'Dangerous weapon'" means any firearm, whether loaded or unloaded, or any device designed as a weapon and capable of producing death or great bodily harm, or other device or instrumentality which, in the manner it is used or intended to be used, is calculated or likely to produce death or great bodily harm." MINN. STAT. ANN. § 609.022, subd. 6 (West 1991). *See also State v. Graham*, 336 N.W.2d 335, 366-37 (Minn. 1985) *and LaMere v. State*, 278 N.W.2d 552, 555 (Minn. 1979).

**24. Mississippi** - In 1984, the Mississippi Code provided that:

> "A person is guilty of aggravated assault if he (a) attempts to cause serious bodily injury to another, or causes such injury purposely, knowingly or recklessly under circumstances manifesting extreme indifference to the value of human life; or (b) attempts to cause or purposely or knowingly causes bodily injury to another with a deadly weapon or other means likely to produce death or serious bodily harm; and, upon conviction, he shall be punished by imprisonment in the county jail for not more than one (1) year or in the penitentiary for not more than twenty (20) years. [other penalties cited for aggravated assault upon a law enforcement officer or fireman]."

MISS. CODE ANN. § 97-3-7 (1990). The Mississippi Code did not define "serious bodily injury."

In 1992, the Mississippi Supreme Court stated that "[a] statute is not unconstitutionally vague unless people of common intelligence must guess at its meaning and differ as to its application. Section 97-3-7(2) is not unconstitutionally vague, particularly when applied in a case involving brutal injuries . . . . In more ambiguous cases, we suggest that prosecutors and trial courts refer to the definition of 'serious bodily injury' set out in the Model Penal Code."

*Fleming v. State*, 604 So.2d 280, 293 (Miss. 1992) (citations omitted).

In *Davis v. State*, 530 So.2d 694 (Miss. 1988), the Supreme Court of Mississippi expressly approved the following "deadly weapon" jury instruction where the criminal conduct at issue occurred on May 13, 1984:

> A deadly weapon may be defined as any object, article or means which, when used as a weapon is, under the existing circumstances, reasonably capable or likely to produce death or serious bodily harm to a human being upon whom the object, article or means is used as a weapon.

Id. at 700 (stating that the above-referenced "is the legally correct definition of deadly weapon").

**25. Missouri** - In 1984, MO. ANN. STAT. § 565.050 (West 1989) provided "[a] person commits the crime of assault in the first degree if he attempts to kill or knowingly causes or attempts to cause serious physical injury to another person."

In 1984, MO. ANN. STAT. § 565.060 (West 1989) provided that:

"1. A person commits the crime of assault in the second degree if he:

(1) Attempts to kill or knowingly causes or attempts to cause serious physical injury to another person under the influence of sudden passion arising out of adequate cause; or

(2) Attempts to cause or knowingly causes physical injury to another by means of a deadly weapon or dangerous instrument; ..."

The Missouri Code defined "serious physical injury" as "physical injury that creates a substantial risk of death or that causes serious disfigurement or protracted loss or impairment of the function of any part of the body." MO. ANN. STAT. §§ 565.061(26) & 565.002(6) (West 1989). "'Deadly weapon' means any firearm, loaded or unloaded, or any weapon from which a shot, readily capable of producing death or serious physical injury may be discharged, or a switchblade knife, dagger, billy, blackjack or metal knuckles." MO. ANN. STAT. § 565.061(10) (West 1989). A "dangerous instrument" was defined as "any instrument, article or substance, which, under the circumstances in which it is used, is readily capable of causing death or other serious physical injury." MO. ANN. STAT. § 565.061(9) (West 1989). "'Physical injury' means physical pain, illness, or any impairment of physical condition." MO. ANN. STAT. § 565.061(20) (West 1989).

  **26.** **Montana** - In 1984, MONT. REV. CODE ANN. § 45-5-202 (1984) provided:

> "(1) A person commits the offense of aggravated assault if he purposely or knowingly causes serious bodily injury to another.
>
> (2) if he purposely or knowingly causes:
>
> (a) bodily injury to another with a weapon;
>
> (b) reasonable apprehension of serious bodily injury in another by use of a weapon; or
>
> (c) bodily injury to a peace officer or a person who is responsible for the care or custody of a prisoner.
>
> (3) A person convicted of aggravated assault shall be imprisoned in the state prison for a term of not less than 2 years or more than 20 years and may be fined not more than $50,000, except as provided in 46-18-222."

MONT. REV. CODE ANN. § 45-2-101(59) (1984) defined "serious bodily injury" as "bodily injury which creates a substantial risk of death or which causes serious permanent disfigurement or protracted loss or impairment of the function or process of any bodily member or organ. It includes serious mental illness or impairment." *See State v. George*, 203 Mont. 124 (1983).

MONT. REV. CODE ANN. § 46-18-221 (1984) imposed additional punishment for using a "dangerous weapon" "while engaged in the commission of [an] offense," and § 45-2-101 (71) provided that "'weapon' means any instrument, article, or substance which, regardless of its primary function, is readily capable of being used to produce death or serious bodily injury."

**27.** **Nebraska** - NEB. REV. STAT. § 28-308 (1) (1984) provided: "A person commits the offense of assault in the first degree if he intentionally or knowingly causes serious bodily injury to another person." NEB. REV. STAT. § 28-309 (1) (1984), provided in relevant part that:

"(1) A person commits the offense of assault in the second degree if he:
    (a) Intentionally or knowingly causes bodily injury to another person with a dangerous instrument; or
    (b) Recklessly causes serious bodily injury to another person with a dangerous instrument."

"Serious bodily injury shall mean bodily injury which involves a substantial risk of death, or which involves substantial risk of serious permanent disfigurement, or protracted loss or impairment of the function of any part or organ of the body." NEB. REV. STAT. § 28-109 (20) (1984) (enacted 1977).

NEB. REV. STAT. § 28-109 (7) (1984) provided that "'deadly weapon' shall mean any firearm, knife, bludgeon, or other device, instrument, material, or substance, whether animate or inanimate, which in the manner it is used or intended to be used is capable of producing death or serious bodily injury."

**28.** **Nevada** - NEV. REV. STAT. § 200.481 (1984) provided:

"1. As used in this section:

    (a) "Battery" means any willful and unlawful use of force or violence upon the person of another . . . .

2. Any person convicted of a battery, other than a battery committed by an adult upon a child which constitutes child abuse, shall be punished:

> (a) If the battery is not committed with a deadly weapon, and no substantial bodily harm to the victim results, except under circumstances where a greater penalty is provided in NRS 197.090, for a misdemeanor. . .
>
> (b) If the battery is not committed with a deadly weapon, and substantial bodily harm to the victim results, for a gross misdemeanor. . . .
>
> (d) If the battery is committed with the use of a deadly weapon by imprisonment in the state prison for not less than 2 years nor more than 10 years. . . . "

The Nevada Code did not define "substantial bodily harm" until April 1985. "Substantial bodily harm" was defined as "1. Bodily injury which creates a substantial risk of death or which causes serious, permanent disfigurement or protracted loss or impairment of the function of any bodily member or organ; or 2. Prolonged physical pain." NEV. REV. STAT. 0.060 (1985). The Nevada Supreme Court set forth an identical definition in 1977. *See Gibson v. State*, 590 P.2d 158, 158 (Nev. 1979).

**29.    New Hampshire** - In 1984, the New Hampshire criminal code classified first degree assault as a class A felony and indicated that a person committed first degree assault when he:

"I. Purposely causes serious bodily injury to another; or

II. Purposely or knowingly causes bodily injury to another by means of a deadly weapon."

N.H. REV. STAT. ANN. § 631:1 (1984).

The Code defined "deadly weapon" and "serious bodily injury" as follows:

"V.. 'Deadly weapon' means any firearm, knife or other substance or thing which, in the manner it is used, intended to be used, or threatened to be used is known to be capable of producing death or serious bodily injury.

VI. 'Serious bodily injury' means any harm to the body which causes sever, permanent or protracted loss of or impairment to the health or of the function of any part of the body."

N.H. REV. STAT. ANN. § 625:11 (1984).

**30.     New Jersey** - N.J. STAT. ANN. § 2C:12-1(b) (effective 1981) provided: "A person is guilty of aggravated assault if he:

(1) Attempts to cause serious bodily injury to another, or causes such injury purposely or knowingly or under circumstances manifesting extreme indifference to the value of human life recklessly causes such injury, or

(2) Attempts to cause or purposely or knowingly causes bodily injury to another with a deadly weapon; or

(3) Recklessly causes bodily injury to another with a deadly weapon; or

(4) Knowingly under circumstances manifesting extreme indifference to the value of human life points a firearm. . . , at or in the direction of another, whether or not the actor believes it to be loaded . . . ."

"'Serious bodily harm' means bodily harm which creates a substantial risk of death or which causes serious, permanent disfigurement or protracted loss or impairment of the function of any bodily member or organ or which results from aggravated sexual assault or sexual assault." N.J. STAT. ANN. § 2C:3-11(d) (enacted 1978).

Under New Jersey law, the term "deadly weapon" included any device "which in the manner it is fashioned would lead the victim reasonably to believe it to be capable of producing death or serious bodily injury." *State v. Mieles*, 199 N.J. Super 29, 40, 488 A. 235, 240 (N.J.

Super. Ct. App. Div. 1985), quoting N.J. STAT. ANN. § 2C:11-1(c) (1982).

31. **New Mexico** - N.M. STAT. ANN. § 30-3-2 (A) (1978) provided that "Aggravated assault" includes "unlawfully assaulting or striking at another with a deadly weapon." N.M. STAT. ANN. § 30-3-5 (1978) provided:

> "§ 30-3-5. Aggravated battery
>
> A. Aggravated battery consists of the unlawful touching or application of force to the person of another with intent to injure that person or another.
>
> B. Whoever commits aggravated battery, inflicting an injury to the person which is not likely to cause death or great bodily harm, but does cause painful temporary disfigurement or temporary loss or impairment of the functions of any member or organ of the body, is guilty of a misdemeanor.
>
> C. Whoever commits aggravated battery inflicting great bodily harm or does so with a deadly weapon or does so in any manner whereby great bodily harm or death can be inflicted is guilty of a third degree felony."

"'[G]reat bodily harm' means an injury to the person which creates a high probability of death; or which causes serious disfigurement; or which results in permanent or protracted loss or impairment of the function of any member or organ of the body ." N.M. STAT. ANN. § 30-1-12 (A) (1978). Part B of this statute provided:"'[D]eadly weapon' means any firearm, whether loaded or unloaded; or any weapon which is capable of producing death or great bodily harm, including but not restricted to any types of daggers, brass knuckles, switchblade knives, bowie knives, poniards, butcher knives, dirk knives and all such weapons with which dangerous cuts can be given, or with which dangerous thrusts can be inflicted, including swordcanes, and any kind of sharp pointed canes, also slingshots, slung shots, bludgeous; or any other weapons with which dangerous wounds can be inflicted.'"

**32.** **New York** - N.Y. PENAL LAW § 120.05(1)(2) and (4) (1965) provided as follows:

"A person is guilty of assault in the second degree when:

1. With intent to cause serious physical injury to another person, he causes such injury to such person or to a third person; or

2. With intent to cause physical injury to another person, he causes such injury to such person or to a third person by means of a deadly weapon or a dangerous instrument; or

. . . .

4. He recklessly causes serious physical injury to another person by means of a deadly weapon or a dangerous instrument."

N.Y. PENAL LAW § 120.10 (1965) provided as follows:

"A person is guilty of assault in the first degree when:

1. With intent to cause serious physical injury to another person, he causes such injury to such person or to a third person by means of a deadly weapon or a dangerous instrument; or

2. With intent to disfigure another person seriously and permanently, or to destroy, amputate or disable permanently a member or organ of his body, he causes such injury to such person or to a third person; or

3. Under circumstances evincing a depraved indifference to human life, he recklessly engages in conduct which creates a grave risk of death to another person, and thereby causes serious physical injury to another person; or

4. In the course of and in furtherance of the commission or attempted commission of a felony or of immediate flight therefrom, he, or another participant if there be any, causes serious physical injury to a person other than one of the participants."

N.Y. PENAL §§ 10 (10) and (13) provided as follows:

> "'Serious physical injury' means physical injury which creates a substantial risk of death, or which causes death or serious and protracted disfigurement, protracted impairment of health or protracted loss or impairment of the function of any bodily organ.
>
> . . . .
>
> 'Dangerous instrument' means any instrument article or substance, including a "vehicle" as that term is defined in this section, which, under the circumstances in which it is used, attempted to be used or threatened to be used, is readily capable of causing death or other serious physical injury."

**33.     North Carolina** - In 1984, N.C. GEN. STAT. § 14-33 (1984), provided in relevant part as follows:

> "(a) Any person who commits a simple assault or a simple assault and battery or participates in a simple affray is guilty of a misdemeanor punishable by a fine not to exceed fifty dollars ($50.00) or imprisonment for not more than 30 days.
>
> (b) Unless his conduct is covered under some other provision of law providing greater punishment, any person who commits any assault, assault and battery, or affray is guilty of a misdemeanor punishable by a fine, imprisonment if, in the course of the assault, assault and battery, or affray, he:
>
>> (1) Inflicts, or attempts to inflict, serious injury upon another person or uses a deadly weapon . . . ."

**34.     North Dakota** - In 1984, N.D. CENT. CODE § 12.1-17-02 (1984) provided as follows: "Aggravated assault. A person is guilty of a Class C felony if that person:

>> 1. Willfully causes serious bodily injury to another human being;
>>
>> 2. Knowingly causes bodily injury or substantial bodily injury to another human being with a dangerous weapon or other weapon, the possession of which under the circumstances indicates an intent or readiness to inflict serious bodily injury;

3. Causes bodily injury or substantial bodily injury to another human being while attempting to inflict serious bodily injury on any human being; or

4. Fires a firearm or hurls a destructive device at another human being."

"'Serious bodily injury' means bodily injury which creates a substantial risk of death or which causes serious permanent disfigurement, unconsciousness, extreme pain, permanent loss or impairment of the function of any bodily member or organ" N.D. CENT. CODE § 12.1-01-04(29) (1984).

N.D. CENT. CODE § 12.1-01-04(6) provided:

"'Dangerous weapon' means, but is not limited to, any switchblade or gravity knife, machete, scimitar, stiletto, sword, or dagger; any billy, blackjack, sap, bludgeon, cudgel, metal knuckles, or sand club; any slungshot; any bow and arrow, crossbow, or spear; any weapon which will expel, or is readily capable of expelling, a projectile by the action of a spring, compressed air, or compressed gas including any such weapon, loaded or unloaded, commonly referred to as a BB gun, air rifle, or $CO_2$ gun; and any projector of a bomb or any object containing or capable of producing and emitting any noxious liquid, gas, or substance."

35. **Ohio** - In 1984, OHIO REV. CODE ANN. § 2903.11 made it a crime for anyone to knowingly "(1) Cause serious physical harm to another; (2) Cause or attempt to cause physical harm to another by means of a deadly weapon or ordinance. . . ."

OHIO REV. CODE ANN. § 2901.01 (E) provided that:

(E) "'Serious physical harm to persons' means any of the following:

(1) Any mental illness or condition of such gravity as would normally require hospitalization or prolonged psychiatric treatment;

(2) Any physical harm which carries a substantial risk of death;

(3) Any physical harm which involves some permanent incapacity, whether partial or total, or which involves some temporary, substantial incapacity;

(4) Any physical harm which involves some permanent disfigurement, or which involves some temporary, serious disfigurement;

(5) Any physical harm which involves acute pain of such duration as to result in substantial suffering, or which involves any degree of prolonged or intractable pain."

OHIO REV. CODE ANN. § 2923.11(A) provided that:

"'Deadly weapon' means any instrument, device or thing capable of inflicting death, and designed or specially adapted for use as a weapon, or possessed, carried, or used as a weapon."

*See State v. Hicks*, 14 Ohio App. 3d 25, 26, 469 N.E. 2d 992, 993 (Ohio Ct. App. 1984).

36. **Oklahoma** - In 1984, OKLA. STAT. tit. 21, § 646, provided as follows:

"§ 646. Aggravated assault and battery defined

A. An assault and battery becomes aggravated when committed under any of the following circumstances:

1. When great bodily injury is inflicted upon the person assaulted; or

2. When committed by a person of robust health or strength upon one who is aged, decrepit, or incapacitated, as defined in Section 641 of this title.

B. For purposes of this section "great bodily injury" means bone fracture, protracted and obvious disfigurement, protracted loss or impairment of the function of a body part, organ or mental faculty, or substantial risk of death.

OKLA. STAT. tit. 21, § 645, provided as follows:

"§ 645. Assault, battery, or assault and battery with dangerous weapon.

Every person who, with intent to do bodily harm and without justifiable or excusable cause, commits any assault, battery, or assault and battery upon the person of another with any sharp or dangerous weapon, or who, without such cause, shoots at another, with any kind of firearm or air gun or other means whatever, with intent to injure any person, although without the intent to kill such person or to commit any felony, upon conviction is guilty of a felony punishable by imprisonment in the State Penitentiary not exceeding ten (10) years, or by imprisonment in a county jail not exceeding one (1) year."

In *Smith v. State*, 79 Okla. Crim. 1 (Okla. Crim. App. 1944), the court ruled that a "dangerous weapon" within this section is one likely to produce death or great bodily injury by use made of it or one which endangers life or inflicts great bodily harm in the manner in which it is used or attempted to be used.

37. **Oregon** - In 1984, OR. REV. STAT. included the following assault statutes:

"**163.165 Assault in the third degree**
- (1) A person commits the crime of assault in the third degree if the person:
  - (a) Recklessly causes serious physical injury to another by means of a deadly or dangerous weapon;
  - (b) Recklessly causes serious physical injury to another under circumstances manifesting extreme indifference to the value of human life; or
  - (c) Recklessly causes physical injury to another by means of a deadly or dangerous weapon under circumstances manifesting extreme indifference to the value of human life.
- (2) Assault in the third degree is a Class C felony.

. . . .

**163.175 Assault in the second degree**
- (1) A person commits the crime of assault in the second degree if the person:
  - (a) Intentionally or knowingly causes serious physical injury to another; or
  - (b) Intentionally or knowingly causes physical injury to another by means of a deadly or dangerous weapon; or

(c) Recklessly causes serious physical injury to another by means of a deadly or dangerous weapon under circumstances manifesting extreme indifference to the value of human life.

. . . .

**163.185 Assault in the first degree**

(1) A person commits the crime of assault in the first degree if the person intentionally causes serious physical injury to another by means of a deadly or dangerous weapon."

OR. REV. STAT. § 161.015 (1)(2) and (7) included the following definitions.

(1) "'Dangerous weapon' means any instrument, article or substance which under the circumstances in which it is used, attempted to be used or threatened to be used, is readily capable of causing death or serious physical injury.

(2) "Deadly weapon" means any instrument, article or substance specifically designed for and presently capable of causing death or serious physical injury."

. . . .

(7) "'Serious physical injury' means physical injury which creates a substantial risk of death or which causes serious and protracted disfigurement, protracted impairment of health or protracted loss or impairment of the function of any bodily organ."

38. **Pennsylvania** - In 1984, PA CONS. STAT. ANN. § 2702(a) provided in relevant part as follows:

"**§ 2702 Aggravated assault**

(a) **Offense defined** - A person is guilty of aggravated assault if he:

(1) attempts to cause serious bodily injury to another, or causes such injury intentionally, knowingly or recklessly under circumstances manifesting extreme indifference to the value of human life;

(2) attempts to cause or intentionally, knowingly or recklessly causes serious bodily injury to a police officer making or attempting to make a lawful arrest or to an operator of a vehicle used in public transportation while operating such a vehicle;

(3) attempts to cause or intentionally or knowingly causes bodily injury to a police officer making or attempting to make a lawful arrest;

(4) attempts to cause or intentionally or knowingly causes bodily injury to another with a deadly weapon; . . . "

18 PA. CONS. STAT. ANN. § 2301 included the following definitions:

"'**Bodily injury.**' Impairment of physical condition or substantial pain.

'**Deadly weapon.**' Any firearm, whether loaded or unloaded, or any device designed as a weapon and capable of producing death or serious bodily injury, or any other device or instrumentality which, in the manner in which it is used or intended to be used, is calculated or likely to produce death or serious bodily injury.

'**Serious bodily injury.**' Bodily injury which creates a substantial risk of death or which causes serious, permanent disfigurement, or protracted loss or impairment of the function of any bodily member or organ."

**39.** **Rhode Island** - In 1984, R.I. GEN. LAWS § 11-5-2 (enacted 1956) provided as follows:

"Every person who shall make an assault or battery, or both, with a dangerous weapon, or with acid or other dangerous substance. . . . shall be punished. . . . ."

Under this provision, a dangerous weapon included any object that under the circumstances in which it is used is likely to cause death or serious bodily injury. *See State v. Zangrilli*, 440 A.2d 710 (R.I. 1982); *State v. Jackson*, 752 A.2d 5 (R.I. 2000).

**40.** **South Carolina** - Under South Carolina law as in effect in 1984, assault and battery were generally considered common law offenses. "An `assault' [was] an unlawful attempt, coupled with a present ability, to commit a violent injury upon the person of another. A 'battery' [was] the successful accomplishment of such attempt. While there [was] no statutory definition of the offense of 'assault and battery' in this state, [there were] three degrees: 1) assault and battery with intent to kill and murder; 2) assault and battery of a high and aggravated nature, and 3) simple assault and battery." State v. Jones, 130 S.E. 747, 751 (S.C. 1925).

In 1969, the South Carolina General Assembly classified assault and battery with intent to kill as a felony offense. The remaining degrees of assault and battery were misdemeanors. State v. Hill, 254 S.C. 321, 329, 175 S.E. 2d 227, 231 (S.C. 1970). In 1984, S.C. CODE ANN. § 16-3-610 provided as follows:

"§ 16-3-610 Assault with concealed weapon.

> If any person be convicted of assault, assault and battery, assault or assault and battery with intent to kill or manslaughter and it shall appear upon the trial that the assault, assault and battery, assault or assault and battery with intent to kill or manslaughter shall have been committed with a deadly weapon of the character specified in § 16-23-460 carried concealed upon the person of the defendant so convicted the presiding judge shall, in addition to the punishment provided by law for such assault, assault and battery, assault or assault and battery with intent to kill or manslaughter, inflict further punishment upon the person so convicted by confinement in the Penitentiary for not less than three months nor more than twelve months, with or without hard labor, or a fine of not less than two hundred dollars or both fine and imprisonment, at the discretion of the judge.

S.C. CODE ANN. § 16-3-620 provided as follows:

"§ 16-3-620 Assault and battery with intent to kill.

> The crime of assault and battery with intent to kill shall be a felony in this State and any person convicted of such crime shall be punished by imprisonment not to exceed twenty years."

S.C. CODE ANN. § 16-23-460 provided in relevant part, for the forfeiture of "a dirk, slingshot, metal knuckles, razor or other deadly weapon usually used for the infliction of personal injury concealed upon his person. . . ."

In *State v. Campbell*, 287 S.C. 377, 379, 339 S.E. 2d 109 (Sup. Ct. 1985), the Supreme Court of South Carolina stated that "A deadly weapon is generally defined as 'any article, instrument or substance which is likely to produce death or great bodily harm'", quoting *State v. Sturdivant*, 304 N.C. 293, 283 S.E. 2d 719 (1981).

**41. South Dakota** - In 1984, S.D. CODIFIED LAWS § 22-18-1.1 (Michie 1987), proscribed "aggravated assault" as follows :

"Any person who:

> (1) Attempts to cause serious bodily injury to another, or causes such injury, under circumstances manifesting extreme indifference to the value of human life;
>
> (2) Attempts to cause or knowingly causes, bodily injury to another with a dangerous weapon;
>
> (3) Attempts to cause or knowingly causes any bodily injury to a law enforcement officer or other public officer engaged in the performance of his duties; or
>
> (4) Assaults another with intent to commit bodily injury which results in serious bodily injury;
>
> (5) Attempts by physical menace with a deadly weapon to put another in fear of imminent serious bodily harm. . . .

is guilty of aggravated assault. Aggravated assault is a Class 4 felony."

The term "serious bodily injury" was not defined by statute in 1984. In *State v. Janisch*, 290 N.W. 2d 473, 476 (1980), the Supreme Court of South Dakota held that the term "serious bodily injury" as referred to in the assault statute "is such injury as is grave and not trivial, and gives rise to apprehension of danger to life, health or limb." A statutory definition for "serious bodily injury" was added in 2005, and provided: "'Serious bodily injury,' such injury as is grave and not trivial, and gives rise to apprehension of danger to life, health, or limb." S.D. CODIFIED LAWS § 22-1-2(44.1) (2005). In 1984, the term "dangerous weapon" or "deadly weapon" was defined in S.D. CODIFIED LAWS § 22-1-2(9) (Michie 1987) as follows: "any firearm, knife or device, instrument, material or substance, whether animate or inanimate, which is calculated or designed to inflict death or serious bodily harm, or by the manner in which it is used is likely to inflict death or serious bodily harm."

**42.    Tennessee** - The Tennessee Code punished "aggravated assault." The aggravated assault statute was amended in 1984. The 1984 amendment added subsection (b)( 5) to the statute. TENN. CODE ANN. § 39-2-101 stated as follows:

"Aggravated Assault – (a) As used in this section, unless the context otherwise requires:

> (1) "Bodily injury" includes a cut, abrasion, bruise, burn, or disfigurement; physical pain; illness or impairment of the function of a bodily member, organ, or mental faculty;
>
> (2) "Serious bodily injury" means bodily injury which involves a substantial risk of death, unconsciousness; extreme physical pain; protracted and obvious disfigurement; or protracted and obvious disfigurement; or protracted loss or impairment of the function of a bodily member or organ.

(b) Any person who:
> (1) Attempts to cause or causes serious bodily injury to another willfully, knowingly or recklessly under circumstances manifesting extreme indifference to the value of human life;
>
> (2) Attempts to cause or willfully or knowingly causes bodily injury to

another with a deadly weapon;

(3) Assaults another while displaying a deadly weapon or while the victim knows such person has a deadly weapon in his possession; or

(4) Being the parent or custodian of a child or the custodian of an adult, willfully or knowingly fails or refuses to protect such child or adult from an aggravated assault described in (1),(2), or (3) above;

(5) After having been enjoined or restrained, by a diversion order, condition of probation or other court order from initiating contact with a person, is twice convicted of committing a battery on such person; provided, however, the battery described in this subdivision shall not constitute aggravated battery unless the defendant had actual knowledge that he or she was prohibited by an injunction, court order or condition of probation from initiating contact with the victim of the battery is guilty of the offense of aggravated assault regardless of whether the victim is an adult, a child, or the assailant's spouse.

is guilty of the offense of aggravated assault regardless of whether the victim is an adult, a child, or the assailant's spouse.

(c) Aggravated assault shall be punished by not less than two (2) nor more than ten (10) years imprisonment."

The term "deadly weapon" was not defined by statute. In *State v. Bolin*, 678 S.W.2d 40, 41 (Sup. Ct. 1984), "deadly weapon" was defined as "any weapon or instrument which from the manner in which it is used or attempted to be used is likely to produce death or great bodily injury."

**43.** **Texas** The Texas Penal Code includes a provision punishing aggravated assault. As in effect in 1984, the aggravated assault statute in TEX. PENAL CODE ANN. § 22.02 (Vernon 1989), provided as follows:

"(a) A person commits an offense if the person commits assault as defined in Section 22.01 of this code and the person:

(1) causes serious bodily injury to another, including the person's spouse;

(2) causes bodily injury to a peace officer or a jailer or guard employed at a municipal or county jail or by the Texas Department of Corrections when the person knows or has been informed the person assaulted is a peace officer, jailer, or guard:

(A) while the peace officer, jailer, or guard is lawfully discharging an official duty;  or

(B) in retaliation for or on account of an exercise of official power or performance of an official duty as a peace officer, jailer, or guard;  or

(3) causes bodily injury to a participant in a court proceeding when the person knows or has been informed the person assaulted is a participant in a court proceeding:

(A) while the injured person is lawfully discharging an official duty;  or

(B) in retaliation for or on account of the injured person's having exercised an official power or performed an official duty as a participant in a court proceeding;  or

(4) uses a deadly weapon.

(b) The actor is presumed to have known the person assaulted was a peace officer if he was wearing a distinctive uniform indicating his employment as a peace officer.

(c) An offense under this section is a felony of the third degree. . . ."

The terms "bodily injury," "deadly weapon," and "serious bodily injury" were defined by statute. As in effect in 1984, TEX. PENAL CODE ANN. § 1.07 stated as follows:

"(a) In this code: . . .

(7) 'Bodily injury' means physical pain, illness, or any impairment of physical condition. . . .

(11) 'Deadly weapon' means:

(A) a firearm or anything manifestly designed, made, or adapted for the purpose of inflicting death or serious bodily injury; or

(B) anything that in the manner of its use or intended use is capable of causing death or serious bodily injury. . .

(34) 'Serious bodily injury' means bodily injury that creates a substantial risk of death or that causes death, serious permanent disfigurement, or protracted loss or impairment of the function of any bodily member or organ. . . .

(b) The definition of a term in this code applies to each grammatical variation of the term."

44. **Utah** - As in effect in 1984, UTAH CODE ANN. 1953 § 76-5-103 (1988) prohibited "aggravated assault" as follows:

"(1) A person commits aggravated assault if he commits assault as defined in Section 76-5-102 and:

(a) He intentionally causes serious bodily injury to another; or

(b) He uses a deadly weapon or such means or force likely to produce death or serious bodily injury.

(2) Aggravated assault is a felony of the third degree."

In 1984, UTAH CODE ANN. 1953 § 76-1-601, defined the terms "bodily injury," "serious bodily injury," and "deadly or dangerous weapon" as follows:

> "(8) 'Bodily injury' means physical pain, illness, or any impairment of physical condition.
>
> (9) 'Serious bodily injury' means bodily injury that creates or causes serious permanent disfigurement, protracted loss or impairment of the function of any bodily member or organ or creates a substantial risk of death.
>
> (10) 'Deadly or dangerous weapon' means anything that in the manner of its use or intended use is likely to cause death or serious bodily injury."

**45.     Vermont** - The Vermont aggravated assault statute was enacted and became effective in 1971. VT. STAT. ANN. tit. 13, § 1024 (1989) provided as follows:

"(a) A person is guilty of aggravated assault if he:

> (1) attempts to cause serious bodily injury to another, or causes such injury purposely, knowingly or recklessly under circumstances manifesting extreme indifference to the value of human life; or
>
> (2) attempts to cause or purposely or knowingly causes bodily injury to another with a deadly weapon; or
>
> (3) for a purpose other than lawful medical or therapeutic treatment, he intentionally causes stupor, unconsciousness, or other physical or mental impairment or injury to another person by administering to him, without his consent, a drug, substance or preparation capable of producing the intended harm; or
>
> (4) with intent to prevent a law enforcement officer former performing a lawful duty, he causes physical injury to any person.

(b) A person found guilty of violating a provision of subsection (a)(1) or (2) of this section shall be imprisoned for not more than 15 years or fined not more than $10,000.00 or both.

(c) A person found guilty of violating a provision of subsection (a)(3) or (4) of this section shall be imprisoned for not more than five years or fined not more than $5,000.00 or both."

The terms "bodily injury," "serious bodily injury" and "deadly weapon" are defined in VT. STAT. ANN. tit. 13, § 1021(1989). This statute was enacted in 1972. As in effect in 1984, these terms were defined as follows:

"For the purpose of this subchapter:

(1) 'Bodily injury' means physical pain, illness or any impairment of physical condition;

(2) 'Serious bodily injury' means bodily injury which creates a substantial risk of death or which causes serious, permanent disfigurement, or protracted loss or impairment of the function of any bodily member or organ;

(3) 'Deadly weapon' means any firearm, or other weapon, device, instrument, material or substance, whether animate or inanimate which in the manner it is used or is intended to be used is known to be capable of producing death or serious bodily injury."

**46.** **Virginia** - Apparently, in 1984, Virginia did not have an aggravated assault or simple assault statute that is substantially similar to the MPC's definition of assault resulting in serious bodily injury. In Virginia, assault was an offense at common law and was a misdemeanor. "An assault is any attempt or offer with force or violence to do a corporeal hurt to another, whether from malice or wantonness, as by striking at him in a threatening or insulting manner, or with such other circumstances as denote at the time an intention, coupled with a present ability, of actual violence against his person, as by pointing a weapon at him when he is within reach of it. When the injury is actually inflicted it amounts to a battery, which includes an assault, and this, however small it maybe, as by spitting in a man's face, or in any way touching him in anger, without lawful provocation." *Hardy and Curry v. Commonwealth*, 17 Gratt. 592, 58 Va. 592 (1867). "An assault . . . is an attempt or offer with force and violence to do some bodily hurt to another, whether from wantonness or malice, by means calculated to produce the end if carried into execution, as by striking at him with a stick or other weapon, or without a weapon, though he be not struck, or even by raising up the arm or cane in a menacing manner . . . or any similar act, accompanied with circumstances denoting an intention, coupled with a present ability, of using actual violence against the person of another." *Berkeley v. Commonwealth*, 88 Va. 1017, 14 S.E. 916 (1892).

VA. CODE ANN. § 18.2-51 (Michie 1982) prohibits shooting, stabbing, etc., with intent to maim, kill, etc. This statute was enacted in 1950 with amendments in 1960 and 1975. As in effect in 1984, it stated as follows:

> "If any person maliciously shoot, stab, cut, or wound any person or by any means cause him bodily injury, with the intent to maim, disfigure, disable, or kill, he shall, except where it is otherwise provided, be guilty of a Class 3 felony. If such act be done unlawfully but not maliciously, with the intent aforesaid, the offender shall be guilty of a Class 6 felony."

VA. CODE ANN. § 18.2-54 (Michie 1982) was enacted in 1950 and, as in effect in 1984, provided that

> "On any indictment for maliciously shooting, stabbing, cutting or wounding a person or by any means causing him bodily injury, with intent to maim, disfigure, disable or kill him, or of causing bodily injury by means of any acid, lye or other caustic substance or agent, the jury or the court trying the case without a jury may

find the accused not guilty of the offense charged but guilty of unlawfully doing such act with the intent aforesaid, or of assault and battery if the evidence warrants."

Prior to the enactment of Section 18.2-54, the Supreme Court of Virginia held that assault was a common law offense that was punishable as a misdemeanor but that assault was not punishable under the provisions of the maiming statute. *Jones v. Commonwealth*, 184 Va. 679, 36 S.E. 2d 571 (1946).

**47.    Washington** - The Criminal Code in Washington was revised in 1986. The former assault in the first degree statute, WASH. REV. CODE § 9A.36.010 (1977), is set forth below. The text of these assault statutes were also cited in *State v. Adlington-Kelly*, 95 Wash.2d 917 (1981).

The former assault in the first degree statute stated as follows:

"(1) Every person, who with intent to kill a human being, or to commit a felony upon the person or property of the one assaulted, or of another, shall be guilty of assault in the first degree when he:
> (a) Shall assault another with a firearm or any deadly weapon or by any force or means likely to produce death; or
> (b) Shall administer to or cause to be taken by another, poison or any other destructive or noxious thing so as to endanger the life of another person.

(2) Assault in the first degree is a class A felony."

The former assault in the second degree was set forth at WASH. REV. CODE § 9A.26.020 (1977) as follows:

"(1) Every person who, under circumstances not amounting to assault in the first degree shall be guilty of assault in the second degree when he:

(a) With intent to injure, shall unlawfully administer to or cause to be taken by another, poison or any other destructive or noxious thing, or any drug or medicine the use of which is dangerous to life or health; or

(b) Shall knowingly inflict grievous bodily harm upon another with or without a weapon; or

(c) Shall knowingly assault another with a weapon or other instrument or thing likely to produce bodily harm; or

(d) shall knowingly assault another with intent to commit a felony.

(2) Assault in the second degree is a class B felony."

As in effect in 1984, the terms "deadly weapon" and "bodily injury" were defined in WASH. REV. CODE § 9A.04.110 (1977) as follows:

"(4) 'Bodily injury' or 'physical injury' means physical pain, illness, or an impairment of physical condition. . . .

(6) 'Deadly weapon' means any explosive or loaded or unloaded firearm, and shall include any other weapon, device, instrument, article, or substance, include a "vehicle" as defined in this section, which, under the circumstances in which it is used, attempted to be used, or threatened to be used, is readily capable of causing death or serious bodily injury."

The term "grievous bodily injury" is "any serious hurt or injury or injury that is seriously painful or hard to bear. It need not be a permanent injury." *State v. Osborne*, 669 P.2d 905, 910 (1983). In *State v. Salinas*, 549 P.2d 712, 719 (1976), the Supreme Court of Washington found the following jury instruction to adequately state the law. "You are instructed that the words `grievous bodily harm' include a hurt or injury calculated to interfere with the health or comfort of the person injured; it need not necessarily be an injury of a permanent character. By `grievous' is meant atrocious, aggravating, harmful, painful, hard to bear, serious in nature."

**48.     West Virginia** - The West Virginia Code prohibits malicious or unlawful assault. Prior to 1984, this statute was last amended in 1978. As in effect in 1984, W. VA. CODE, § 61-2-9 (1987) prohibited the following:

> "(a) If any person maliciously shoot, stab, cut or wound any person, or by any means cause him bodily injury with intent to maim, disfigure, disable or kill, he shall, except where it is otherwise provided, be guilty of a felony, and, upon conviction, shall be punished by confinement in the penitentiary not less than two nor more than ten years. If such act be done unlawfully, but not maliciously, with the intent aforesaid, the offender shall be guilty of a felony, and, upon conviction, shall, in the discretion of the court, either be confined in the penitentiary not less than one nor more than five years, or be confined in jail not exceeding twelve months and fined not exceeding five hundred dollars.
>
> (b) Assault. -- If any person unlawfully attempts to commit a violent injury to the person of another or unlawfully commits an act which places another in reasonable apprehension of immediately receiving a violent injury, he shall be guilty of a misdemeanor, and, upon conviction, shall be confined in jail for not more than six months, or fined not more than one hundred dollars, or both such fine and imprisonment.
>
> (c) Battery. -- If any person unlawfully and intentionally makes physical contact of an insulting or provoking nature with the person of another or unlawfully and intentionally causes physical harm to another person, he shall be guilty of a misdemeanor, and, upon conviction, shall be confined in jail for not more than twelve months, or fined not more than five hundred dollars, or both such fine and imprisonment."

**49.     Wisconsin** - In 1984, Wisconsin prohibited aggravated battery as follows:

> "(1) Whoever causes bodily harm to another by an act done with intent to cause bodily harm to that person or another without the consent of the person so harmed is guilty of a Class A misdemeanor.
>
> (1m) Whoever causes great bodily harm to another by an act done with intent to cause bodily harm to that person or another without the consent of the person so harmed is guilty of a Class E felony.

(2) Whoever causes great bodily harm to another by an act done with intent to cause great bodily harm to that person or another with or without the consent of the person so harmed is guilty of a Class C felony.

(3) Whoever intentionally causes bodily harm to another by conduct which creates a high probability of great bodily harm is guilty of a Class E felony. A rebuttable presumption of conduct creating a high probability of great bodily harm arises:

>(a) If the person harmed is 62 years of age or older; or

>(b) If the person harmed has a physical disability, whether congenital or acquired by accident, injury or disease, which is discernible by an ordinary person viewing the physically disabled person."

WIS. STAT. ANN. § 940.19 (1989).

WIS. STAT. § 939.63 provided for an enhanced penalty "[i]f a person commits a crime while possessing, using or threatening to use a dangerous weapon." WIS. STAT. § 941.20 proscribed "[e]ndangering safety by use of a dangerous weapon."

The terms "bodily harm," "dangerous weapon," and "great bodily harm" were defined in WIS. STAT. § 939.22 (1983-1984). As in effect in October 1984, this provision stated as follows:

>"(4) 'Bodily harm' means physical pain or injury, illness, or any impairment of physical condition. . . .

>(10) 'Dangerous weapon' means any firearm, whether loaded or unloaded; any device designed as a weapon and capable of producing death or great bodily harm; any electric weapon, as defined in § 941.295(4); or any other device or instrumentality which, in the manner it is used or intended to be used, is calculated or likely to produce death or great bodily harm. . . .

(14) 'Great bodily harm' means bodily injury which creates a high probability of death, or which causes serious permanent disfigurement, or which causes a permanent or protracted loss or impairment of the function of any bodily member or organ or other serious bodily injury."

**50.     Wyoming -**     Wyoming prohibits aggravated assault and battery.    This statute, WYO. STAT. ANN. § 6-2-502 (Michie 1988), was amended in 1984 with an effective date of June 5, 1984.  As amended, the statute provided in relevant part as follows:

"(a) A person is guilty of aggravated assault and battery if he:

(i) Causes serious bodily injury to another intentionally, knowingly or recklessly under circumstances manifesting extreme indifference to the value of human life;

(ii) Attempts to cause, or intentionally or knowingly causes bodily injury to another with a deadly weapon;

(iii) Threatens to use a drawn deadly weapon on another unless reasonably necessary in defense of his person, property or abode or to prevent serious bodily injury to another; or

(b) Aggravated assault and battery is a felony punishable by imprisonment for not more than ten (10) years."

WYO. STAT. ANN. § 6-1-104 (Michie 1988), defined the terms "bodily injury," "deadly weapon," and "serious bodily injury" as follows:

"(a) As used in W.S. 6-1-101 through 6-10-203 unless otherwise defined:

(I) 'Bodily injury' means physical pain, illness or any impairment of physical condition; . . .

(iv) 'Deadly weapon' means but is not limited to a firearm, explosive or incendiary material, motorized vehicle, an animal or other device, instrument, material or substance, which in the manner it is used or is intended to be used is reasonably capable of producing death or serious bodily injury; . . .

(x) 'Serious bodily injury' means bodily injury which creates a substantial risk of death or which causes miscarriage, severe disfigurement or protracted loss or impairment of the function of any bodily member or organ."

# APPENDIX D
# Model Section 1959 Indictments

January 2004

**Exhibit C**

**MODEL "Stand-alone" 18 U.S.C. § 1959 Counts**: There are four sample variations to the first count of this five-count indictment. The remaining counts incorporate and reallege portions of the Count One. Sample I includes enterprise allegations similar to those used in violent gang RICO indictments/informations. This form of pleading is especially effective when the prosecutor wishes to get more of his or her story before the court. The remaining samples contain varying degrees of information. While OCRS will, in appropriate circumstances, approve a "bare bones" count, each 1959 count must contain at least three paragraphs: the "enterprise" paragraph, a paragraph setting out the racketeering activity that the enterprise "engaged in," and the "charging" paragraph.

If the proposed charging instrument contains a 1959 murder offense that occurred on or after September 13, 1994, that offense may be a capital offense requiring compliance with the Attorney General's Protocol for Capital Offenses. If you have questions regarding such an offense, please contact OCRS.

If you have questions regarding the preparation of your indictment/information or your 1959 prosecutive memorandum, please contact OCRS' Assistant Chief Amy Chang Lee (202/514-6882) or any member of the RICO Unit (202/514-1214) or consult the U.S. Attorney's manual at 9-110.800 through 9-110.816.

**COUNT ONE, SAMPLE I**

UNITED STATES DISTRICT COURT
DISTRICT OF _____

- - - - - - - - - - - - - - - - - - - - - - - - - - - -X

UNITED STATES OF AMERICA  :

    -v.-  :

                                                 <u>INDICTMENT/INFORMATION</u>

                      :

                      :

        Defendant(s).  :

- - - - - - - - - - - - - - - - - - - - - - - - - - - -X

<u>Violent Crimes In Aid Of Racketeering Activity</u>

<u>COUNT ONE</u>

<u>Conspiracy to Murder (name of victim)</u>

The [Grand Jury or United States Attorney] charges:

<u>The Enterprise</u>

1. At various times relevant to this Indictment/Information, [name of defendant(s)], the defendant, and others known and unknown, were members and associates of the [name of enterprise], a criminal organization whose members and associates engaged in acts of violence, including murder, attempted murder, robbery, extortion and narcotics distribution, and which operated principally in _____ .

2. This criminal organization, including its leadership, membership, and associates, constituted an enterprise as defined in Title 18, United States Code, Section 1959(b)(2),

that is, a group of individuals associated in fact that engaged in, and the activities of which affected, interstate and foreign [where applicable] commerce. The enterprise constituted an ongoing organization whose members functioned as a continuing unit for a common purpose of achieving the objectives of the enterprise.

<u>Purposes of the Enterprise</u>

3. The purposes of the enterprise included the following:

a. Enriching the members and associates of the enterprise through, among other things, murder, extortion, robbery, and distribution of narcotics.

b. Preserving and protecting the power, territory and profits of the enterprise through the use of intimidation, violence, threats of violence, assaults and murder.

c. Promoting and enhancing the enterprise and its members' and associates' activities.

d. Keeping victims in fear of the enterprise and in fear of its members and associates through threats of violence and violence.

## Means and Methods of the Enterprise

4. Among the means and methods by which the defendants and their associates conducted and participated in the conduct of the affairs of the enterprise were the following:

    a. Members of the enterprise and their associates used, attempted to use, and conspired to use extortion, which affected interstate commerce.

    b. Members of the enterprise and their associates committed, attempted and threatened to commit acts of violence, including murder, robbery and extortion, to protect and expand the enterprise's criminal operations.

    c. Members of the enterprise and their associates promoted a climate of fear through violence and threats of violence.

    d. Members of the enterprise and their associates used and threatened to use physical violence against various individuals.

    e. Members of the enterprise and their associates trafficked in heroin.

5. The above-described enterprise, through its members and associates, engaged in racketeering activity as defined in Title 18, United States Code, Sections 1959(b)(1) and 1961(1), namely, acts involving [murder, etc.] in violation of [name of

state(s) law with statutory citation]¹ and narcotics trafficking in violation of Title 21, United States Code, Sections 841(applicable subsections) and 846,² and acts indictable under Sections 1503 (obstruction of justice) and 1951 (extortion), of Title 18, United States Code.

      6.    In or about the spring of      , in the District of   [state]   , as consideration for the receipt of, and as consideration for a promise and an agreement to pay,

---

[1] Generally, OCRS no longer requires inclusion of a specific state citation in *this* paragraph of the 1959 count. See 18 U.S.C. § 1961(1)(A) specifying certain state offenses that may be charged as racketeering activity if, among other things, the alleged state offense is "an act involving" one of the enumerated state offenses. Therefore, alleging racketeering activity violative of a single statutory section or sub-section may have the unintended effect of restricting racketeering activity to that single statutory violation. For example, state X proscribes every degree of murder as a separate, discrete statutory violation. Alleging murder as a violation of any one statute in such a state would limit proof of the enterprise's racketeering activity involving murder to that one degree of murder, when in fact the evidence supports enterprise activity involving various degrees of murder.

[2] Alternatively, use the language in 1961(1)(D): offenses involving the felonious manufacture, importation, receiving, concealment, buying, selling, or otherwise dealing in controlled substances or listed chemicals, in violation of (or indictable under) Title 21, United States Code, Sections 841(applicable subsections) and 846.

anything [optional: a thing] of pecuniary[3] value from the [name of enterprise], and for the purpose of gaining

entrance to and maintaining and increasing their positions in the [name of enterprise], an enterprise engaged in racketeering activity,                                                                                     , the defendant, and others known and unknown, unlawfully, and knowingly conspired to murder **[name of victim]**, in violation of [state law/penal code, etc. and statutory cite].[4]

(Title 18, United States Code, Sections 1959(a)(5))
or All in violation of Title 18, United States Code, Section 1959(a)(5).

---

[3]We recommend charging both 1959 purposes/motives (pecuniary gain and the gaining, maintaining, increasing motive). <u>See</u> <u>United States v. Thai</u>, 29 F.3d 785 (2d Cir. 1994), where the court rejected the government's argument that the defendant's acts were to maintain and increase his position in the enterprise in which he was a leader because the only evidence (unexpectedly) of motive was that the defendant committed the crime only because he was offered $10,000 to do so.

[4] If overt acts are required to establish an element of the underlying offense, they must be proven at trial. The jury must be instructed on all elements, including the necessity of proving overt acts. In such cases, OCRS recommends pleading overt acts. Each overt act must be limited to a single, discrete act or event free of conclusions, legal or otherwise.

**SAMPLE II**

```
UNITED STATES DISTRICT COURT
DISTRICT OF _____
- - - - - - - - - - - - - - - - - - - - - - - - - - - X

UNITED STATES OF AMERICA       :

        -v.-                   :
                                         INDICTMENT/INFORMATION
                               :

                               :
         Defendant(s).         :
- - - - - - - - - - - - - - - - - - - - - - - - - - - X
```

<u>Violent Crimes In Aid Of Racketeering Activity</u>

<u>COUNT ONE</u>

<u>Conspiracy to Murder (name of victim)</u>

The [Grand Jury or United States Attorney] further charges:

At all times relevant to this [Indictment or Information]:

1. The defendant(s) [name(s)], together with other persons, known and unknown, were members and associates of a criminal organization, that is, an enterprise, as defined in Title 18, United States Code, Section 1959(b)(2), namely the [name of enterprise], a group of individuals associated in fact that was engaged in, and the activities of which affected, interstate and foreign commerce. The enterprise constituted an ongoing organization whose members functioned as a continuing unit for a common purpose of achieving the objectives of the enterprise.

2. The defendant [ name ] was the leader [lieutenant, enforcer, etc.] of the [name of enterprise]. Defendant [or name of defendant] controlled the membership and discipline of the [name of enterprise].

3. The primary goal of [A purpose of, etc.] the [name of enterprise] was to [e.g.] earn money for its members through the sale of retail quantities of heroin, cocaine, etc., principally in the [geographical location--streets, etc.], extortion, robbery, whatever. Members of the [name of enterprise] made regular purchases of heroin/cocaine, etc. and packaged the heroin/cocaine, etc. for sale at [location], the [name of enterprise]'s designation location, or "spot."

4. Members and associates of the enterprise used violence, which at times included murder, to promote and protect the enterprise's drug trafficking enterprise operation/business [extortion business, etc.]; to discipline enterprise workers who had violated enterprise rules/code; to punish enterprise workers who had fallen into disfavor; to punish enterprise workers who had been disloyal; to retaliate against rival gangs; and to promote and enhance its prestige, reputation and position with respect to others [the community, etc.].

5. The above-described enterprise, through its members and associates, engaged in racketeering activity as defined in Title 18, United States Code, Sections 1959(b)(1) and 1961(1),

namely, acts involving [murder, etc.] in violation of [name of state(s) law with statutory citation]⁵ and narcotics trafficking in violation of Title 21, United States Code, Sections 841(applicable subsections) and 846,⁶ and acts indictable under Sections 1503 (obstruction of justice) and 1951 (extortion), of Title 18, United States Code.

6. In or about the spring of          , in the District of    [state]   , as consideration for the receipt of, and as consideration for a promise and an agreement to pay, anything [a thing] of pecuniary⁷ value from the [name of

---

⁵Generally, OCRS no longer requires inclusion of a specific state citation in **this** paragraph of the 1959 count. See 18 U.S.C. § 1961(1)(A) specifying certain state offenses that may be charged as racketeering activity if, among other things, the alleged state offense is "an act involving" one of the enumerated state offenses. Therefore, alleging racketeering activity violative of a single statutory section or sub-section may have the unintended effect of restricting racketeering activity to that single statutory violation. For example, state X proscribes every degree of murder as a separate, discrete statutory violation. Alleging murder as a violation of any one statute in such a state would limit proof of the enterprise's racketeering activity involving murder to that one degree of murder, when in fact the evidence supports enterprise activity involving various degrees of murder.

⁶Alternatively, use the language in 1961(1)(D): offenses involving the felonious manufacture, importation, receiving, concealment, buying, selling, or otherwise dealing in controlled substances or listed chemicals, in violation of (or indictable under)] Title 21, United States Code, Sections 841(applicable subsections) and 846.

⁷We recommend charging both 1959 purposes/motives (pecuniary gain and the gaining, maintaining, increasing motive). See United States v. Thai, 29 F.3d 785 (2d Cir. 1994), where the court rejected the government's argument that the defendant's acts were
(continued...)

enterprise], and for the purpose of gaining entrance to and maintaining and increasing their positions in the [name of enterprise], an enterprise engaged in racketeering activity,

, the defendant, and others known and unknown, unlawfully, and knowingly conspired to murder **[name of victim]**, in violation of [state law/penal code, etc. and statutory cite].

(Title 18, United States Code, Sections 1959(a)(5))
or All in violation of Title 18, United States Code, Section 1959(a)(5).

---

[7](...continued)
to maintain and increase his position in the enterprise in which he was a leader because the only evidence (unexpectedly) of motive was that the defendant committed the crime only because he was offered $10,000 to do so.

**COUNT 1, SAMPLE III**

UNITED STATES DISTRICT COURT
DISTRICT OF _____

- - - - - - - - - - - - - - - - - - - - - - - - - - - - - - -X

UNITED STATES OF AMERICA      :

     -v.-      :

                                        INDICTMENT/INFORMATION
                        :

                        :
     Defendant(s).      :

- - - - - - - - - - - - - - - - - - - - - - - - - - - - - -X

<u>Violent Crimes In Aid Of Racketeering Activity</u>

<u>COUNT ONE</u>

<u>Conspiracy to Murder (name of victim)</u>

The [Grand Jury or United States Attorney] charges:

At all times relevant to this [Indictment or Information]:

1.  The defendant(s) [name(s)], together with other persons, known and unknown, were members and associates of a criminal organization, that is, an enterprise, as defined in Title 18, United States Code, Section 1959(b)(2), namely the [name of enterprise], a group of individuals associated in fact that engaged in, and the activities of which affected, interstate and foreign commerce. The enterprise constituted an ongoing organization whose members functioned as a continuing unit for a common purpose of achieving the objectives of the enterprise. A

primary purpose of the enterprise was to earn money for its members and associates through [e.g., extortion of local merchants, etc.].

2.   The above-described enterprise, through its members and associates, engaged in racketeering activity as defined in Title 18, United States Code, Sections 1959(b)(1) and 1961(1), namely, acts involving [murder, etc.] in violation of [name of state(s)] law [statutory cite(s)][8] and narcotics trafficking in violation of Title 21, United States Code, Sections 841 (can also add applicable subsections) and 846,[9] and acts indictable under Sections 1503 (obstruction of justice) and 1951 (extortion), of Title 18, United States Code.

3.   In or about the spring of _____, in the District of [state], as consideration for the receipt of,

---

[8]Generally, OCRS no longer requires inclusion of a specific state citation in **this** paragraph of the 1959 count. See 18 U.S.C. § 1961(1)(A) specifying certain state offenses that may be charged as racketeering activity if, among other things, the alleged state offense is "an act involving" one of the enumerated state offenses. Therefore, alleging racketeering activity violative of a single statutory section or sub-section may have the unintended effect of restricting racketeering activity to that single statutory violation. For example, state X proscribes every degree of murder as a separate, discrete statutory violation. Alleging murder as a violation of any one statute in such a state would limit proof of the enterprise's racketeering activity involving murder to that one degree of murder, when in fact the evidence supports enterprise activity involving various degrees of murder.

[9]Alternatively, use the language in 1961(1)(D): offenses involving the felonious manufacture, importation, receiving, concealment, buying, selling, or otherwise dealing in controlled substances or listed chemicals, in violation of (or indictable under) Title 21, United States Code, Sections 841(applicable subsections) and 846.

and as consideration for a promise and an agreement to pay, anything [optional: a thing] of pecuniary[10] value from the [name of enterprise], and for the purpose of gaining entrance to and maintaining and increasing their positions in the [name of enterprise], an enterprise engaged in racketeering activity,

, the defendant, and others known and unknown, unlawfully, and knowingly conspired to murder **[name of victim]**, in violation of [state law/penal code, etc. and statutory cite].

(Title 18, United States Code, Sections 1959(a)(5))
or All in violation of Title 18, United States Code, Section 1959(a)(5).

---

[10] We recommend charging both 1959 purposes/motives (pecuniary gain and the gaining, maintaining, increasing motive). See <u>United States v. Thai</u>, 29 F.3d 785 (2d Cir. 1994), where the court rejected the government's argument that the defendant's acts were to maintain and increase his position in the enterprise in which he was a leader because the only evidence (unexpectedly) of motive was that the defendant committed the crime only because he was offered $10,000 to do so.

COUNT 1, SAMPLE IV

UNITED STATES DISTRICT COURT
DISTRICT OF _____

- - - - - - - - - - - - - - - - - - - - - - - - - - - - -X

UNITED STATES OF AMERICA          :

    -v.-                              :

                                                         INDICTMENT/INFORMATION
                                :

                                :

        Defendant(s).         :

- - - - - - - - - - - - - - - - - - - - - - - - - - - - -X

<u>Violent Crimes In Aid Of Racketeering Activity</u>

<u>COUNT ONE</u>

<u>Conspiracy to Murder (name of victim)</u>

The [Grand Jury or United States Attorney] charges:

At all times relevant [pertinent, material] to this indictment [information]:

    1.   The defendant(s) [add names], together with other persons, known and unknown, were members and associates of a criminal organization whose members and associates engaged in [list criminal activities, e.g, acts of violence, including murder, kidnapping and robbery, extortion, narcotics trafficking, etc. [no statutory cites required here].

    2.   This criminal organization, including its leadership, membership, and associates, constituted an enterprise

as defined in Title 18, United States Code, Section 1959(b)(2), that is, a group of individuals associated in fact that engaged in, and the activities of which affected, interstate and foreign [where applicable] commerce. The enterprise constituted an ongoing organization whose members functioned as a continuing unit for a common purpose of achieving the objectives of the enterprise.

3. The above-described enterprise, through its members and associates, engaged in racketeering activity as defined in Title 18, United States Code, Sections 1959(b)(1) and 1961(1), namely, acts involving [murder, etc.] in violation of [name of state(s)] law [statutory cite(s)][11] and narcotics trafficking in violation of Title 21, United States Code, Sections 841(applicable subsections) and 846,[12] and acts indictable under Sections 1503

---

[11]Generally, OCRS no longer requires inclusion of a specific state citation in **this** paragraph of the 1959 count. See 18 U.S.C. § 1961(1)(A) specifying certain state offenses that may be charged as racketeering activity if, among other things, the alleged state offense is "an act involving" one of the enumerated state offenses. Therefore, alleging racketeering activity violative of a single statutory section or sub-section may have the unintended effect of restricting racketeering activity to that single statutory violation. For example, state X proscribes every degree of murder as a separate, discrete statutory violation. Alleging murder as a violation of any one statute in such a state would limit proof of the enterprise's racketeering activity involving murder to that one degree of murder, when in fact the evidence supports enterprise activity involving various degrees of murder.

[12]Alternatively, use the language in 1961(1)(D): offenses involving the felonious manufacture, importation, receiving, concealment, buying, selling, or otherwise dealing in controlled substances or listed chemicals, in violation of (or indictable under) Title 21, United States Code, Sections 841(applicable
(continued...)

(obstruction of justice) and 1951 (extortion), of Title 18, United States Code.

4. In or about the spring of         , in the District of   [state]   , as consideration for the receipt of, and as consideration for a promise and an agreement to pay, anything [optional: a thing] of pecuniary[13] value from the [name of enterprise], and for the purpose of gaining entrance to and maintaining and increasing their positions in the [name of enterprise], an enterprise engaged in racketeering activity,                                      , the defendant, and others known and unknown, unlawfully, and knowingly conspired to murder **[name of victim]**, in violation of [state law/penal code, etc. and statutory cite].

(Title 18, United States Code, Sections 1959(a)(5))
or All in violation of  Title 18, United States Code, Section 1959(a)(5).

---

[12](...continued)
subsections) and 846.

[13]We recommend charging both 1959 purposes/motives (pecuniary gain and the gaining, maintaining, increasing motive). See United States v. Thai, 29 F.3d 785 (2d Cir. 1994), where the court rejected the government's argument that the defendant's acts were to maintain and increase his position in the enterprise in which he was a leader because the only evidence (unexpectedly) of motive was that the defendant committed the crime only because he was offered $10,000 to do so.

## COUNT TWO

### Murder of [name of victim]

The [Grand Jury or the United States Attorney] further charges:

1. Paragraphs _____ of Count One [i.e., the enterprise paragraphs and the "engaged in racketeering activity" paragraph--usually all the paragraphs of the first Section 1959 charge except the charging paragraph] of this Indictment/Information are realleged and incorporated by reference as though fully set forth herein.

2. In or about _____, in the _____ District of [state] _____, as consideration for the receipt of, and as consideration for a promise and agreement to pay, anything of pecuniary value from the [enterprise name], and for the purpose of gaining entrance to and maintaining and increasing his position in the [enterprise name], an enterprise engaged in racketeering activity, [name of defendant], the defendant, unlawfully, and knowingly [e.g., murdered] [name of victim] in violation of [state law and citation] [Optional: ,that is, the defendant (add brief statement of facts or add brief statement of facts incorporating words of state statute)].

(Title 18, United States Code, Sections 1959(a)(1) and 2 [as appropriate].)

OR   All in violation of . . .[14]

---

[14]Note:  See 18 U.S.C. § 1959(a)(1), (2), (3), (4), (5), or (6) for appropriate offense, i.e., (1) murder or kidnaping; (2) maiming (rarely used/approved); (3) assault with a dangerous weapon or assault resulting in serious bodily injury; (4) threatening to commit a crime of violence; (5) attempting or conspiring to commit murder or kidnaping; and (6) attempting or conspiring to commit a crime involving maiming, assault with a dangerous weapon or an assault resulting in serious bodily injury.

## COUNT THREE

**Assault Resulting in Serious Bodily Injury upon [name of victim]**

The [Grand Jury or the United States Attorney] further charges:

1. Paragraphs _____ of Count One [i.e., the enterprise paragraphs and the engaged in racketeering activity paragraph of the first Section 1959 charge] of this Indictment/Information are realleged and incorporated by reference as though fully set forth herein.

2. In or about _____, in the _____ District of [state] _____, as consideration for the receipt of, and as consideration for a promise and agreement to pay, anything of pecuniary value from the [enterprise name], and for the purpose of gaining entrance to and maintaining and increasing his position in the [enterprise name], an enterprise engaged in racketeering activity, [name of defendant], the defendant, unlawfully, and knowingly assaulted, and aided and abetted an assault, resulting in serious bodily injury upon [name of victim, etc.] in violation of [state and cite].

(Title 18, United States Code, Sections 1959(a)(3) and 2 [as appropriate].)

or All in violation of . . .

## COUNT FOUR

**Assault with a Dangerous Weapon upon [name of victim]**

The United States Attorney further charges:

1. Paragraphs _____ of Count One [i.e., the enterprise paragraphs and the engaged in racketeering activity paragraph of the first Section 1959 charge] of this Indictment are realleged and incorporated by reference as though fully set forth herein.

2. In or about _____, in the _____ District of [state], as consideration for the receipt of, and as consideration for a promise and agreement to pay, anything of pecuniary value from the [enterprise name], and for the purpose of gaining entrance to and maintaining and increasing his position in the [enterprise name], an enterprise engaged in racketeering activity, [name of defendant], the defendant, unlawfully, [willfully,] and knowingly assaulted with a dangerous weapon [that is, identify weapon--optional] and aided and abetted the assault with a dangerous weapon of/against [name of victim, etc.] in violation of [state and cite].

(Title 18, United States Code, Sections 1959(a)(3) and 2 [as appropriate].)

or All in violation of . . .

## COUNT FIVE

**Conspiring to Commit An Assault with a Dangerous Weapon upon [name of victim]**

The [Grand Jury or the United States Attorney ] further charges:

1. Paragraphs _____ of Count One [i.e., the enterprise paragraphs and the engaged in racketeering activity paragraph of the first Section 1959 charge] of this Indictment are realleged and incorporated by reference as though fully set forth herein.

2. In or about _____, in the _____ District of [state] _____, as consideration for the receipt of, and as consideration for a promise and agreement to pay, anything of pecuniary value from the [enterprise name], and for the purpose of gaining entrance to and maintaining and increasing his position in the [enterprise name], an enterprise engaged in racketeering activity, [name of defendant], the defendant, unlawfully and knowingly conspired to commit an assault with a dangerous weapon [that is, identify weapon--optional] against [name of victim, etc.] in violation of [state and cite].

(Title 18, United States Code, Sections 1959(a)(6) .)

or All in violation of Section 1959(a)(6) of Title 18, United States Code.

## COUNT SIX

### Assault With a Dangerous Weapon Upon [name of victim] Resulting in Serious Bodily Injury

The [Grand Jury or the United States Attorney] further charges:

1. Paragraphs _____ of Count One [i.e., the enterprise paragraphs and the engaged in racketeering activity paragraph of the first Section 1959 charge] of this Indictment/Information are realleged and incorporated by reference as though fully set forth herein.

2. In or about _____, in the _____ District of [state] _____, as consideration for the receipt of, and as consideration for a promise and agreement to pay, anything of pecuniary value from the [enterprise name], and for the purpose of gaining entrance to and maintaining and increasing his position in the [enterprise name], an enterprise engaged in racketeering activity, [name of defendant], the defendant, unlawfully and knowingly committed an assault with a dangerous weapon resulting in the serious bodily injury of [name of victim], in violation of [state and cite], [optional: that is, the defendant forcibly stole jewels and cash from (name of victim) by the use of a firearm, and in the course of the robbery discharged his firearm, thereby causing serious bodily injury to (victim)].

(Title 18, United States Code, Sections 1959(a)(3) and 2 [as appropriate].)

or All in violation of . . .

## COUNT SEVEN

### Kidnaping of [name of victim]

The [Grand Jury or the United States Attorney] further charges:

1. Paragraphs _____ of Count One [i.e., the enterprise paragraphs and the engaged in racketeering activity paragraph of the first Section 1959 charge] of this Indictment/Information are realleged and incorporated by reference as though fully set forth herein.

2. In or about _____, in the _____ District of [state] _____, as consideration for the receipt of, and as consideration for a promise and agreement to pay, anything of pecuniary value from the [enterprise name], and for the purpose of gaining entrance to and maintaining and increasing his position in the [enterprise name], an enterprise engaged in racketeering activity, [name of defendant], the defendant, unlawfully, [willfully,] and knowingly kidnaped [name of victim], in violation of [state and cite], [optional: that is, the defendant (add brief statement of facts or add brief statement of facts incorporating words of state statute).

(Title 18, United States Code, Sections 1959(a)(1) and 2 [as appropriate].)

or All in violation of . . .

_____
United States Attorney

January 2004

**Exhibit A**

**Model Indictment/Information: 18 U.S.C. §§ 1962(c) and (d), 1959**
(Association in Fact Enterprise: Purposes, Manner/Means, Racketeering Acts, charging paragraph; RICO conspiracy; Section 1959 (Enterprise paragraph, Racketeering Activity paragraph, charging paragraph)). This outline/format is also applicable to non-violent RICOs. Please contact OCRS if you need copies of file-stamped RICO/1959 (or Section 1959 only) cases to use as "go-bys."

```
UNITED STATES DISTRICT COURT
         DISTRICT OF
- - - - - - - - - - - - - - - - -X
UNITED STATES OF AMERICA         :

       -v.-                      :      INDICTMENT/INFORMATION

                                 :

                                 :

         Defendant.              :
- - - - - - - - - - - - - - - - -X
```

COUNT ONE

The [Grand Jury or United States Attorney] charges:

The Enterprise

1. At various times relevant to this Indictment/Information, [name of defendant(s)], the defendant, and others known and unknown, were members and associates of the [name of enterprise], a criminal organization whose members and associates engaged in acts of violence, including murder,[1] attempted murder, robbery, extortion and narcotics distribution,

---

[1] If you propose charging any offense that could be charged as a capital offense under any federal statute, you must contact the Capital Case Unit of the Criminal Division as soon as possible.

and which operated principally in the (e.g., [ name of section] of [name of city]).

2. The [enterprise name], including its leadership, membership and associates [or members and associates], constituted an "enterprise," as defined by Title 18, United States Code, Section 1961(4) (hereinafter "the enterprise"), that is, a group of individuals associated in fact. The enterprise constituted an ongoing organization whose members functioned as a continuing unit for a common purpose of achieving the objectives of the enterprise. This enterprise was engaged in, and its activities affected,[2] interstate and foreign commerce.

## Purposes of the Enterprise

3. The purposes of the enterprise included the following:

a. Enriching the members and associates of the enterprise through, among other things, murder, extortion, robbery, the operation of illegal gambling businesses and distribution of narcotics.

b. Preserving and protecting the power, territory and profits of the enterprise through the use of intimidation, violence, threats of violence, assaults and murder.

c. Promoting and enhancing the enterprise and its

---

[2]Punctuation is statutory. See e.g., 18 U.S.C. § 1962(c) ("any enterprise engaged in, or the activities of which affect, interstate or foreign commerce").

members' and associates' activities.

d. Keeping victims in fear of the enterprise and in fear of its members and associates through threats of violence and violence.

<u>Roles of the Defendants</u> [3]

4. The defendants participated in the operation and management of the enterprise.

a. The defendant _____ was a leader of the enterprise who directed other members of the enterprise in carrying out unlawful and other activities in furtherance of the conduct of the enterprise's affairs.[4]

b. Under the direction of the leader [or leaders] of the enterprise, the defendants _____ participated in unlawful and other activities in furtherance of the conduct of the

---

[3] OCRS recommends that indictments also include allegations describing the organization and structure of the enterprise (whether hierarchical or lateral (e.g., a coalition) and its decision-making mechanism along with the enterprise's leadership and responsibilities attributed to the various positions in the enterprise. In addition, where there are multiple defendants, AUSAs should include this "Role of the Defendants" section. Especially in Ninth Circuit prosecutions, there should be a brief description of the organizational structure of the enterprise and allegations concerning each defendant's "operation and management" of the enterprise. See <u>Reves v. Ernst & Young</u>, 113 S. Ct. 1163 (1993).

[4] After this sentence, the indictment/information can also allege more specific information about the roles/positions of the leaders of the enterprise.

enterprise's affairs.[5]

## Means and Methods of the Enterprise

5. Among the means and methods by which the defendants and their associates conducted and participated in the conduct of the affairs of the enterprise were the following:

a. Members of the enterprise and their associates used, attempted to use, and conspired to use extortion, which affected interstate commerce.

b. Members of the enterprise and their associates committed, attempted and threatened to commit acts of violence, including murder, robbery and extortion, to protect and expand the enterprise's criminal operations.

c. Members of the enterprise and their associates promoted a climate of fear through violence and threats of violence.

d. Members of the enterprise and their associates used and threatened to use physical violence against various individuals.

e. Members of the enterprise and their associates trafficked in heroin.

---

[5] After this sentence, the indictment/information can also allege more specific information about the roles/positions of the lower-level members of the enterprise.

## The Racketeering Violation

6. From [approximately;, in or about         , through in or about      ; etc.]     until        , [with both dates being approximate and inclusive] in the           District of            and elsewhere,                                                        the defendant(s),                       together with others known and unknown [to the grand jury known and unknown, etc.], being persons employed by and associated with the [name of enterprise, or if no name, the enterprise] described above, [which was] an enterprise engaged in, and the activities of which affected, interstate and foreign **[where applies]** commerce, unlawfully, and knowingly conducted and participated, directly and indirectly, in the conduct of the affairs of that enterprise through a pattern of racketeering activity, that is, through the commission of [the following; the following acts; Racketeering Acts One through Five as set forth in paragraphs Seven through Eleven below].

## The Pattern of Racketeering Activity

7. The pattern of racketeering activity as defined in Title 18, United States Code, Sections 1961(1) and 1961(5), consisted of the following acts:

8. Racketeering Act One--
   Conspiracy To Murder [name of victim A]

On or about          , in the      District of       , [name of defendant(s)]      , the defendant, and others known and unknown, unlawfully and knowingly conspired to murder _____, a member of the [enterprise name], in violation of [state code cite & sections].[6]

---

[6] If overt acts are required to establish an element of the charged state offense, they must be proven at trial. The jury must be instructed on all elements, including the necessity of proving overt acts. In such cases, OCRS recommends pleading overt acts. Each overt act must be limited to a single, discrete act or event free of conclusions, legal or otherwise. In order to comply with *Apprendi*, all facts, including overt acts, necessary to establish an element of the charged offense must be pled where the racketeering act in question carries with it a life sentence, thus implicating RICO's increased maximum sentence.

9. Racketeering Act Two--
   Murder of [name of victim B]

On or about           , in the        District of         , [name of defendant]   , the defendant, and others known and unknown, unlawfully, intentionally and knowingly murdered[7]                , a member of the [enterprise name], in violation of [state code cite & sections, including, if appropriate, aiding and abetting statute].

10. Racketeering Act Three--
    Conspiracy To Murder, Attempted Murder of Victim C[8]

The defendant [defendants named below] committed the following acts, any one of which [either of which] alone constitutes the commission of Racketeering Act Three:

   a.  On approximately [In or about]         , in the         and             Districts of  [state(s)], [name of

---

[7]Pursuant to the Apprendi v. New Jersey, 530 U.S. 466 (2000), track the language of the state statute if the racketeering act is one that provides the basis for a life sentence under RICO.

[8]If the conspiracy to murder and the murder pertain to the same victim, the conspiracy and murder must be charged as alternative charges in the same act of racketeering ("sub-predicated"). If there is one conspiracy to kill several individuals, one act will consist of the conspiracy to murder sub-predicated with one murder and any attempts. In most cases, other murders (which were also objects of the conspiracy) may stand as separate acts of racketeering (one for each murder after the first sub-predicated murder). This sub-predication is required pursuant to OCRS' "single-episode" policy.

All sub-predicated acts must be preceded by the following: The defendant [the defendants named below] committed the following acts, any one of which [either of which] alone constitutes Racketeering Act [insert number]:

defendant(s)]                    , the defendant, and others known and unknown, unlawfully and knowingly conspired to murder [victim], in violation of [cite(s)].

b. On or about                    , in the District of [state],          [name of defendant(s)]          , the defendant, and others known and unknown, unlawfully, intentionally and knowingly attempted to murder an individual identified herein as "Victim #1, in violation of [state cites].

11. Racketeering Act Four--
Conspiracy to Distribute Heroin

From approximately     , through in or about       , both dates being approximate and inclusive, in the          District of            and elsewhere,

, the defendant, and others known and unknown, unlawfully, intentionally and knowingly combined, conspired, confederated and agreed together and with each other to distribute and possess with intent to distribute one kilogram and more of mixtures and substances containing detectable amounts of heroin[9] and thereby violated [OR contrary to] the narcotics laws of the United States, to wit, Title 21, United States Code, Sections 812, 841(a)(1) and 841(b)(1)(A), in violation of Title 21, United States Code, Section 846.   OR, e.g.,:

---

[9] Pursuant to Apprendi, specify the quantity of drugs if the racketeering act is one that provides the basis for a life sentence under RICO.

From approximately [in or about]          , until [up to and including, through in or about]          , both dates being approximate and inclusive, in the          District of          and elsewhere,                              ,the defendant, and others known and unknown, unlawfully, intentionally and knowingly combined, conspired, confederated and agreed together and with each other to [violate Title 21, United States Code, Sections 812, 841(a)(1) and 841(b)(1)(A)], that is, to distribute and possess with intent to distribute one kilogram and more of mixtures and substances containing detectable amounts of heroin, in violation of Title 21, United States Code, Section 846.

(Title 18, United States Code, Section 1962(c).)

[OR  All in violation of . . . , etc.]

NOTE: There is no overt act requirement for RICO conspiracy. United States v. Salinas, 522 U.S. 52, 63 (1997).[10]

## The Racketeering Conspiracy

### COUNT TWO

The Grand Jury further charges:

1. Paragraphs ___ through ___ in Count ___ [i.e., the enterprise (including its purpose and means and methods) or the substantive RICO count excluding the paragraphs setting forth the charging language] are hereby realleged and incorporated as if fully set forth herein. [The acts of racketeering can be incorporated here, or see below at asterisk.]

2. From [in or about and between _____ through _____], both dates being approximate and inclusive, within the _____ District(s) of _____ and elsewhere, the defendants (list the defendants), together with other persons known

---

[10] On December 2, 1997, the Supreme Court unanimously affirmed the Fifth Circuit's holding in United States v. Salinas, 522 U.S. 52 (1997), (case below, United States v. Marmolejo, 89 F.3d 1185 (5th Cir. 1996), resolving the conflict among the circuits concerning whether a RICO conspiracy defendant must have "agreed to personally commit" two acts of racketeering (the rule in the First, Second, and Tenth Circuits). The Court held that, to be found guilty of a conspiracy to commit a RICO violation, a defendant need not personally commit or agree to commit two predicate acts (two acts of racketeering). See 522 U.S. at 64 ("The RICO conspiracy statute, § 1962(d), broadened conspiracy coverage by omitting the requirement of an overt act; it did not, at the same time, work the radical change of requiring the Government to prove each conspirator agreed that he would be the one to commit two predicate acts").

and unknown, being persons employed by and associated with the __ _____, an enterprise, which engaged in, and the activities of which affected, interstate [and foreign, if it applies] commerce, knowingly, and intentionally conspired to violate 18 U.S.C. § 1962(c), that is, to conduct and participate, directly and indirectly, in the conduct of the affairs of that enterprise through a pattern of racketeering activity, as that term is defined by 18 U.S.C. § 1961(1) and (5). The pattern of racketeering activity through which the defendants agreed to conduct the affairs of the enterprise consisted of the acts set forth in paragraphs __ through __ of Count One of this Indictment, which are incorporated as if fully set forth herein* [or, acceptable in some circumstances: set forth below, etc.].

It was a [further] part of the conspiracy that the defendant agreed that a conspirator would commit at least two acts of racketeering activity in the conduct of the affairs of the enterprise.

All in violation of Title 18, United States Code, Section 1962(d).

## Violent Crimes In Aid Of Racketeering Activity
### COUNT THREE

Murder of _____

The [Grand Jury or United States Attorney] further charges:

1. At all times relevant to this [Indictment or Information], the [name of enterprise], as more fully described in Paragraphs One through Four of Count One of this Indictment/Information,[11] which are realleged and incorporated by reference[12] as though set forth fully herein, constituted an enterprise as defined in Title 18, United States Code, Section 1959(b)(2), namely the [name of enterprise], that is, a group of individuals associated in fact which was engaged in, and the activities of which affected, interstate and foreign commerce. The enterprise constituted an ongoing organization whose members functioned as a continuing unit for a common purpose of achieving the objectives of the enterprise.

2. At all times relevant to this [Indictment or

---

[11] Include all paragraphs that describe or allege the enterprise, including the paragraphs setting forth the enterprise purposes (always plural) and the means and methods of the enterprise.

[12] You may allege instead the incorporation of the appropriate paragraphs from the RICO count as the opening paragraph of the first Section 1959 count as long as it (the paragraph of incorporation) is followed by this or a substantially similar enterprise paragraph. Recommended variations for pleading Section 1959 are available from OCRS.

Information], the above-described enterprise, through its members and associates, engaged in racketeering activity as defined in Title 18, United States Code, Sections 1959(b)(1) and 1961(1), namely, acts involving [murder, etc.] in violation of [name of state law and citations][13] and narcotics trafficking in violation of Title 21, United States Code, Sections 841 and 846,[14] and acts indictable under Sections 1503 (obstruction of justice) and 1951 (extortion), of Title 18, United States Code.

3. In or about the spring of          , in the District of    [state]   , as consideration for the receipt of, and as consideration for a promise and an agreement to pay, [a

---

[13]Generally, OCRS no longer requires a specific state citation in **this** paragraph of the 1959 count. See 18 U.S.C. § 1961(1)(A) specifying certain state offenses that may be charged as racketeering activity if, among other things, the alleged state offense is "an act involving" one of the enumerated state offenses. Therefore, alleging racketeering activity violative of a single statutory section or sub-section may have the unintended effect of restricting racketeering activity to that single statutory violation. For example, state X proscribes every degree of murder as a separate, discrete statutory violation. Alleging murder as a violation of any one statute in such a state would limit proof of the enterprise's racketeering activity involving murder to that one degree of murder, when in fact the evidence supports enterprise activity involving various degrees of murder.

[14]Alternatively, use the language in Section 1961(1)(D): offenses involving the felonious manufacture, importation, receiving, concealment, buying, selling, or otherwise dealing in controlled substances or listed chemicals, in violation of (or indictable under), Title 21, United States Code, Sections 841 (applicable subsections) and 846.

thing, anything] of pecuniary[15] value from the [name of enterprise], and for the purpose of gaining entrance to and maintaining and increasing his position in the [name of enterprise], an enterprise engaged in racketeering activity, **[name of defendant]**, the defendant, and others known and unknown, unlawfully, and knowingly murdered **[name of victim]**, in violation of [citation, state code].

(Title 18, United States Code, Sections 1959(a)(1))
[OR All in violation of . . . .] [See 18 U.S.C. § 1959(a)(1)-(6) for enumerated offenses; also charge 18 U.S.C. § 2 and state abetting and abetting as appropriate.]

---

[15] We recommend charging both purposes (pecuniary gain and gaining, maintaining, increasing position in the enterprise). See United States v. Thai, 29 F.3d 785 (2nd Cir. 1994), where the court rejected the government's argument that the defendant's acts were to maintain and increase his position in the enterprise in which he was a leader because the only evidence (unexpectedly) of motive was that the defendant committed the crime only because he was offered $10,000 to do so.

## COUNT FOUR

The United States Attorney further charges:

A. Paragraphs 1 and 2 of Count Three of this Indictment [i.e., the paragraphs setting out the enterprise and the enterprise racketeering activity as alleged in the first Section 1959 count OR re-allege the original enterprise paragraphs--see n. 7 above] are realleged and incorporated by reference as though fully set forth herein.

B. From            through           , both dates being approximate and inclusive,    in the District of [state] , as consideration for the receipt of, and as consideration for a promise and agreement to pay, [a thing, anything] of pecuniary value from the [enterprise name], and for the purpose of gaining entrance to and maintaining and increasing his position in the [enterprise name], an enterprise engaged in racketeering activity,

[**name of defendant**]   , the defendant, unlawfully, and knowingly attempted to murder [**name of victim**], in violation of [citation, state code].

(Title 18, United States Code, Sections 1959(a)(5))
[OR All in violation of . . . .]

_____
United States Attorney

www.ingramcontent.com/pod-product-compliance
Lightning Source LLC
Chambersburg PA
CBHW080651190526
45169CB00006B/2071